SOCIALISM WITH A NORTHERN ACCENT

Radical traditions for modern times

SOCIALISM WITH A NORTHERN ACCENT

Radical traditions for modern times

Paul Salveson

London Lawrence & Wishart 2012

Lawrence and Wishart Limited
99a Wallis Road
London
E9 5LN

First published 2012

British Library Cataloguing in Publication Data.
A catalogue record for this book is available from the British Library

ISBN 9781 907103 391

Text setting E-type, Liverpool
Printed and bound by MPG Biddles, Kings Lynn

Contents

Foreword

Paul Salveson's book is an important account of Labour's traditional, community-based values, with many lessons for today. These values were born out of the industrial struggle in the North, which was long and bitter. It was working-class people who created the trade unions, co-operatives and municipal bodies as foundations of our communities that still endure. Within the Labour Party and the wider labour movement we have always held dear to our traditional values of community, democracy and justice, but there has also been a constant process of change and adaptation to modern conditions.

Interestingly, Paul points out that in the North, Scotland and Wales, different socialist cultures emerged from different experiences. Each had a different response to industrial development, but all developed strong community solidarity, an essential component of the 'Northern Socialism' which the book describes. Paul gives proper recognition to the under-recognised role of women in creating this Northern socialist culture, which gave it a particular emphasis and direction.

Such regional differences and experiences lead Paul to make an interesting point. Socialism in the South was to a certain extent economics-based, reflecting the influence of Sidney and Beatrice Webb, with an element of Marxism. However, the picture was quite different in the North, where neither the Webbs nor Marxism made much headway. The socialism that emerged in the 1890s was about values and community. It was about using working-class power at local level – in the council, work-place and in the co-op store. I was fascinated by Paul's account of the cultural side of our movement in the North: the choirs, cycling clubs, galas and garden parties. We've a distinctive heritage and we're proud of being 'down to earth'. We've never much liked jargon, or, for that matter, snobbery.

That difference reminds me of an example from my own experience. When I attended Labour's Ruskin College, Oxford, as a Northern trade union activist, on one occasion I became involved in arguments with a white-collar industrial activist from somewhere 'down south', who dismissed me as a 'lumpen proletarian'. It was months before I discovered he was insulting me.

Paul is a supporter of the traditional values he describes in the book, though he recognises that they are not enough on their own to win the next general election. He advocates greater regional decentralisation, a strengthening of local government and municipal enterprise, co-operatives, a new unionism and a greater accountability in the economy on the part of capital.

Paul's suggestion of a 'radical regionalism' forming part of Northern socialism should be the start of a new debate. He proposes electoral reform and coalitions with other progressive forces, linked with an approach to a genuinely sustainable development that can move us away from free-market capitalism.

Socialism with a Northern Accent joins other recent publications on Labour's future that have shifted the debate from Left v Right, Old Labour v New Labour to a different and certainly more colourful level. We've had Red Labour, Blue Labour and now Purple Labour. So: 'Northern Labour' – why not? Just don't give it a colour.

Some of these new debates share a common view that the last Labour government's record was a failure, despite the achievements of getting millions more back to work, a reduction of poverty, Sure Start, the minimum wage, an outstanding record of investment in health and education and a decade of sustainable economic growth with the lowest inflation and interest rates for decades. It was the state's power, through government, that made it possible to achieve this.

Does anyone think the present pensions problems can be solved without state intervention? Climate Change and the global economic financial crisis affects all countries and demands collective state intervention to provide a global solution to a global problem. All these objectives require an enabling state - of some form or other - to get us through the huge challenges facing the world in the coming period. Let's debate the nature of how we change the state and improve its accountability - but we must never divorce Labour from that 'enabling state' role.

Some of the recent interventions suggest that Labour cannot win the next general election on its own record or values, and some of the prescriptions (not in this book I have to say) are nearer to Tory/Liberal Democrat policy – such as 'Housing Asbos', elected mayors and other measures. To justify the process for future coalitions we don't need to water down our own values and policies to accommodate this kind of nonsense.

I'm so pleased that this debate will now take place with Paul's 'Northern Socialist' contribution. Hopefully it strengthens the case for retaining our traditional values while debating the modern setting into which we place them. So let's stop apologising every minute and replace that with pride in our history. Paul's 'Socialism with a Northern Accent' encourages us to do just that and is an essential read.

John Prescott

Acknowledgements

M any friends and colleagues have helped with the work which went into writing this book, over many years. I'm especially grateful to John Walton, who pored over the draft in detail and offered lots of useful observations (as well as spotting a few typographical howlers), and to Denis Pye, Dave Walsh, Hester Dunlop, Barry Winter, Andy Croft and Nigel Todd.

An early inspiration for this book was that dialectical unity, Eddie and Ruth Frow.

Several institutions have been extremely helpful. They include:

Working Class Movement Library, Salford
People's History Museum, Manchester
Bolton Public Library
Rossendale Community History Team (Lancashire County Council)
Chetham's Library, Manchester
University of Huddersfield Library and Archives

Cover illustration: Victor Grayson leads Colne Valley Socialists on a procession to celebrate the opening of Scapegoat Hill Socialist Club, May 1908. Photo courtesy of University of Huddersfield Library and Archives and Colne Valley Labour Party.

Introduction

This book has been written in Slaithwaite, part of Huddersfield's Colne Valley. We still have a few working mills here, producing the top quality woollens for which the area became famous in the nineteenth century. Colne Valley elected its first Independent Labour Party councillor, George Garside, as early as 1892 – before the party was officially formed; and the valley holds a special place in socialist history because of the stunning victory by Victor Grayson at a parliamentary by-election in 1907, on a programme of 'undiluted socialism'. Socialists, feminists and even anarchists from across the North of England came to Colne Valley to help in Grayson's campaign, and the victory was the result of twenty years of hard campaigning work. Historian and former Colne Valley MP David Clark, who has described the network of socialist clubs, choirs, and all-round political campaigning that was the background to Grayson's election, argues that Colne Valley was the highest expression of the 'ethical socialist' movement which swept the North before the First World War. The argument of this book is that we need to recapture some of that values-led socialism in our politics today.

Grayson was defeated in 1910, but Labour went on to hold the Colne Valley for long stretches up to the present day.[1] Although the shape of this Pennine constituency has changed, and its demographics are much altered, it remains a strongly contested seat. The Conservatives won it from Labour in 2010 and at various times since 1910 it has been held by Liberals, including the pacifist Richard Wainwright.

Many of the issues facing Labour nationally are found here in Colne Valley, in microcosm. This is no safe seat for anyone, and throws several challenges at the Labour Party. How do we retain the support of a shrinking, but still important, traditional working-class base? How can Labour appeal to a professional middle class which has developed in the last twenty years, attracted by the Pennine landscape, the sense of community and tradition – and the ease of the commute to Leeds and Manchester? How can it meet the needs of the local Asian communities, many of whose fathers came to Yorkshire to work in the mills, as well as the most recent incomers, young people from Poland, Slovakia and other Eastern European countries?

The Labour Party must rebuild itself as a popular political force which makes the best of its past achievements and relates to people's present-day identities and aspirations. It must be seen as a comfortable home to all of these different sections of the community. The long march back to popularity and power will need to involve many different, complementary, approaches which recognise the changed nature of Britain – most of which are reflected here in Colne Valley.

There is much in the British socialist tradition that has been forgotten or ignored, and which runs counter to state centralism, in particular a stress on grass-roots solutions, co-operation and an emphasis on local culture. Applied imaginatively, these traditions open up the possibility of creating a popular democratic culture which reflects different but complementary regional and national identities across Britain. Our comrades in Wales have gone furthest in that direction, with a 'twenty-first century socialism to a Welsh recipe', in the words of former Wales Labour leader Rhodri Morgan. The proof of that particular pudding was shown in the sweeping electoral victories at the Assembly elections in 2010. But popular democracy is about more than winning elections; and the Welsh government is putting the socialist recipe into practice in dozens of different ways that make a positive difference to people's lives, and a reality of that much abused term 'sustainable development'.

LOST TRADITIONS

This book aims to uncover some of the lost radical and socialist traditions which were largely specific to the North of England, and suggests ways of making some of those traditions relevant for today. Despite an increasingly global economy and media, people still doggedly identify with their region, their locality, their community. Politics should be about giving a strong voice to each of those levels, and move away from the centralised governance that holds sway within England.

Labour and its sister Co-operative Party have always had a streak of decentralism and localism running through them, in the latter case a very strong one. But the assumptions within and outside the party have often been counter to this. 'Old Labour' was regarded by many as the party of centralisation and state ownership, as exemplified by the post-war Attlee government. The reality was much more complex. There were debates over different forms of social ownership, regional devolution and grassroots democracy taking place throughout the 1940s and 1950s, as well as in much earlier periods.

I'm attempting here to highlight that alternative tradition, and to offer some ideas for how it can relate to a modernising socialist agenda. Socialists – be they Labour Party members, Greens or non-aligned radicals – should have an awareness of their heritage that can help inspire campaigning today. So this book isn't simply aimed at Labour Party members, or even 'the left' as traditionally understood. We need to learn from other traditions, as – hopefully – others can learn from our achievements. Even the Conservative's 'Big Society' owes much to the co-operative tradition and the community-building work of social-ists over many decades: Oscar Wilde was right that imitation is the sincerest form of flattery. But the Coalition's abuse of voluntary action by using it to plaster over the cracks caused by swingeing cuts is already resulting in growing cynicism amongst many community activists.

This book is not just a review of historical trends, and neither does it attempt to be a history of socialism in the North of England. Instead it draws on examples of radical politics and culture in the North over the last two hundred years that are, to a greater or lesser degree, distinctive to the region, and have lessons for us today. It argues that new forms of regional and local democracy, social enterprise and community empowerment are needed, and a new political practice. These should be based on a consciousness of our radical heritage, above all the ILP tradition of ethical socialism and the 'larger socialism' preached by Edward Carpenter before the First World War. A 'larger socialism' for today will be very different to that of the late nineteenth century, but ought to emphasise the enduring values of justice, democ-racy, equality and community that the ILP pioneers held so dear. As John Prescott has said, traditional values in a modern setting.

ENGLAND AND 'THE NORTH'

Whilst my focus is on 'the North', the argument is not a sterile north versus south one. It is about recognising the different streams and rivers within a wider British sea. I would love to see books appearing on the radical traditions in the South West, London, the East of England and the Midlands. Each region, each nation, has its own story to tell. Within Wales and Scotland there is already a much stronger awareness of their socialist history, culture and tradition, and there's much that the English regions can learn from them.

There are some that argue that Labour should engage more with 'Englishness'. The difficulty with that suggestion is that 'England' is a large nation which has historically been dominated by London and the South East. That irritating phrase, 'quintessentially English,' is in reality the romanticised image of an England only to be found in the south, and even then not in the marginalised communities of inner London and other major towns cities of the South and South West, such as Bristol, Southampton, Plymouth and Brighton. Jeremy Paxman, in his entertaining exploration of our national life, asked where the ideal 'England' was:

> You could instantly rule out places like Northumberland and Yorkshire ... Come to think of it, you could probably rule out anywhere north of a line from the Severn to the Trent. For not only is this imagined England rural rather than urban, it is southern rather than northern.[2]

A progressive political focus should be on Britain as part of a wider Europe, and, within that, on the UK nations and English regions, in a strong, collaborative and vibrant federation.

Labour needs to cultivate a patchwork of regional and national identities, both political and cultural, as part of a wider 'Britishness', celebrating a diverse, confident and progressive Britain of regions and nations. Socialism 'with a Northern accent' must be complemented by progressive politics in other English regions, and Scotland and Wales, each of which reflects their own distinctive traditions.

So where is 'The North'? For the purposes of my argument it comprises three regions: North West, Yorkshire and the Humber, and the North East. These are called, in dull technocratic jargon, 'standard planning regions'. They each have their distinctive facets, whilst sharing some common experiences – and they face similar shared challenges over the coming years as a result of the disproportionate effect of Coalition cuts on the North as a whole.

Most of the primary research behind this book was done in Lancashire, and to a lesser extent Yorkshire. The North East needs more detailed treatment than I have been able to provide, and it is fair to say that the socialism of the Durham and Northumberland coalfields was quite different from that of the Lancashire and Yorkshire textile districts. Cleveland, too, had its own distinctive politics and culture, rooted in the ironstone mining communities and the iron and steel industry. West Cumbria and the Furness area also has its own rich heritage.

So plenty of difference; but they each have things in common, and there is scope for more co-operation between these three Northern regions. In the final chapter of this book I debate the idea of a Northern 'super-region', which could take power out of the centre and relate as an equal to the devolved governments in Wales and Scotland as part of a federal Britain.

A new Northern politics can learn a lot from the achievements of socialists and radicals over the last two hundred years, to help create a vibrant, inclusive culture which is democratic, decentralised and diverse. In particular, the political culture that grew up around the Independent Labour Party between the early 1890s and the First World War has many lessons for us today. Far from its 'ethical socialism' being vague, or possessing – according to Stanley Pierson – 'little intellectual coherence', it had strong and universal values of community, solidarity and peace at its heart.[3] It achieved much more, through ILP socialists on local councils, than any of the 'scientific socialists' in the early British Marxist groups such as the Social Democratic Federation. Much of this book is a critical celebration of the achievements of the ILP and non-party socialist organisations such as *The Clarion* network – and a consideration of ways in which some of their passion can be rekindled in a modern context. At a time when the role of the state is being debated, the ILP's view, which combined a strong role for a central state in ensuring universal welfare provision and ownership of some industries, coupled with vibrant municipal state enterprise and an enhanced role for co-operatives, has much to offer us today.

The ILP was born and grew in the industrial North. As E.P. Thompson has argued, fulminating against London-centric history:

the ILP grew from the bottom up; its birthplaces were in those shadowy parts known as 'the provinces' ... Its first council seat was won in the Colne Valley; its first authentic parliamentary challenges came in Bradford and Halifax: its first conference showed an enormous preponderance of strength in the North of England.[4]

MANY STREAMS MAKE THE RIVER

British socialism contains many distinctive traditions; we're lucky to have such a rich and diverse heritage. The focus here is on the North of England, but it isn't any 'better' or worse than the strong traditions of Scotland, Wales, London and other English regions. The socialism which grew up in the South Wales valleys is different from that of the central belt of Scotland, or the politics of inner London; all are valid and all should be cherished. The point is that there *are* differences, and the socialism which emerged in the 1890s is not reducible to Fabian horse-trading in London clubs or the hallowed confines of Westminster.

In 1895, Robert Blatchford, that flawed genius of socialist propaganda, wrote:

> if you asked a London Socialist for the origin of the new movement he would refer you to Karl Marx and other German Socialists. But so far as our northern people are concerned I am convinced that beyond the mere outline of State Socialism Karl Marx and his countrymen have had but little influence. No; the new movement here, the new religion, which is Socialism, and something more than Socialism, is the result of the labours of Darwin, Carlyle, Ruskin, Dickens, Thoreau and Walt Whitman.[5]

Putting aside Blatchford's strident anti-Germanism, he has a point; and he is actually making a stronger statement than Thompson. Not only was the early ILP much more strongly rooted in the industrial North than in, say, London and Birmingham, it was actually a *different* sort of politics from that of other regions. Something very distinctive emerged in the industrial towns and cities of the North before the First World War, which helped shape the world we live in now, and helped form the modern Labour Party. Martin Pugh, in his history of the Labour Party, makes a similar point, after noting the immense variations in local political culture in the nineteenth century:

> The inevitable result was a patchy geographical advance during Labour's early history and a movement that acquired pronounced

local and regional characteristics. The tactics that worked in Lancashire were less relevant in County Durham; Labour was not the same party in London as it was in Yorkshire ...[6]

This book attempts to give at least a feel of that broad, regional, values-driven socialism so different from the centralist approaches of the Fabians and SDF.

PIONEERS, OH PIONEERS! NORTHERN HEROES AND HEROINES

All the past we leave behind,
We debouch upon a newer mightier world, varied world,
Fresh and strong the world we seize, world of labor and the march,
Pioneers! O pioneers!

Walt Whitman

The socialism which emerged in the North during the 1890s had roots not only in the radical Liberalism of a previous generation, but amongst the handloom weavers of Pennine Lancashire and Yorkshire a century before – radical democrats inspired by revolutionary France and the writings of Tom Paine. They had later formed a sizeable section of the Chartist movement of the late 1830s and 1840s. This was a radicalism quite specific to the Pennines; it put down roots in the small handloom-weaving communities in Lancashire and the West Riding. It was located in that dramatic moorland landscape between the towns of Rochdale and Ashton to the west and Huddersfield and Halifax to the east. Samuel Bamford in Lancashire and Ben Rushton in the West Riding typified that rich culture (see Chapter 1).

By the time of the Napoleonic Wars, that culture was being fatally undermined by rampant industrial capitalism. The Luddite revolts in 1812 were a desperate attempt to protect not only living standards but a whole way of life. By the 1840s handloom weaving was a dying trade, with thousands thrown into poverty.[7] Some of the weavers – and many of their children – were forced to take work in the factories, though some of that culture and political radicalism went with them, exploding into Chartism. The life of Rochdale Chartist Tom Livsey was not untypical: he moved from Owenite socialism through Chartism to co-operation and Liberalism in the 1850s.[8]

Those radical traditions were never entirely forgotten. The 'socialist revival' in Lancashire and Yorkshire venerated the surviving 'old Chartists'. Socialists like Allen Clarke wrote about Chartism, in both fiction and journalism. The 'new socialism' which swept the industrial North in the late 1880s and early 1890s understood who its predecessors were.

The North, particularly from the mid-1880s to the early 1900s, produced a crop of remarkable visionaries, most of whom remain 'hidden from history'. The importance of Edward Carpenter has recently been re-established thanks to the work of Sheila Rowbotham, but Allen Clarke, Caroline Martyn, Victor Grayson, Ethel Carnie, and Robert Blatchford remain virtually forgotten.[9] Major influences on northern socialism, such as Walt Whitman and British propagandists including Blatchford, Snowden, Glasier and Carpenter himself, have hardly been acknowledged.[10]

Traditional 'labour history' has a strange obsession with Sidney and Beatrice Webb, those earnest collectors of 'facts' and advocates of 'the inevitability of gradualism' who established the tiny Fabian Society, with its handful of almost entirely London-based members. It's interesting to read socialist periodicals of the 1890s – be it the jolly *Clarion*, the more serious *Labour Leader, Justice* or *Workman's Times*, or indeed the plethora of local socialist newspapers like the *Huddersfield Worker* and *Rochdale Labour News*, and see how often the Webbs pop up. Hardly at all. The people who do appear, time after time, are Hardie, Hyndman, 'cultural icons' like Whitman, Carlyle and Ruskin, as well as William Morris and Edward Carpenter. At the risk of being accused of parochialism, I would argue that the reason for the importance attributed to the Webbs in much historical writing is that they shared the same kind of world as the people who were writing the history: middle-class, London-based, and elitist. E.J. Hobsbawm, writing back in the early 1960s, notes their ability to 'blow their own trumpet', helped by having, in 1892, at the peak of their influence, some 10 per cent of their membership employed as journalists. Their claims to have played a major part in forming the modern Labour Party, or for that matter the ILP, are unfounded.[11]

A number of historical figures have a habit of popping up in different parts of this book, most of whom were associated with the ILP. They include Allen Clarke, Katharine Bruce Glasier and Selina Cooper. Clarke straddled a key period in socialism's development –

the 1890s to the 1920s – and his career offers some quite different perspectives to those gleaned from conventional socialist history. He was a socialist of a distinctly libertarian hue, a lover of the country-side and a keen cyclist, a dabbler and dreamer who used a Lancashire regional identity to promote his idea of socialism. Selina Cooper, overlapping in time, represented the often uneasy combination of municipal socialism, feminism, trades unionism and opposition to war. Both were born into the Northern working class and exemplify its finest traditions. Katherine Bruce Glasier, dubbed 'the grand-mother of the Independent Labour Party' in the 1940s, personified that values-driven socialism, with a strong 'spiritual' tinge, rather than a dry, statist economics-based one. Whilst this book is largely chronological, I devote a separate chapter to this rich socialist culture which emerged in the North between the late 1880s and the First World War.

Socialism is not the only political culture from which we should learn. There is a wider radical tradition which should be celebrated and built upon. Thomas Newbigging, a radical Liberal from the Rossendale Valley, is also quoted extensively in this book. A great democrat, defender of Irish freedom and lover of his native Lancashire, Newbigging deserves to be rescued from obscurity.[12] As he said in 1886 to a packed meeting in Pendleton Town Hall, Salford:

> We owe every shred of our English liberty to men and women who were called demagogues and agitators, and viler names than these ...
> The truth is, we need more agitators.

Paul Salveson, Slaithwaite, West Yorkshire October 2011

NOTES

1. See Paul Salveson, *Looking Forward – Looking Back: Colne Valley Labour Party 1891-2011*, 2011; and Cyril Pearce, *Colne Valley Labour Party: Souvenir Centenary History* 2001.
2. Jeremy Paxman, *The English: portrait of a people*, 2nd ed. 1999, pp156-7. See Chapter 8 for a fuller discussion of 'The English Question'.
3. Stanley Pierson, *Marxism and the Origins of British Socialism*, 1973, p140.
4. E.P. Thompson, 'Homage to Tom Maguire', in John Saville (ed.), *Essays in Labour History*, 1972, p277.

5. Robert Blatchford, 'The New Party in the North', in A. Reid (ed), *The New Party*, 1895, pp13-4.

6. Martin Pugh, *Speak for Britain: a new history of the Labour Party*, 2010, p10.

7. See Geoff Timmins, *The Last Shift: the decline of handloom weaving in the nineteenth century Lancashire*, 1993.

8. Livsey has been sadly neglected by historians but Margaret Rebecca Lahee's *The Life and Times of Alderman T. Livsey*, 1866, is a remarkable early biography.

9. For Clarke see Paul Salveson, *Lancashire's Romantic Radical: the Life and Writings of Allen Clarke/Teddy Ashton*, 2009. Jill Liddington, *The Life and Times of a Respectable Rebel: Selina Cooper*, 2000, is an excellent biography of an important figure in Lancashire socialism. For Carpenter, Sheila Rowbotham's *Edward Carpenter: A Life of Liberty and Love*, 2008, is monumental. *The Life and Letters of Caroline Martyn*, by Lena Wallis, has recently been republished with an introductory biography. Little has been written about Blatchford since Laurence Thompson's biography, *Robert Blatchford: Portrait of an Englishman*, 1951. Grayson has several biographies, including David Clark's *Victor Grayson: Labour's Lost Leader*, 1985; and Reg Groves, *The Strange Case of Victor Grayson*, 1975.

10. Little has been written about either John Bruce Glasier or Katharine Bruce Glasier (who outlived him by several decades), despite their central importance to the growth of British socialism. Laurence Thompson's *The Enthusiasts*, 1971, is a quirky but affectionate account of their lives.

11. E.J. Hobsbawm, 'The Fabians Reconsidered', in *Labouring Men*, 1963. Hobsbawm's essay was an extended review of Alan Macbriar's *The Fabians and British Socialism*, 1962, which reaches a similar conclusion.

12. Newbigging deserves a full biography. A good feel for his views can be gleaned from his *Speeches and Addresses*, published in 1887 but very hard to find today.

PART I

The Heroic Age of Northern Socialism

1. Democratic Struggles: Peterloo and Chartism

On 15 August 2010 a small group of socialists gathered in the open space outside Manchester Central, the exhibition centre that was once a great railway terminus, to commemorate one of the most important events in nineteenth-century politics – the Peterloo Massacre.

They were standing on what was once St Peter's Fields, an open space on the edge of the first city of the industrial revolution. On Sunday 16 August 1819 some 60,000 working men and women, many with their children, had gathered from all parts of Lancashire and the West Riding, to hear Henry 'Orator' Hunt and to demand universal suffrage. They were peaceful, and in carnival mood – many contemporary accounts describe the marchers decked out in their 'Sunday best'. Yet within a few minutes carnival turned to carnage as the local yeomanry were let loose on the crowd, hitting out blindly with their sabres as they tried to get to the stage where Hunt was speaking. At least seventeen people died and hundreds were seriously wounded. The impact of the massacre was huge, outraging liberal opinion across the country. The yeomanry were congratulated by the local establishment on their 'bravery', and nobody ever faced charges for what was state-sponsored murder on a large scale; no Saville Commission was set up to establish what happened on that day, though the similarities with our more recent 'Bloody Sunday' are uncannily similar – even to the extent of one of the cavalry alleging he heard gun shots coming from the marchers.

Several broadsheet ballads were written about the massacre, including 'The Peterloo Massacre' by Michael Wilson (see p21). Wilson was a participant in the demonstration and it would seem that one of his friends, 'Sam o'Dick's', was left for dead. The song was still heard being sung in the last years of the nineteenth century in the Stalybridge area.[1]

The Peterloo Massacre

Come, Robin, sit deawn an' aw'll tell thee a tale
Boh, first, prithee, fill me a bobbin' o'ale
Aw'm as drey mon, as soot, an' aw'm hurt i'mi crop
Havin' left Sam o'Dick's where aw fear he mun stop

Chorus:
For the gentlemen cavalry
Cut 'em down cleverly;
Real Royal Yeomanry!
Cavalry brave!

Mr Hunt new coom forrad an' spoke a few words,
When the Peterloo cut-my-throats shaken'd their swords,
Aw thowt sure en of they were runnin' their rigs,
Till aw seed moor nor twenty lay bleedin' like pigs.

Boh let's tae a peep o'these Peterloo chaps,
'At ma'es sich a neyse abeawt cullers an' caps,
See what they'n composed on, and then we may judge,
For it runs i'mi moind 'ot their loyalty's fudge.
Theer's the taxman, exciseman, placeman, an'preycher,
    that hum;
The fat-guted landlord, o'licence in fear
Cuts the throats o'his neybours who buy his bad beer

Michael Wilson

THE LIFE OF A RADICAL: SAMUEL BAMFORD

Samuel Bamford was one of the great figures of early nineteenth-century working-class culture. He embodied the radicalism – and intellectual culture – of the handloom-weaving communities which flourished across the Pennines in the late eighteenth and early nineteenth centuries. Writing in the early 1800s of the handloom weavers, Bamford asked:

> And what shall I say of the working class? That they are the most intelligent of any island – in the world ... they are the greatest readers; can shew the greatest number of good writers; the greatest number of sensible and considerate public speakers. They can shew a greater number of botanists; a greater number of horticulturalists; a greater number who are acquainted with the abstruse sciences; the greatest number of poets, and a greater number of good musicians, whether choral or instrumental.[i]

Bamford was born into this highly cultured community in 1788, in what was then the small village of Middleton on the outskirts of Manchester. His father was a weaver and admirer of Tom Paine. Bamford himself became a weaver in his early twenties and followed the family tradition of devouring the works of Paine. In 1816 he formed a local reform club in Middleton and became active in the surrounding area. His activities came to the attention of the authorities who arrested him for treason in March 1817, but he was acquitted on the grounds of insufficient evidence.

The highpoint of Bamford's political career came two years later when he led a large number of people from Middleton to attend the meeting at St Peter's Fields. After the massacre that followed, Bamford was one of several men who were arrested and charged with 'assembling with unlawful banners at an unlawful meeting for the purpose of inciting discontent', and he was sentenced to one year's imprisonment.

After his release he did not return to political life, but attempted to supplement his income from weaving with selling poetry, writing in both standard English and dialect. His *Early Days* and *Passages in the Life of a Radical* provide an invaluable source for working-class life in Lancashire in the early nineteenth century. Always something of a tetchy character, and easily given to offence, Bamford refused to take part in the Chartist movement, and even enrolled as a special constable, to the disgust of his radical friends.

i. Samuel Bamford, *Walks in South Lancashire*, 1844, pp14-15.

The impact of Peterloo echoed throughout the nineteenth century. Immediately, it stimulated demands for radical reform; during the Chartist period of the late 1830s and 1840s, 'Remember Peterloo' was a rallying cry against the establishment. Radical Liberals, in the 1870s and 1880s, recalled the massacre in their speeches, and later, socialists in the North of England would refer to the massacre as a symbol of the depths to which the ruling class would sink in its attempt to thwart 'the will of the people'. Peterloo was the most important event in a series of developments in the first half of the nineteenth century which culminated in the Chartist movement.

THE RADICAL BACKGROUND TO PETERLOO

The North of England was the crucible of the Industrial Revolution – coal mining, textiles, and iron and steel were the major industries which emerged from the 1760s and transformed Britain. With them came an industrial working class. By the late 1790s there were strong trade unions in centres such as Manchester, Newcastle, Sunderland and Sheffield, with increasing support for the radical political ideas expounded by Tom Paine and bolstered by the democratic ideals of the French revolution. In Newcastle, Thomas Spence was one of the foremost radicals, a man well ahead of his time. He pre-dated Paine and wrote a pamphlet called *The Rights of Man* followed by a further publication on *The Rights of Infants*. He was a member of Newcastle Philosophical Society but was thrown out in 1775, following an incendiary speech. He was a friend of the French Jacobin Marat who lived in Newcastle between 1770 and 1776, working as a doctor and vet. So it could be argued that the French revolution was actually inspired by Geordies! Spence was also a formative influence on the Chartist movement in the North-East. There is an active Thomas Spence Society in Newcastle today, and a plaque in his memory was unveiled in the city in 2010.[2]

E.P. Thompson, in *The Making of the English Working Class*, charted the development of this radical political tradition up to the emergence of Chartism in the late 1830s.[3] Whilst many parts of Britain had their radical strongholds, the breadth of support for radical political ideas between the 1790s and the 1830s was strongest in the North. Up to 1832 very few men had the vote (and of course no women). Even the emerging industrial middle class were disenfranchised, and this offered the basis for a cross-class coalition in the reform movements of the 1820s.

The radical movements of the early nineteenth century saw extensive use of poetry to express working people's aspirations for reform. The influence of Robert Burns, with his radical, plebeian and democratic poetry, using Scots working-class vernacular, was enormous. It gave working people the self confidence to write, and write about things that mattered to them, in the way that they spoke every day. The pages of *The Northern Star* are full of examples of working people's poetry, as are most of the other Chartist publications of that time.

The North also had its own subversive caricaturists, such as 'Tim Bobbin' – or John Collier – known as 'The Lancashire Hogarth'. Collier was 'the father of Lancashire dialect literature' and used his literary and artistic skills to poke fun at local dignitaries.[4] The hand-loom weavers of Lancashire and the West Riding were highly creative across a range of fields, with many accomplished musicians as well as writers, botanists and mathematicians amongst their number, as Samuel Bamford observed in his 1844 *Walks in South Lancashire*. Tom Paine's *The Rights of Man* was widely read and contemporary accounts record well-read copies in many a weaver's cottage. A highly articulate and self-educated radicalism flourish during the few decades of prosperity as the spinning industry became automated in the 1780s and created a huge demand for weaving.

As E.P. Thompson describes:

> a unique blend of social conservatism, local pride and cultural attainment made up the way of life of the Yorkshire and Lancashire weaving community ... there was certainly a leaven amongst the northern weavers of self-educated and articulate men of considerable attainments.[5]

Throughout the late eighteenth and early nineteenth century, informal and at times illegal networks of radical discussion groups helped lay the seed for the revolutionary movements of the 1820s and 1830s. *The Huddersfield Examiner* published a semi-fictional story in 1883 about radical life in the Holme Valley in the early years of the century:

> There was in Honley, many years ago, and still is, a room which was known to the inhabitants as 'Th'Garrit' ... a cave of Abdullam where gathered the originals of the district, whether cobblers, given then as

now somewhat to freethinking in matters religious, radicals, admirers of Robert Owen ... men who cared little for the opinions of 'stick-in-the-muds' and a great deal for the education of their children and t'Rights of Man' ... weavers, dyers, farmers, all who were not quite agreed that the world as it ran was the best world that could be, met to devise improvements and point out where and what remedies might be made.[6]

The period of prosperity in the weaving communities was brief and by the early nineteenth century many weavers were living in dire poverty as power looms and factory production steadily replaced their often home-based handlooms. At the extreme end of working-class protest were the 'Luddite' disturbances in Lancashire and Yorkshire in 1812. These outbreaks, a reflection of the extreme poverty facing the weavers by this time, were ruthlessly suppressed, and many of the leaders were executed. Two events – the burning of a mill at Westhoughton, near Bolton, and the assassination of an unpopular mill owner in Huddersfield – led to the execution of several local people, including, in Westhoughton, a boy aged twelve, who was hung at Lancaster.[7] These judicial murders left an enduring sense of injustice which fuelled support for the Chartist movement years later, and even radicalism in the 1860s. J.T. Staton, the radical Bolton dialect writer, recalled the Westhoughton executions in an election sketch published in his *Bowtun Loominary* in 1853, attacking the Tories:

> Remember now Westhoughton mill
> How many there you stooped to kill
> Think of that infant voice so shrill
> That at Lancaster you hung.[8]

Luddism was more than just a crude reaction to rapid industrialisation. It was a revolt against the loss of the community and culture described by Samuel Bamford, and had parallels with the reaction of mining communities in the 1980s to what was a loss not just of mining jobs but of entire communities and their way of life.

Highly politicised handloom-weavers, such as Benjamin Rushton of Halifax, George White of Bradford and Richard Pilling of Manchester, formed the leadership of a wider radical movement which swept the North. Thompson, referring to the emergence of a politically skilled

BENJAMIN RUSHTON, HANDLOOM WEAVER AND CHARTIST

Halifax was one of the strongest centres of radicalism throughout the nineteenth century, and Benjamin Rushton was the central figure in the local Chartist movement. He was employed at Ovenden, near Halifax, as a fancy worsted weaver, and wove pieces for Crossley's, the large carpet manufacturer whose mills are now the Dean Clough arts and business complex. His political activity probably stretched back to the Peterloo period, but the first recorded instance of him as a political leader was in 1831, when he chaired a meeting of over two hundred workers in Ovenden, demanding greater reform than what was being offered by the Reform Bill then going through parliament. In particular, the meeting wanted universal suffrage, annual parliaments and a secret ballot.[i]

Rushton took on a leadership role at the start of the Chartist movement in Halifax, formally moving support for the Charter at a meeting in July 1838. In October of that year he attended the huge Chartist demonstration at Peep Green, leading the Halifax contingent. The following year he spoke at the biggest-yet Chartist demonstration, at Hartshead Moor. Perhaps his most famous role was chairing the mass meeting on Blackstone Edge in July 1846, attended by 30,000 Chartists from both sides of the Pennines. He was not a violent demagogue, and advised the striking workers in August 1842 to 'keep the peace and do violence to no man'. Though brought up as a Methodist, he became increasingly hostile to established religion. He was a regular preacher at the 'Chartist Chapel' in Littletown, in the Spen Valley.

Rushton died in poverty in 1853, the weaving industry having gone into rapid decline. But his funeral was one of the largest of any working-class leader in the nineteenth century. Five special trains ran from Bradford, and the local paper estimated that between 6000 and 10,000 people attended the event, with the procession taking nearly two hours to pass through the town. In accordance with his wishes, there was no religious service and his epitaph was taken from the works of Robert Burns.

Halifax has never forgotten Rushton and its Chartist heritage. A gathering of old Chartists took place in 1885, organised by the local Liberal Party, and Rushton's memory was toasted. A further meeting took place in 1953, on the centenary of his death, with another in 1976. In 2006 the town held a Chartist festival, and the Calderdale Youth parliament framed their own 'People's Charter'. Each year, on May Day, a celebration of the 'great meeting' is held on Blackstone Edge.

i. John Hargreaves, *Benjamin Rushton, Handloom Weaver and Chartist*, 2007.

radical working-class leadership in the 1830s, argues that 'the Lancashire radicalism of 1816-20 was in great degree a movement of weavers, and the making of these later leaders was in communities of this kind'.[9] Many of them were also to take on key roles in the later Chartist movement.

Th'Owd Handloom Weyvers o'Barnsley

God help th'owd handloom weyvers,
Theyn woven hard an' long,
An naah ther owd an starving,
An' well, aw think it's wrang

They'n woven cloath for princes,
They'n woven cloth for men,
They done soa mich for little,
At naah ther baght thersen

God help em i' ther owd age,
For poverty's ther lot,
An if poor fowk can't help em,
They'll ha a chance to rot

Ther starvin' naah i'Barnsley,
Ther lots too bad to tell,
So send em help, an handy,
An aw'll send some misel

Ben Turner[10]

THE EMERGENCE OF CHARTISM

Radical movements multiplied in the North during the 1820s and ultimately coalesced into the Chartist Movement, with its six demands focused around universal suffrage. Across Britain, the nature of the movement varied immensely. It's over-simplistic to say that London and the South espoused a more moderate, non-violent approach whilst the industrial North was prepared to take the more insurrectionary route – there are elements of both in regions across Britain, and the most notable 'rising' was in Newport, South Wales, in 1839.

TOM LIVSEY: A GRADELY RADICAL

Rochdale, some fifteen miles over the Pennines from Huddersfield, shared many of its Yorkshire neighbour's radicalism. It is famous as the town where modern co-operation took off, with the establishment of the 'Rochdale Pioneers' in 1844, though co-operative shops of a more ephemeral existence had existed in Rochdale fifteen years before that. Tom Livsey's political career encompassed co-operation, Chartism and ultimately Liberalism. Born in 1817, the son of a publican, he became politically active in his teens and was at the forefront of radical politics in Rochdale for over twenty-five years; he almost succeeded in being elected mayor of the town.

Allen Clarke's novel of Co-operation and Chartism, *The Men Who Fought for Us*, features Livsey extensively.[i] Clarke introduces him to the reader as the Chartist General Strike of 1842 is gathering strength:

> A fine, handsome young man named Tom Livsey, aged about twenty-seven, yet, young as he was, a member of the Board of Guardians and beloved by the poor for his kind ways.

At the 'Chartist and Socialist Meeting', Livsey argues with those who want to escalate the strike, pointing out the heavy military presence in the town:

> They'd rejoice if we'd only no more gumption than kick up a bit of a bother, an' give 'em the opportunity they're waiting for. We're hurtin' 'em far more by doin' nowt than doin' summat just now ...

Later in the tale, Clarke tells us more about Livsey. At the age of twenty-two he and some others founded the Chartist Club in Rochdale, and he made his first speech to commemorate the birthday of the great radical Henry Hunt. He subsequently became the leader of Chartism in Rochdale, though was astute enough to avoid being provoked into violence. His youthful political education appears to have been through his relationships with Owenite socialists, such as the family friend John Schofield

One of the most remarkable things about Livsey is his biography. It was written by Margaret Rebecca Lahee, who lived for many years in Rochdale after emigrating from Ireland. Lahee was the earliest published woman writer in dialect, and clearly a writer of radical sentiments. *The Life and Times of the Late Alderman T. Livsey* was published in 1866 and, like Allen Clarke, Lahee uses Livsey's broad Lancashire speech to create a picture of a working-class politician who was at the very heart of his community.

Livsey was also involved in local campaigns for religious freedom, refusing to pay Church rates, and in scores of other local campaigns to improve life for Rochdale's working class, not least the struggle against the New Poor Law. As Lahee commented:

> His spirit was like an avalanche carrying all before it; no barrier was too great for his energies to surmount; no scheme for the improvement of his town and its people too stupendous for him to undertake.

Livsey represented the Castleton Ward on the Board of Guardians, and within a short time of being elected became its chairman. He and his colleagues on the Board soon came up against the Poor Law Commissioners, when they led a Poplar-style revolt over the distribution of poor relief, and the policy of separating families and throwing them into the workhouse. The London-based Commissioners took the Rochdale Guardians to court – and lost, though the battle continued until 1858.

When Livsey wasn't doing battle with the Poor Law Commissioners he was active in early municipalisation projects. As early as 1843 Rochdale Corporation succeeded in taking over the local gas company, following public outrage over profiteering. When Livsey became chairman of the Gas Committee the municipally-owned company started to make a healthy profit, and at the same time made substantial improvements to the Corporation's street lighting.

Livsey's role in the co-operative movement is well documented by Lahee; he was present at some of the early discussions in the local Chartist rooms that led to the formation of the Rochdale Equitable Pioneers Society. He was outraged at the 'exclusive dealing' that was used to attempt to strangle the new society, arguing that:

> your best plan will be to co-operate, bring your combined influence to bear upon the question, let heart and soul be in the task, til you are able to build corn mills and cotton mills of your own ...

Livsey died on 25 January 1864, at the age of forty-eight. He straddles the years of Chartism and Liberalism, and is a great example of an early working-class politician in a local authority. His battles against the Poor Law Commissioners prefigure the campaigns against unemployment relief in Poplar, East London, by ninety years.

i. Allen Clarke, *The Men Who Fought For Us*, 1918, p63. The novel was published by the Co-operative Printing Society in Manchester.

Bolton, Bradford and Huddersfield; and the 'General Strike' of 1842, undoubtedly strongest in the textile districts of the North, was accompanied by some sporadic violence.[11] In Sheffield, Samuel Holberry and other Chartists planned an armed insurrection in 1840 but were betrayed by an informer. Holberry died in prison two years later. More than 50,000 people attended the funeral procession in his native city, and today he is commemorated by a water fountain in the city's Peace Gardens.

Northern Chartism was based on an alliance of two forces, one in decline and the other in its early stages of growth: the handloom weavers and the factory proletariat. As we have seen, some of the individual hand-loom weavers – Benjamin Rushton is a good example – had the experience and independence to take on a wider role within the movement. Many of these local working-class leaders had been schooled in Owenite socialism in the 1820s, and had dabbled in early forms of co-operation.

Chartism also found strong support on Tyneside, with enthusiastic backing for the ultimate general strike, or 'sacred month', which would usher in the new world. In 1839 the Scots Chartist leader Abram Duncan asked a large gathering of women Chartists in Newcastle 'were they ready to make a sacred month of it, and take to the hillside?' The unanimous response was 'We will!'.[12] During the 1842 strike there was solid support in the Durham coalfield, though Newcastle itself remained aloof. Small mining villages like Winlaton witnessed confrontations between soldiers and strikers. In Cleveland, several small flax growing and weaving communities were centres of Chartist support.

THE RADICAL PRESS

The early radical movement was supported by a strong, semi-under-ground press. The history of the radical press goes back to the Diggers and Levellers of the seventeenth century, but it was in the early nineteenth century that radical journalism really took off – aided by improvements in printing technology, but above all by the creation of a mass readership for radical newspapers, despite restricted literacy. Over the last two hundred years there have only been two genuinely popular, mass circulation radical newspapers. The first of these was Feargus O'Connor's *Northern Star*, which began publication in 1837, and was initially edited from Leeds (the second was Blatchford's *Clarion*, edited in Manchester, of which more later).[13]

By the 1820s the North already had many newspapers of a broadly radical persuasion and in support of demands for reform. *The Leeds Mercury* was one of the most important, but there were others. They were mainly aimed at a middle-class liberal readership. One important precursor to the *Northern Star* was *The Manchester Observer*, which aimed at a specifically radical working-class readership, and was published in the years between 1816 and 1820. According to a Home Office report it was 'designed to inflame the minds of the lower orders'. Stanley Harrison, in his *Poor Men's Guardians*, notes that it had a circulation of over 3000, which increased by a further thousand after Peterloo. There were also other radical papers which had smaller circulations and an even more ephemeral existence, such as John Carlile's *Republican* or John Wade's *Gorgon*. In the 1830s, *The Poor Man's Guardian*, edited by Henry Hetherington, had a strong circulation in the northern industrial districts. Stanley Harrison notes that it:

> ... hammered out of the diverse trends of Owenism and the Co-operative Movement, trade union organization and the whole rich inheritance inherited from the American, French and Irish revolutions via Cobbett and Paine, a distinctive self-consciousness for the new [working] class.[14]

The Poor Man's Guardian ceased publication in 1835, but had laid some of the seeds which were soon to flower in the greatest radical working-class movement of the nineteenth century – Chartism.

The Chartist movement, so strongly rooted in the North of England, needed its own voice to counter the attacks from the Tory Press. James Bronterre O'Brien, who had edited *The Poor Man's Guardian* since 1832, was urged by Yorkshire Tory radical Richard Oastler 'to put the soul of *The Poor Man's Guardian* into *The Northern Star*'.[15] By May 1838, just a few months after its first issue, *The Northern Star* was selling 48,000 copies a week, a phenomenal achievement for any radical paper. It was relatively expensive, at fourpence ha'penny, and contained densely written reports of Chartist activities across the country, but particularly in the North. It also had a strong coverage of international events, including news from France, Ireland and the USA. Stanley Harrison described its success as follows:

> For the superior vigour and longevity of the Northern Star there were many reasons, including the fact that the majority of its readers lived in the strife-torn centres of the new industrialism. Its position as undisputed head of the rebel press fraternity, its accessibility to most views in the movement, and its effective editorship, were other causes of the great lead it had other Chartist newspapers.[16]

There were also many other publications, such as *The Southern Star*, edited by O'Brien, and the Newcastle-based *Northern Liberator*.

The Northern Star was much more than a series of accounts of political gatherings. It invariably carried features on the arts, and encouraged a new generation of radical poets such as W.J. Linton by publishing a weekly poetry section. Karl Marx was the German correspondent for the paper, and this introduced his writings to a British working-class readership for the first time.

Circulation fluctuated with the fortunes of the Chartist Movement. The period around the great campaigns of 1839 saw the paper exceeding the circulation of *The Times*, with over 40,000 audited sales. However, this number hugely underestimates the paper's influence. Many accounts have survived of how *The Northern Star* was read in groups, often by a local leader who had the necessary literacy skills to both read and declaim the contents.

The Lancashire dialect writer Ben Brierley later recalled that in the 1840s, when he was a young man in Failsworth, a weaving community on the east side of Manchester, he was required to spend his Sundays reading the paper to a group of older Chartists. It was subscribed to by his father and five others:

> Every Sunday morning these subscribers met at our house to hear what prospect there was of the 'expected smash-up' taking place. It was my task to read aloud so that all could hear at the same time ...[17]

But in 1852, at a time when the Chartist movement had declined to become no more than a small sect, *The Northern Star* – 'the publishing phenomenon of the nineteenth century' – came to an end.[18] The next thirty years was a relatively barren time for the radical press in the

North, though *The Newcastle Weekly Chronicle* kept the standard of radicalism flying in the North-East. However, the 1880s was to see a renaissance of radical working-class newspapers, in tandem with the revival of socialist politics. Once again, the movement was primarily in the North of England.

WOMEN FIND THEIR VOICE: THE FEMALE POLITICAL UNIONS AND CHARTISM

The active involvement of women in Northern democratic struggles goes back to Peterloo and earlier. Accounts of the great Manchester demonstration of 16 August 1819 give us a picture of the extent of working-class women's involvement in the reform movement. Samuel Bamford, leader of the Middleton radicals, described how the Middleton and Rochdale contingent comprised some 6000 men, led by a column of two hundred women. In the events which followed, many women were amongst the casualties.

For some years before Peterloo, Lancashire women had formed their own organisations. Samuel Bamford tells of women attending radical meetings and voting alongside men: 'female political unions were formed, with the chairwoman, committees, and other officials'.[19] By the 1830s women – and young girls – had become an important part of the factory working class. Women were employed in a number of roles, including weaving and parts of the spinning process, though the pattern across Lancashire and Yorkshire varied, and some towns had a tradition of women ceasing to work on getting married, while in other towns they carried on at the loom or warper. What clearly did start to happen was the shaping of a collective consciousness, which would ultimately lead to strong support for the vote from working-class women in Lancashire and Yorkshire.

Women's involvement in Northern Chartism has been the subject of recent research and there is clear evidence that women played an active part in the movement. In the small West Riding town of Elland, for example, working-class women formed a Female Radical Association in 1838, initially to fight the New Poor Law, which was seen as a direct attack on women's rights. The leading figure in the association was Elizabeth Hanson, wife of Abram Hanson, a well-known Chartist speaker. (One of their sons was baptised as 'Fergus O'Connor Hanson.)

Women's suffrage was not part of the Chartist programme, but there was an assumption that once male suffrage had been won women's emancipation would soon follow. Chase estimates that around 100 women Chartist associations had been formed by 1839, spread across the country but with a strong presence in the North.[20] Certainly, *The Northern Star* carried frequent reports of women's activity in the movement. On 12 November 1842, for example, it reported on a meeting of the National Charter Association at Kirkheaton, a small weaving community near Huddersfield, noting that 'at the class nine females came forward and enrolled their names as members of the association'.[21]

THE FIRST RADICAL WORKING-CLASS PARTY

The Chartists have often been vilified as a disorganised rabble, while Feargus O'Connor has been described as an Irish 'demagogue'. This says more about the class and racial prejudices of some historians than it does about Chartism. More recent historical research – culminating in Malcolm Chase's *Chartism: A New History* (2007) – has shown Chartism to be a remarkably broad movement with a highly sophisticated political leadership, at both national and local level. The National Charter Association was in effect the first mass radical party in British history, and it fielded candidates in both national and local elections. It was at its strongest in the North: Manchester and the cotton towns, Bradford and the West Riding. In some of the new industrial towns, such as Middlesbrough, there was also strong support for the Charter, with activity centring on the 'Working Men's Reading Room', which included a well-stocked library of radical books and pamphlets.

Even with the restricted franchise the movement succeeded in getting some of its leaders elected. There is little doubt that the establishment of the day saw Chartism as a huge threat, and mobilised accordingly. Whilst there was no further catastrophe on the scale of Peterloo, thousands of special constables were mobilised for the major Chartist demonstrations, and preparations were made to violently suppress the movement. It is a testament to the skills of the Chartist leaders that this was averted. When the movement's momentum faltered, it was not because of repression but followed on from the failure of the 1848 petition and monster demonstration on Kennington

Common, London. By the early 1850s Chartism had became more of a radical sect than a mass movement.

Many of its leaders, including Ernest Jones, Rochdale's Tom Livsey and Bolton's James Kirkman, subsequently became involved in the Liberal Party, but there were further attempts to revive the movement. In December 1857 the 'Northern Reform Union' was established in Newcastle, in the city's Chartist Hall, with the central objective of universal manhood suffrage.[22] And when socialism revived in the 1880s, Hyndman's programme was, quite consciously, an adaptation of the 'six points' of the Charter, with land nationalisation and home rule for Ireland as additional themes.

EARLY MODELS OF CO-OPERATION

Alongside the movements for political reform in the first half of the nineteenth century, a strong network of co-operative societies developed, with particularly strong roots in the Northern industrial towns. But the full history of these societies has yet to be written, and they have become overshadowed by the success of the 'Rochdale model' of co-operation which began in the mid-1840s.[23] The early co-operative societies often involved the same people that were active in the fight for political democracy and trades unionism, and were seen as revolutionary institutions, creating a new society within the bosom of the old. They were inspired by the mill owner and philanthropist Robert Owen, who set out a comprehensive vision of a future world in his *A New View of Society*, published in 1817. Owen's basic philosophy was that people were shaped by their surroundings. Give them healthy, educative surroundings and good working conditions, and you would create 'a happy and moral people'. He believed that by building communities founded on these principles the new society would be born. A remarkably wide range of people, including the Duke of Kent, became convinced by Owen's ideas. But Owenism was far from being a purely 'top down' movement inspired by the great and the good. Many working-class people decided to create their own co-operative societies, with modest initial goals but with a longer-term aim of creating socialist societies. In larger towns, Owenite 'halls of science' were established as centres for discussion, education and entertainment.[24]

G.J. Holyoake, one of the leaders of nineteenth-century co-operation, called the Owenites 'world makers'. Dozens of co-operative societies were formed across England, with a concentration in the industrial North, involved in retailing and manufacturing, but, as one delegate to the 1832 Co-operative Congress made clear, 'the grand ultimate object of all co-operative societies, whether engaged in trading, manufacturing, or agricultural pursuits, is community in land'.[25]

This set the tone of pre-Rochdale co-operation. It was very much a radical grass-roots movement, with the ultimate objective of creating a socialist society from the bottom up. Establishing socialist or communistic societies within the bosom of capitalism would ultimately lead to the transformation of all society. However, there was also a short-term advantage to be had from co-operation. Thousands of working-class families, especially in the expanding industrial towns, were being exploited by shopkeepers selling adulterated food at high prices. In the words of one co-operator, Dr King of Brighton, 'the wagon of joint shop-keeping is hitched to the star of a noble social ideal'.[26]

Sidney Pollard estimates that by the early 1830s at least five hundred co-operative shops had been established, and in 1834 the shops movement became part of a much bigger Owenite project, involving Robert Owen's visionary scheme to create a 'Grand National Moral Union of the Useful and Productive Classes'. This had some similarities to later syndicalist ideas (see Chapter 4), and envisaged unions of workers – initially in the building trade – taking over the running of their industries. Despite claiming a membership of 800,000, however, the Union collapsed by the end of the year, and many of the co-operative shops collapsed with it. In some cases, the trading co-operatives then transformed themselves into conventional joint-stock companies.

The energies of many of the 'ideological' Owenites went into establishing 'Halls of Science' in a large number of towns, as places of education and debate. One Owenite community that was established at Queenwood, in Hampshire, lasted until 1846. But as Pollard notes, the 'ignominious failure' of this project marked the end of the first phase of co-operation.[27]

However, a parallel attempt to create a co-operative community was the Chartist Land Scheme of the 1840s, inspired and led by O'Connor.[28] The idea was to buy a plot of land that would be held in common, with each individual family owing its own house and garden. The first community, established in Worcestershire, was named

'O'Connorville'. It had some initial success, but ultimately the colony disintegrated. The plots of land proved too small to support agriculture, and the new residents often had little experience of farming. The site is now an expensive housing estate.

The picture that emerges of Northern radicalism in the period that began with the Luddites and Peterloo, and ended with the decline of Chartism in the early 1850s, is of a remarkably diverse movement, which had the struggle for democracy at its centre. The early co-operative ventures, so strong in the Northern textile centres, were as much about creating self-sufficient and self-governing working-class communities as providing affordable and nutritious food. Chartism was more than a focus for working-class industrial grievances; it was a beacon for political reform that would enable working-class people to elect their own representatives in Parliament, who would legislate in their interests. Women as well as men played a full and active part in all the main radical movements of this period, with 'female political unions' formed in many towns and villages of the North around the time of Peterloo, and women also playing a prominent role in the Chartist movement.

NOTES

1. John Harland (ed.), *The Songs of the Wilsons*, 1865, pp25-6. The Stalybridge reference is in Samuel Hill, *Old Stalybridge Songs and their Singers*, 1906.
2. For Thomas Spence see Malcolm Chase, 'Paine, Spence, Chartism and "the Real Rights of Man"' (2008 Eric Paine Memorial Lecture), *The Journal of Radical History of the Thomas Paine Society*, 2008, volume 9, issue 3, pp1-14; also K. Armstrong (ed.), *The Hive of Liberty – The Life and Works of Thomas Spence 1750-1814*, 2010.
3. E.P. Thompson, *The Making of the English Working Class*, 1963. Thompson wrote most of the book while he was living in the West Riding and reflects this regional perspective.
4. See Jean and Peter Bond, *Tim Bobbin Lives! The Life and Times of a Lancashire Legend*, 1986, and permanent exhibition in Rochdale Public Library. The emergence of Lancashire dialect literature has been chronicled in Marta Vicinus, *The Industrial Muse*, 1974; and Paul Salveson, unpublished PhD, *Region, Class, Culture: Lancashire Dialect Literature 1746-1935*, University of Salford 1993.
5. Thompson, op. cit., p323; Roger Elbourne, *Music and Tradition in Early Industrial Lancashire 1780-1840*, 1980, gives a superb account of the hand-loom weavers' musical culture.

6. Alan Brooke, *Honley Socialist Club: popular socialism in a textile village 1891-1927*, 1992. Brooke quotes from a romance entitled 'Beaumont's Lad' published in the *Huddersfield Examiner* during 1883.

7. E.P. Thompson, op. cit., has much on the Luddites; and see also Brooke and Kipling, op. cit.; Bob Davies, *The Luddites of Westhoughton*, 1972, is strong on local detail of the Lancashire risings; and the Wagon and Horses pub in Westhoughton has some window panels depicting scenes from the attacks on the local mill. Frank Peel's *The Risings of the Luddites, Chartists and Plug-Drawers* (2nd ed. 1887) is an interesting Yorkshire based account. Alan Brooke and Lesley Kipling's *Liberty or death: Radicals, republicans and Luddites 1793-1823*, 1993, is an excellent account of radical movements in the Huddersfield/Kirklees area.

8. *Bowtun Loominary*, 29 January 1853.

9. Thompson, op. cit., pp325-6.

10. Ben Turner, *Dialect and other pieces from a Yorkshire Loom*, 1909, p41.

11. See Mick Jenkins, *The General Strike of 1842*, 1980.

12. Malcolm Chase, *Chartism: a new history*, 2007, p79.

13. See Stanley Harrison, *Poor Men's Guardians: a survey of the struggle for a democratic newspaper press 1763-1973*, 1974, for a good outline of the history of the radical press.

14. Harrison, op. cit., p83.

15. Ibid., p83.

16. Ibid., p119.

17. Ben Brierley, *Home Life and Recollections of a Life*, n.d. (c 1880), p23.

18. Chase, op. cit., p16.

19. Samuel Bamford, *Passages in the Life of a Radical*, Vol. 2, 1903 edition, p141.

20. Chase, op. cit., p41.

21. *Northern Star*, 12 November 1842.

22. See Royden Harrison, *Before the Socialists: Studies in Labour and Politics*, 1965.

23. See Sidney Pollard, 'From Community Building to Shopkeeping', in A. Briggs and J. Saville (ed.), *Essays in Labour History*, 1967.

24. Alan Brooke, *The Hall of Science: co-operation and socialism in Huddersfield 1830-1848*, 1993, has a valuable description of the Huddersfield 'Hall of Science', which is still standing.

25. Pollard, op. cit., pp77-8.

26. Ibid., p83.

27. Ibid., p88.

28. See Chase, op. cit., pp247-254, for an account of the scheme.

2. Between Chartism and Socialism

Chartism petered out as a mass movement after the great but ultimately ineffective demonstrations of 1848. In several towns of the North it was already in decline, after the heroic years of the late 1830s and early 1840s. The first phase of the Co-operative Movement was also at an end. Many northern towns had their venerated 'old Chartists', and even a few Owenites, some of whom lived to see the franchise extended to all men over thirty in 1884. These veterans remained active in local political activities as well as trades unions, though the heady days of mass meetings on Blackstone Edge had long since passed. Allen Clarke, in his novel *The Knobstick* (an old Lancashire word for 'blackleg'), describes an old Chartist, 'Joe Carklan', probably based on an historical figure called 'Radical Grimshaw' who was well known in Bolton political circles through to the 1880s. Here, as the storm clouds of the 1887 engineers' strike loom, Carklan is looking back to the 1840s: 'In them days men were full o'reform, and meant to alter every bad arrangement and right every wrong; but their enthusiasm deed away as soon as their ballies were full'.[1]

INHERITOR OF THE CHARTIST TRADITION: RADICAL LIBERALISM

Liberalism absorbed much of the energies of Chartism in the North (and co-operation took the rest). Thus, as we have seen, Tom Livsey, leader of the local Chartist movement in Rochdale, went on to become a key figure in the Liberal Party, in a classic example of the transition from Chartism to Liberalism that took place in the 1850s and 1860s.[2] But the radical flame that had originated in the Pennine weaving communities in the 1790s, inspired by Paine and the French Revolution, never completely died. It was ultimately to re-ignite in the socialist revival of the late 1880s, which was based on the principles of independence and free thought, and included a strong degree of individualism. For many years this flame was kept alight in the various movements which coalesced around the Liberal Party.

Liberalism and Co-operation were easy bedfellows, often sharing company with Methodism, particularly in the North-East and parts of Yorkshire and Lancashire. Both Lancashire and Yorkshire produced a Liberal political culture that retained strong radical elements, harking back to Chartism and Peterloo. This culture chimed well with the culture of working-class independence and 'respectability' that became particularly strong as the North's pre-eminence as the industrial heartland of the world became firmly established. Thus, in Cleveland, staunch Liberal Joseph Toyn was the driving force behind the local co-operative movement and leader of the Cleveland Miners Association.[3]

However, Liberalism was based on a social compromise. Many of its key figures were major employers in the Northern towns, and their interests were not always the same as their working-class, trade-unionised, fellow Liberals. In many Lancashire towns, particularly Blackburn and Oldham, large numbers of working men also voted Conservative, reflecting the appeal of a 'beer and Britannia' politics; and this working-class Toryism continued to resonate in many Lancashire towns throughout much of the twentieth century. To a degree the Labour Party adapted to this, rather than challenging it.[4]

Thomas Newbigging was one of Lancashire's most respected radical Liberals in the 1870s and 1880s (see opposite). In the North East, Joseph Cowen, MP for Newcastle between 1873 and 1886, bestrode Radical Liberalism like a colossus.

Although born into a wealthy family, and having inherited his father's parliamentary seat, Cowen felt most at home amongst the miners and keelmen of Newcastle, aping their dress and dialect.[5] He was a strong advocate of Irish Home Rule and co-operation, and chaired the 1883 Co-operative Congress when it was held in Newcastle. During his time as MP in the early 1870s, the *Newcastle Weekly Chronicle* serialised the autobiography of the great Chartist leader John Frost, and this helped to maintain memories of the movement, which then fed into the new socialism of the 1880s.

In Cleveland too there was a thriving radical culture, based around republican clubs and the ironstone miners' organisations. There was a strong Irish influence in the area, and a Fenian Club existed amongst

A GREAT NORTHERN LIBERAL: THOMAS NEWBIGGING

The Rossendale Valley has produced some remarkably talented writers and politicians, and none more so than Thomas Newbigging, in many ways the personification of the Northern radical Liberal tradition. One of Lancashire's most respected radical Liberals in the 1870s and 1880s, a fervent champion of Irish freedom and a strong democrat, Newbigging provides yet another link from Owenism through Liberalism towards socialism.

Of Scots Presbyterian origins, Newbigging was born in Glasgow in 1833. His parents had been brought up in New Lanark, Robert Owen's socialist community to the south of Glasgow, where they had met and married. They then settled in Glasgow in the early 1830s, when his father was appointed manager of a large cotton mill. After some years in Galloway the family moved to Lancashire in 1844.

At the age of twenty-three Newbigging was appointed manager of the Rossendale Union Gas Company, based in Bacup at the head of the Rossendale Valley. He went on to become one of Britain's leading gas engineers, spending some years in Brazil, and writing the standard text for the gas industry – *The Gas Manager's Handbook*, published in 1881.

But it was his extensive non-professional interests which mark Newbigging out as exceptional. He was author of *The History of the Forest of Rossendale*, a work which has yet to be surpassed for its detailed historical account of the area; and he was also a talented poet, strongly influenced by Burns. His *Poems and Songs* combine traces of both Lancashire and Scots vernacular. Like many middle-class intellectuals of his day, he was fascinated by dialect, and, with Henry Cunliffe, he wrote a *Glossary of Rochdale-cum-Rossendale Words and Phrases*. He was a member of the Manchester Literary Club and many other literary circles, and was a good friend of the famous Lancashire dialect poet Edwin Waugh.[i]

Newbigging's parental background seems to have instilled a strong social awareness in him from an early age. His politics were Liberal, but on its extreme radical edge. In 1886 he was adopted as the Liberal 'Home Rule' candidate for Rossendale, and six verbatim reports of his election speeches were published in 1887. Whilst not a great deal has been written about Newbigging, this collection of his political speeches includes the six from the 1886 contest and a further twelve from the rest of 1886 and from 1887. The election speeches were all made in Rossendale, but the subsequent ones were made in several locations across Lancashire and Yorkshire, including Salford, Manchester and Huddersfield.

The central theme of the election speeches is Ireland. Newbigging was a passionate believer in Irish freedom, seeing Home Rule as a stepping stone to complete national independence. He was a strong supporter and ally of fellow Rossendalian Michael Davitt (see below). At a speech at the Co-operative Hall in Rawtenstall, Newbigging spoke of the leader of the Irish Land League as having 'imbibed many of his ideas of freedom in breathing the air of the Rossendale Hills'. At a speech in Eccles he again returned to the Irish Question, observing that 'the history of Ireland and its connection with England, both before and since the Act of Union ... is indeed such as to make even a heart of stone bleed'.[ii]

In response to accusations that Davitt and other Irish radicals were 'demagogues and agitators' he cited the English radical tradition: 'We owe every shred of our English liberty to men who were called demagogues and agitators, and viler names than these ... the truth is we need more agitators'. He attacked Tory attempts to 'play the Orange card', and accused Randolph Churchill of 'opening wide the door of race and religious bigotry'.[iii]

Newbigging was passionate about religious equality, land reform, free education for all and strong local government. He was also an early advocate of devolution for Scotland, Wales and England, as well as Ireland, objecting to 'the unwieldy growth of London', which he saw as sapping talent from the rest of the country. His speech at Failsworth during the 1886 election campaign highlighted the dangerously centralised government in Britain:

> there is a magnetic force of attraction towards the governmental centre of the country. Talent, genius, the possessors of great wealth, the victims of poverty – all converge towards the central core of the nation's life; and when, as in the case of London, the growth becomes stupendous almost beyond conception, there is grave reason for apprehension.[iv]

i. For Waugh and the Manchester Literary Club, see Martha Vicinus, *Edwin Waugh: the ambiguities of self-help*, 1984.
ii. Thomas Newbigging, *Speeches and Addresses*, published in 1887, p71.
iii. *Speeches and Addresses*, p80.
iv. *Speeches and Addresses*, p223.

the miners. These groups affiliated to the International Working Men's Association, where they sided with the anarchist Bakunin against Marx.

The cross-class coalition which characterised Liberalism in many parts of the North began to show signs of stress by the 1880s, as independent working-class politics awoke from its slumbers. But it was a long time before it was fully eclipsed by the Labour Party. The Durham and South Yorkshire coalfields proved particularly strong Liberal territory, well into the twentieth century.

THE UNION MADE US STRONG

Although Chartism had all but disappeared by the early 1850s, many of the trades unions which had supported the Charter's 'six points' were on the ascendant. The North became the focus of the organised labour movement during this period. The industrial revolution centred to a large extent on Lancashire, Yorkshire and the North East, though South Wales, the Midlands and central Scotland were also of great importance. Strong unions emerged in textiles, mining, iron and steel-making, shipbuilding and – slightly later – the railways. The pattern of trade union development was immensely varied. The early miners' unions, concentrated particularly in Yorkshire and County Durham, had sporadic successes followed by annihilation. In textiles, early attempts at unionisation were strenuously resisted, though John Doherty's Grand National Consolidated Trade Union had a spectacular growth in the early 1830s – followed by rapid decline. During the 1840s some of the unions in Lancashire and Yorkshire played an active part in the Chartist Movement, though some of the more skilled workers' unions held aloof.

The pattern which emerged in Lancashire, Yorkshire and the North-East during the 1860s and 1870s was of unionisation of the more skilled sections of the cotton and woollen labour force: predominantly male and relatively well-paid. Alan Fowler and Terry Wyke's history of the Lancashire spinners' union is entitled *The Barefoot Aristocrats*, but the skilled and highly-paid 'minders' worked in their bare feet not out of poverty but because of the oily floors supporting the huge spinning mules.[6] These workers were proud of their craft and enjoyed a high degree of autonomy, employing their own assistant 'piecers'. None of this lent itself to radical politics; many were staunch Conservatives, as epitomised by James Mawdsley, who for many years was leader of the Lancashire cotton spinners.

The area-based miners' unions put down strong roots, and came together nationally in the Miners' Federation of Great Britain.[7] In textiles, both the spinners and then power-loom weavers developed strong organisations that were gradually recognised by the employers. But the apparent industrial harmony was periodically shattered by violent industrial unrest, such as the 1853 Preston Lock-Out and the near-insurrection in Blackburn in 1878, when a mill owner's house was burnt down.[8] The 1887 Bolton engineers' strike saw pitched battles with strike breakers, and soldiers were drafted in to help strike-breakers get to work. This is the story told, in fictional form, in Clarke's *The Knobstick*, which was published a few years after the strike. In mining areas there were also sporadic periods of serious unrest, particularly in the North East, where eviction of miners' families from their homes was common.

By the 1870s, trades councils had been formed in most of the major industrial centres of the North, thereby uniting the main trades unions in particular towns or cities. Manchester Trades Council was one of the first, formed in 1866, two years before the national Trades Union Congress. The Sheffield Association of Organised Trades had been formed as early as 1859, and became Sheffield Trades and Labour Council in 1871. Bradford's Trades Council was formed in 1872, and Newcastle's in 1873. They, and others like them, became powerful institutions in their own right – often, in later years, to the concern of the TUC, which saw them a potential threat to their own power.[9]

The prevailing impression of trades unionism in the North during the 1860s and 1870s is of an increasingly strong but highly localised movement. The textile unions were particularly local in character, reflecting the different wage rates in each of the major spinning and weaving centres. This highly decentralised structure would inevitably have an influence on Northern working-class politics as it emerged in the late 1880s, as seen in the jealously-guarded independence of local socialist organisations.

THE ROCHDALE MODEL OF CO-OPERATION: MUTUAL AID IN PRACTICE

The Co-operative movement soaked up some of the energies of working-class radicalism following the end of Chartism. Rochdale, some ten miles east of Manchester, seems an unlikely place for the start of a world movement which now has over 10 million adherents. Yet the twenty-seven men and one woman who formed the Rochdale Equitable Pioneers Society in 1844 – 'The Rochdale Pioneers' – started a movement which has spread to most countries around the world, and remains one of Britain's biggest retailers and most popular 'brands'.

Rochdale Co-op was different from what had gone before, in the great age of community-building of the 1820s and 1830s, but there were continuities. In Allen Clarke's 1918 novel *The Men Who Fought For Us*, he lists the twenty-eight original members that made up 'the pioneers'. They included men like James Standring, a weaver and socialist (i.e. Owenite), Joseph Smith, a clogger and socialist, and several Chartists, as well as 'Swedenborgians, Radicals, Communists, Rationalists, reformers, or, at least, changers, of all kinds':

> ... as miscellaneous an assortment of what the ordinary average person, who never dreams of looking over the sides of his rut, would call faddists, visionaries, and lunatics as ever gathered together, to discuss, in a small and shabby room, the best means of levering the earth towards the stars. Analysation (sic) of the pioneer group of co-operators shows that it was composed of eight Socialists, five Chartists, two Swedenborgians, one teetotaler, one woman, and eleven other men of reform tendencies. Half a dozen of these, including Ann Tweedale, had been members of the previous Rochdale Co-operative Society, deceased a year or two ... there had been a co-operative society formed on Owenite lines in 1830.[10]

Without the experience of earlier co-operative societies, it seems unlikely that the new departure of 1844 would have happened. Sidney Pollard, writing fifty years after Allen Clarke, notes the importance of the Owenite legacy in inspiring the Rochdale Pioneers: 'their Owenite background is not in doubt ... it emerges clearly from their famous "objects", enunciated at the outset ... the raising of capital in one pound shares, the establishment of a store, the building or purchasing of houses [and] the employment of unemployed members'. Pollard notes in particular the Pioneers' aim that:

> as soon as practicable, this society shall proceed to arrange the powers of production, distribution, education and government, or in

other words to establish a self-supporting home of united interests, or assist other societies in establishing such colonies.[11]

The key difference between the older societies and the Pioneers was their decision to pay dividends to members, after paying interest on capital. This represented a breach with Owenite collectivism, but proved a commercial success. It gave a very powerful inducement to working-class families to join the co-op, offering tangible financial benefits – the legendary 'divi'. A further break from tradition was removing restrictions on membership of the co-op. Anyone could join the Rochdale society.

One might almost argue that the Rochdale Pioneers hit on a successful business model almost by accident. They were clearly more revolutionaries than shopkeepers, but the tide of revolution in the North was beginning to ebb. As we have seen, the Chartist movement had its final fling in 1848, but many of its local organisations had already been in decline for some time.

The men – for Ann Tweedale was an isolated exception at first – were eventually propelled into building what became an immensely successful enterprise that spread across the country. T.W. Mercer, in his celebratory book *Towards the Co-operative Commonwealth*, published in 1936, said:

> If ever workers at the bottom of society resolved to make a gallant attempt to rise together to a much higher level of security and comfort the weavers who pioneered a new co-operative venture in Rochdale were the men! The co-operators had loftier objectives than just selling bread, fresh vegetables and clothing. They aspired to a fully co-operative society…[12]

However, identifying the Pioneers as 'workers at the bottom of society' should be treated with some caution. Most of them were part of a growing 'respectable working class'; and some had a disposable income, though very modest,. Co-operation in the second half of the nine-teenth century was able to develop as a great enterprise because there was a group of educated working men with the time and ability to devote to 'the co-op'. Such men are likely to have been involved in their trades union, the chapel and – increasingly probable in the 1850s and 1860s – the Liberal Party. Many, like Tom Livsey, had been Chartists or Owenites in earlier, more revolutionary, times.

FROM OWENISM TO MODERN SOCIALISM: WATTS, OWEN AND RAMSDEN BALMFORTH

The lives of Watts Balmforth and his sons Owen and Ramsden suggest that there is more continuity than historians have assumed between Owenism – a strong force in the Balmforths' native Huddersfield – and later developments.

Watts Balmforth was born in Huddersfield in 1826 and was sufficiently influenced by Owenite socialism to name his son after the great man. He was too young to have been involved in the Chartist movement, but by 1858 he was on the committee of the West Riding Secular Union.[i] His son Owen attended the Huddersfield Secular Sunday School, which was run by former Owenite David France. (Another pupil was Ben Turner (see p93), who went on to become a leader of the Yorkshire textile unions and a Labour Cabinet Minister.)

In 1873, when still in his teens, Owen Balmforth became secretary of Huddersfield and District Republican Clubs. It is likely that there was a very close relationship between the town's Republican and Secular Clubs, given that both owed their inspiration to Charles Bradlaugh, who visited Huddersfield frequently in the late 1870s and early 1880s. 'Secularism' can in many respects be seen as an embryonic socialist movement; they were certainly at the radical end of Liberalism, and some ultimately joined the socialist movement in the 1880s.

The Balmforth sons went separate ways. Owen remained a stalwart of the Huddersfield Industrial Co-operative Society, writing its 'Jubilee History' in 1910, but remained a Liberal. He was however a strong supporter of the 'new unionism' in the late 1880s and early 1890s, and caused controversy within the Co-operative Society when he proposed financial support for the Manningham Mills strikers in 1891. Ramsden joined the socialist movement, in 1891 speaking on behalf of 'Huddersfield Fabian Society' to local trades unionists, on 'The Religion of Socialism'. The same year saw Ramsden speaking to the Colne Valley Labour Union, a predecessor of the ILP, at Golcar; and he was present at the opening of the nearby Milnsbridge Socialist Club the following year. Ramsden was subsequently elected onto the Huddersfield School Board as a socialist, before becoming a Unitarian minister and emigrating to South Africa. Owen remained in Huddersfield, and became the elder statesman of the co-operative movement.

The lives of Watts and his two sons illustrate the complex continuities between Owenism and modern socialism. As Alan Brooke observed, 'through the bywaters of secularism, republicanism and co-operation the currents of Owenite thought had flowed, sometimes mingling, sometimes submerged to flow into the wellspring of twentieth century Socialism'.[ii]

i. Owen Balmforth, *Jubilee History of Huddersfield Industrial Co-operative Society*, 1910. Nearly every co-operative society published a 'jubilee history'. For example Oldham (1900), Darwen (1910), Pendleton (1910), Accrington (1910).

ii. Alan Brooke, *The Hall of Science: co-operation and socialism in Huddersfield 1830-1848*, 1993, p71.

Whilst the Chartist movement had placed great emphasis on education, with the establishment of Chartist reading rooms in larger towns, such plans were destined to be short-lived. It was the Co-operative movement that really put down deep roots and developed independent non-sectarian working-class education from the 1850s. Virtually every co-operative society had its own library and reading room. Some of the larger societies, such as Accrington, Sunderland, Halifax and Rochdale, would have a network of shops running into double figures. Classes were organised on a huge range of subjects, ranging from the classics to social history, usually with volunteer tutors.

The Rochdale model represented a break from previous co-operative societies, even though it was perhaps not immediately apparent. Perhaps the most obvious change was the opening up of society membership, though the individual 'divi' was a powerful appeal to working people's self-interest.[13] Before long, the Lancashire and Yorkshire textile towns had dozens of local shops, usually with one major store dominating the town centre but with many branches springing up in the outlying communities. In the North East the movement took off not only in the major cities and towns such as Newcastle and Sunderland but also in the pit villages of Durham and Northumberland. Many remain to this day, some still doing good business, though many have vanished or been converted to other uses.

By the 1870s 'the Co-op' was a mature business, controlled by its working-class membership. The directors of the local co-operative societies were largely working-class men, most likely the sons of the original 'Pioneers' of the 1840s and 1850s. They were certainly not revolutionaries. They tended to be drawn from 'the labour aristocracy' – the spinners, engineers and other highly unionised sectors of industry; their fathers may have been hand-loom weavers. This was the first generation of a skilled industrial working class that only knew factory life.

They were cautious with their members' money and suspicious of utopian schemes for 'home colonies' (see below). However, the co-operative societies did play an important role during major industrial disputes, when they would provide credit to strikes' families. Without this support many strikes would have collapsed, with strikers being driven back to work by sheer starvation.

CO-OPERATIVE EDUCATION AND CULTURE

Part of the 'respectable' working-class ethos was education, and many societies – Rochdale was one of the first – created well-stocked libraries, years before Andrew Carnegie's philanthropy and the advent of municipal libraries. Suitably uplifting works by Carlyle, Smiles, Ruskin and other Victorian icons were available to the studious working man and, on some occasions, woman.[14]

Working-class education has an immensely strong tradition in the North of England, rooted in the early days of co-operation, trades unionism and radicalism. Throughout much of the nineteenth century it evolved with little support from the state, based on mechanics' institutes, local co-op reading rooms and mutual improvement classes. The 'dame schools' were an important means of educating working-class children, though with uneven results. Allen Clarke went to a dame school in Bolton in the late 1860s and recalls 'the dame' doing her knitting for most of the school day. However, dame schools have perhaps been too easily condemned – the combination of being non-religious and run by women may have led to them getting an unjustly negative treatment from historians.

Even quite small towns could support substantial co-operative libraries. Thomas Newbigging, who was an active co-operator, spoke at a packed 'soiree' in the town's Co-operative Hall on 4 December 1886, chaired by the mayor. After noting that the society's turn-over had exceeded £100,000 in the previous year – a huge figure at that time – he turned his attention to more uplifting matters:

I am rejoiced to see ... that whilst providing food and clothing for the mortal body you do not neglect food for the mind – the immortal part. One of the grandest treats I have had today is the sight of your noble library, of close on 11,000 volumes, and your reading room is covered with all the leading newspapers, magazines and reviews ... Bacup and Rossendale have reason to be proud of this veritable temple of knowledge that has been reared in their midst.[15]

The co-operative movement encouraged arts groups, dramatic societies, choirs and orchestras. These all came together at the Co-operative Festival, held each year at the Crystal Palace between 1888 and 1905. The movement became part of working-class life in the North, from the cradle to the grave. It fed and clothed you, educated you, and buried you. Increasingly, towards the end of the nineteenth century, it may have employed you. Within the complex of Co-op buildings in Manchester there was a tobacco factory, and offices that employed hundreds of staff. The co-op had its own farms, dairies, bakeries and even coal mines. It never diversified into railways, though it did have a couple of coastal steamers. The CWS's 'Pioneer' brought the first seaborne cargo into Manchester through the Ship Canal in 1896. The Co-op also became involved in actual community building, with the creation of homes and factories forming 'industrial villages', such as that at Shilbottle in Northumberland.

The nineteenth-century co-operative movement, inspired by the Rochdale Pioneers, aimed not only to provide affordable, good quality food and clothing to its members, but to create an alternative society, based on 'home colonies' – or self-governing communities. In reality the Pioneers quietly shelved this objective and got on with the day job, but there remained – over many decades – a tiny but enthusiastic minority who wanted to establish 'heaven on earth' through such co-operative colonies. In a diluted form, the garden cities and villages of the early 1900s were based on similar attempts to create new, democratic communities.

WOMEN IN THE CO-OPERATIVE MOVEMENT

The decline of Chartism into a relatively small sect in the 1850s saw a proportionately larger reduction in women's political role, with most of the women's associations disappearing. Yet the fledgling Co-operative movement attracted strong female support. The 'Rochdale' approach was about providing good quality, affordable produce. As women were the main purchasers in working-class homes, 'the Co-op' had an obvious attraction.

Women as well as men had equal voting rights in the co-operative societies. And as we have seen, Allen Clarke's *The Men Who Fought For Us* highlights the importance of Ann Tweedale – 'solitary and glorious' – as one of the twenty-eight Rochdalians who formed the co-operative society in 1846. (Tweedale had already been involved in earlier attempts at co-operation and was a supporter of the Chartists.) Women did manage to inch their way into the Co-operative movement, but well into the 1890s and early 1900s the committees of Northern societies remained all male.

The Co-operative Women's Guild was formed in 1883, and became a formidable force in promoting co-operation as well as supporting women's suffrage in the early 1900s. It became a way into politics for many working-class women whose presence was not always welcomed at socialist or trades union meetings. Sarah Reddish of Bolton (see pp52-3) became a key figure in the Guild, not just in Lancashire but nationally.

THE INTERNATIONAL CAUSE

Northern working-class politics in the nineteenth century was far from being narrow and inward-looking. A strong tradition of internationalism grew up in the first half of the nineteenth century, in part inspired by the French revolution. E.P. Thompson has documented the huge influence of revolutionary France on the British radical movement. The works of Tom Paine, whose ideas had a direct influence on both the French and American revolutions, were widely disseminated across the industrial North. Numerous accounts of handloom weavers' culture refer to copies of Paine's *Age of Reason* and *Rights of Man* having pride of place on the living-room bookshelf.[16]

This internationalist political culture continued within Chartism, and especially in the 'year of revolution' in 1848. European revolutionaries such as Mazzini, Garibaldi and Kossuth were idolised by many Northern radicals. An interesting footnote to the history of West Riding socialism in the 1880s is the tendency for socialist parents to name their children after revolutionary heroes; hence 'Kossuth Pogson',

SARAH REDDISH: CO-OPERATOR, SOCIALIST AND SUFFRAGIST

It wasn't until after the First World War that women had the parliamentary vote. But some years before this women did win both the vote and the right to stand for election in many local councils. Reddish was a pioneer in winning political representation for women. She was elected to the School Board and as a Poor Law Guardian, and stood – though unsuccessfully – for Bolton town council in 1907. She also played an outstanding role in campaigning against child labour in the mills, and waged a one-woman battle to get improved child health care.

Reddish was born in Bolton in 1849 and left school at the age of 11 to work at home with her mother, a silk weaver.[i] Her father, Thomas, was librarian and secretary to the Bolton Co-operative Education Committee. Sarah later went on to work as a winder and reeler in the local mills, and eventually became a forewoman in a hosiery mill. In 1899 she was appointed part-time organiser of the Women's Trade Union League.

She was a popular public speaker, and travelled with the first women's 'Clarion Van' tour of 1896 (see p86). She also became secretary of the ILP's Bolton West ward branch, although she was in favour of unity with the SDF. An amalgamation of the two local branches did take place in Bolton, and 'Bolton Socialist Party' was formed in September 1898. It is still in existence at its home (since 1905) at 16 Wood Street. Reddish was a member of the Socialist Hall management committee.

Reddish founded the Bolton branch of the Co-op Women's Guild, and was its President for more than twenty years. In 1893 she was appointed organiser for the Northern area of the Guild, a post she held for two years. And she went on to play a leading role in the Women's Co-operative Guild nationally, being elected president in 1897. The official history of the Guild noted that her 'clear, logical and convincing speech came as a revelation of women's power'.[ii]

Reddish played a key role in the women's suffrage movement in Lancashire. In 1903 she, Selina Cooper, Esther Roper, Sarah Dickenson and Eva Gore-Booth formed the Lancashire and Cheshire Women Textile Workers Representation Committee. Two years later she was involved in a major demonstration of Lancashire women cotton workers in London. She was the first woman to be elected to Bolton Education Board in March 1900, and was later elected to the Poor Law Guardians. In 1907 she was also the first woman to stand for Bolton Council, representing women's organisations in the town. She polled a respectable 737 votes but was not elected.

Reddish organised a demonstration on the steps of Bolton Town Hall to protest against the money being spent on the coronation of Edward VII, suggesting the money would have been better spent on feeding the poor. And she organised the 'school for mothers' in Bolton, based on the successful example of a similar project in London, established by Dora Russell. The school was set up in 1908 using co-operative society premises and was a great success: and the model was copied both elsewhere in the town and further afield. She worked closely with Dr John Johnston, one of the local 'Whitmanites' as well as a prominent local doctor (see Chapter 4), and he addressed the first annual general meeting of the school, basing his talk on his book *The Realisation of the Child*. Reddish was also opposed to the First World War, and played an active part in the anti-war movement in Lancashire.

She died, at the age of 78, on 19 February 1928, and is buried at Heaton Cemetery. In 2008 Bolton's Clarion Cycling Club paid homage to her memory and left red flags at her grave. Mary Mullen, writing in *North West Labour History*, described her as:

> a very formidable woman who not only believed in the ideas of Socialism and the promise of a better life for the poor. She devoted her life to bringing about the changes that would help to bring about the ideas she believed in, especially for women and children ... her spirit lives on, the message she preached is as true today as it was in the early days of the twentieth century.[iii]

i. See Mary Mullen, 'Saving Infant Life in Bolton: Women Co-operators to the rescue', in *North West Labour History*, 2010.

ii. Catherine Webb, *The Woman With the Basket: the history of the Women's Co-operative Guild*, 1927, p57.

iii. Mullen, op. cit., p17.

who became a key figure in Colne Valley socialism in the 1890s, and 'William Tell Rushton', grandson of Halifax Chartist Benjamin Rushton.[17]

Ireland was a major touchstone for international solidarity in the nineteenth century, but there were many other issues which English democrats and socialists took to their hearts. In 1848 a huge meeting took place in Bradford's St George's Hall to greet the Hungarian patriot Kossuth, who was on a speaking tour of the country. Support for Hungarian independence, and for Garibaldi and Italian freedom, was particularly strong in the North.

Many socialists and radical Liberals made common cause on international issues in the 1880s and 1890s, including protests against the 'Bulgarian atrocities' (the brutal suppression of a series of uprisings in the Balkans by Turkey, whose Ottoman Empire then still ruled the region). The dialect writer David Taylor, born into a handloom-weaving family in Oldham in 1861, became a co-operator and active Liberal and Unitarian; and he celebrated the opposition of Oldham workers to the Turkish government, at a time when the British Tories were supporting the despotic regime:

> Aw'm gradely fain that Owdham folk
> Are on their feet again
> Contendin' for humanity,
> And liberty of men.
> Aw'm glad to yer them lift their voice
> To swell the leawd protest
> Against these horrid, cruel crimes
> That shook each human breast.[18]

HOME RULE FOR IRELAND

Ireland has been a touchstone of both international solidarity and anti-imperialism in the North of England, across two hundred years and more: the influence of Irish republicanism was strong in the North of England in the early 1800s. Wolfe Tone's rebellion was brutally suppressed following the series of uprisings in Ireland in 1798, but the United Irishmen's tradition of secularism, universal suffrage and national independence echoed throughout the nineteenth century, and linked into the Chartist movement. Many Northern towns and cities had large Irish communities which during different periods made common cause with English radicalism.

Allen Clarke was part of the large Irish community whose numbers had been swelled by emigration during the potato famine of the 1840s. His grandfather was a supporter of the United Irishmen and Robert Emmet, and Clarke and his father inherited some of that Irish revolutionary zeal. Clarke's father was a 'minder', one of the skilled and highly unionised cotton spinners. He took the young Clarke to see

'The Fenian Arch', a play that tells the story of the Manchester Martyrs, three Irishmen who were condemned to death after a policeman was shot – probably accidentally – during their attempt to free two of their Fenian comrades from the van that was escorting them to prison. Clarke commented: 'I should think my father sympathised with the Fenians – though perhaps not with their methods – as the natural outcome of an oppressed race. I know he used to denounce the tyran-nisation of England over Ireland'.[19]

'Home Rule for Ireland' became a key demand of Radical Liberals as well as socialists in the 1880s. Hyndman's SDF regarded Irish freedom as one of its most important aims, and strongly supported Gladstone's Home Rule proposals. As we have seen, Irish Home Rule was the main plank of Thomas Newbigging's Liberal election campaign for Rossendale in 1886. In speech after speech he returns to the iniqui-ties of British rule in Ireland, commenting that a reading of Irish history 'would make a heart of stone bleed'.

The story of Michael Davitt (see p56), honoured as national hero in Ireland but virtually forgotten in Britain, personifies the course of Irish radicalism in the North of England. Davitt was hugely popular in the North of England in his time, idolised by the Irish commu-nity but also widely respected amongst liberals and socialists alike. Thomas Newbigging described him as 'The Lord Nelson of the Irish Party'. Addressing a packed meeting in Davitt's home town of Haslingden, he said:

> You know Michael Davitt. He was reared in your midst, in this very town he grew from youth to manhood. I think he must have imbibed many of his ideas of freedom in breathing the air of the Rossendale hills ... He is a man of unblemished character, and his nobility of soul is ungrudgingly recognised both by friends and opponents.[20]

ANTI-SLAVERY

Perhaps the most legendary example of selfless support for an international cause was that of the Lancashire cotton workers for the anti-slavery cause during the American Civil War. A majority of the Lancashire cotton workers remained solidly in support of the Federal government in the North and emancipation of the slaves, despite the

MICHAEL DAVITT – IRISHMAN AND LANCASTRIAN

Michael Davitt's family were evicted from their cottage in County Mayo during the Irish famine. They moved to Haslingden, a small cotton weaving community in Rossendale, where they lived in the town's 'little Ireland'. Davitt went to work in a local mill at the age of nine but lost his arm in an industrial accident. He was then taken under the wing of the local postmaster, from whom he received the basis of an education.[i]

By the mid-1860s, the younger members of the Irish community were increasingly drawn to the Fenian movement and established secret local groups dedicated to achieving Irish freedom. Davitt became the leader of the Rossendale 'centre', and was soon appointed organiser for Scotland and the North of England. He became involved in arms smuggling activities, and when anti-Catholic mobs attacked St Mary's church in Haslingden in 1868, Davitt and a small group of fellow Fenians fired above the heads of the approaching mob, which then quickly dispersed. He was eventually apprehended and imprisoned.

When Davitt came out of jail he turned from the politics of Fenianism to popular mass struggle on a huge scale. His Irish Land League, which campaigned for the rights of Irish farmworkers and peasants, developed a successful policy of 'passive resistance' in their battles against mass evictions and savage repression, and this later directly inspired Gandhi.

The experience of prison had taken a disastrous toll on Davitt's health and he died in 1906. If forgotten by mainstream British politics, he is remembered by the Lancashire Irish community. In his home town of Haslingden a memorial has been erected which reads:

> This memorial ... marks the site of the home of Michael Davitt, Irish patriot, who resided in Haslingden from 1853 to 1867. He became a great world figure in the cause of freedom and raised his voice and pen on behalf of the oppressed, irrespective of race or creed, that serfdom be transformed to citizenship and that man be given the opportunity to display his God given talents for the betterment of mankind ... Erected by the Irish Democratic League Club, Haslingden (Davitt Branch).[ii]

i. See T.W. Moody, *Davitt and Irish Revolution*, 1984; John Dunleavy, *Davitt's Haslingden*, 2006.

ii. For remains of Davitt's heritage in Haslingden see Paul Salveson, *The People's Monuments: a guide to sites and memorials*, 1987; and Dunleavy, *Davitt's Haslingden*.

Northern blockade of the southern ports that was effectively destroying their livelihoods.[21] In towns like Bolton and Rochdale most of the mills closed during the 'cotton famine'; and tens of thousands of previously well-paid cotton workers were made destitute. William Billington, a working-class writer from Blackburn, used dialect to express the feelings of many workers yearning for the war to end:

> Some factory maisters tokes for t'Seawth
> Wi' a smooth an' oily tongue,
> But iv they'd sense they'd shut their meawth,
> Or sing another song;
> Let liberty not slavery
> Be fostered an' extended –
> Four million slaves mun yet be free,
> An' then t'war will be ended.[22]

Some historians have claimed that Lancashire workers' support for anti-slavery was a myth, and have quoted some of the labour movement press to justify their view. Perhaps the most careful assessment of the arguments has been made by Royden Harrison.[23] Harrison found that there was almost universal support for the Federal cause, and anti-slavery sentiment, amongst the cotton workers, particularly in Lancashire. In one incident that he describes, in Blackburn in 1861, local workers' leader Mortimer Grimshaw tried to get a mass meeting of cotton weavers to support a mediated settlement in America. When the secretary of the Weavers Association intervened and demanded a vote on this suggestion, it went against Grimshaw, with over 4000 hands raised against and a mere dozen in favour. In another incident in a town particularly hard hit by the cotton famine – Stalybridge – unemployed cotton workers passed a vote 'by an immense majority' stating that: 'In the opinion of this meeting, the distress prevailing in the manufacturing districts is mainly owing to the rebellion of the Southern States against the American constitution'.[24]

A sculpture by Jacob Epstein – 'Slave Hold' – is a monument to the cotton workers' support for emancipation, and is on display in Bolton Museum.

THE EMERGENCE OF REGIONAL IDENTITIES

The second half of the nineteenth century saw the emergence of what was, to all intents and purposes, a distinct regional cultural identity in the North – not as a 'Northern' identity per se, but as something that was more than purely local. Lancashire, Cumbria, Yorkshire, Tyneside and Cleveland – each saw the growth of interest in regional traditions. This new awareness had literary and historical elements, and also linked into Liberalism, co-operation and – sometimes – more radical politics. Thus, for example, Samuel Bamford was one of the earliest 'antiquaries' in Lancashire – though the bulk of interest in this field was among the educated middle class.

In the North East, the Newcastle Literary and Philosophical Society was founded as early as 1793, with a magnificent library that still thrives; and the society was associated with a number of advanced causes, including anti-slavery. Dozens of 'lit and phils' were formed in Northern towns and cities during the nineteenth century, most having a strong interest in local and regional culture. These appealed primarily to the liberal middle class. The Newcastle society had an annual subscription of one guinea – far beyond the reach of most workers.

In Cleveland, former Chartist George Tweddell wrote *The Bards and Authors of Cleveland and South Durham*. Tweddell was a supporter of the Cleveland Ironstone Miners' Union and also wrote *The People's History of Cleveland* in 1872. Andy Croft argues that Tweddell was trying to assert an alternative cultural narrative to the metropolitan literary culture of the universities. He quotes Tweddell as saying, 'I could name a local writer for every tick of my watch'.[25]

In Lancashire, working-class dialect writers such as Edwin Waugh and Ben Brierley rubbed shoulders with Manchester's Liberal middle class literati in the Manchester Literary Club. John Harland, a journalist on *The Manchester Guardian*, played a key role in the club and in 1875 produced, with T.T. Wilkinson, *Ballads and Songs of Lancashire* – dedicated to the Manchester Literary Club.

The Yorkshire Dialect Society was formed in 1897, and brought together academic historians and literary scholars such as Professor Joseph Wright and Fred Moorman with trade union activists and socialists such as Ben Turner. Wright straddled the class divide of late Victorian Yorkshire. He was born in Thackley near Bradford in 1855, seventh son of a navvy, and started work in a quarry at the age of six. Later he became a 'doffer' in

Salt's mills in Saltaire. He was unable to read a newspaper until he was fifteen, but went on to become a teacher, learning French, German and Latin, as well as maths and shorthand. He studied for a PhD at the University of Heidelberg on 'Qualitative and Quantitative Changes of the Indo-Germanic Vowel System in Greek'. He became Professor of Comparative Philology at the University of Oxford, but maintained close links with his native Yorkshire. His most important work was the six-volume *English Dialect Dictionary*, published between 1896 and 1905.

The interest in regional history and culture eventually outgrew the confines of the middle-class salons of Manchester, Leeds and Newcastle. By the 1880s working-class newspapers such as the *Cotton Factory Times* and *Yorkshire Factory Times* were publishing dialect poetry and prose, and carrying articles on local and regional history. This reached its apogee with Allen Clarke and his *Teddy Ashton's Northern Weekly*, published between 1896 and 1908, which combined dialect, socialism and regional history (see Chapter 4).

THE BREAK WITH LIBERALISM

By the 1880s there were considerable tensions in the alliance between the Liberals and the labour movement. Whilst some working men, such as Thomas Burt, the North-East miners' leader, were able to gain positions of political power, the door stayed firmly shut for most others. Many trade unionists began to realize that the people they were voting into parliament were the same people they were fighting against for better conditions in the workplace. Allen Clarke, influenced by his Irish nationalist and radical Liberal father, became a socialist in the early 1880s. He was equally critical of 'Tory' and 'Liberal' employers who stood for parliament. He wrote a poem called 'Our Master and MP' (see next page), which pokes fun at those who voted for the very people with whom, as trade unionists, they were battling for a living wage.

The most dramatic rupture between the labour movement and Liberalism came in Bradford, in the early 1890s. A ten-month strike at Manningham Mills, beginning in December 1890, polarised the city. The Liberal establishment – including employers, MPs, councillors and local press – united in their condemnation of the striking textile workers, whose wages had been cut by a one-third. On one occasion the militia violently dispersed the strikers and their supporters, after the Lord Mayor had read out the Riot Act.[27]

Our Master and MP

Longhead's our master
He's money, men and mills
His wheels whirl further faster
His fortune feeds and fills.
Longhead's a keen 'un
Sharp as the devil's claws
Long head's a mean 'un –
An he helps to make our laws

During a strike gigantic
Longhead, wrathful, hot
While with famine we were frantic
Said we all ought to be shot.
He vowed that if he had his way –
He's a nice old turk,
that he'd cure us all in this way
– he'd flog us back to work

Well, not many months after
He put up for MP
And there wasn't any laughter
In our borough of the free –
For he promised workmen glory
If the seat he did but win
And they swallowed all the story
And put the bugger in!

They made him legislator
Thought 'MP' at his name's end
Would turn a local hater
Into a London friend!
So, things settle in their sockets
And for better or for worse,
The man that picks our pockets
Is entrusted with our purse.[26]

A small group of socialists, notably Tom Maguire and Isabella Ford from Leeds, supported the strike and helped give it direction and secure international support. Though the strike was in the end defeated, many workers in Bradford drew the political conclusion that they needed a political party of their own. First they established a local party and, shortly afterwards, the national Independent Labour Party was born, in Bradford, in January 1893.[28]

It took many years before the alliance between Labour and Liberalism was to die completely – not until well after the First World War. But the struggles of the early 1890s, and particularly the Bradford strike, had sown the seed of an independent working-class party, which was to put down strong roots in the North of England. It was to grow in the soil of radical Liberalism and its traditions of free thought, communitarian loyalty and identity, individualism and sense of 'fair play'.

NOTES

1. Allen Clarke, *The Knobstick*, 1891, p173.
2. See Lahee, op. cit., for an account of his later political activities.
3. Andy Croft, *A Writer for Every Tick of My Watch: a History of Writing on Tees-side*, unpublished manuscript, 2011.
4. There is an extensive debate among historians about the strength of working-class conservatism in Lancashire. See Patrick Joyce, *Work, Society and Politics: the culture of the factory in late Victorian England*, 1980; and Martin Pugh, *Speak for England: a new history of the Labour Party*, 2011.
5. See Nigel Todd, *The Militant Democracy: Joseph Cowen and Victorian Radicalism*, 1991, for an account of a remarkable politician.
6. Alan Fowler and Terry Wyke, *The Barefoot Aristocrats*, 1987.
7. See Raymond Challinor, *The Lancashire and Cheshire Miners*, 1972.
8. H.I. Dutton and J.E. King, *Ten Per Cent and No Surrender: The Preston Lock-Out of 1853-4*, 1981; see also Fowler and Wyke, op. cit.
9. For two well-researched trades council histories see J. Mendelson (ed.), *Sheffield Trades and Labour Council 1858-1958*, 1958; and Mary Ashraf, *History of Bradford Trades Council*.
10. Clarke, *The Men Who Fought For Us*, op. cit., pp94-5.
11. Pollard, op. cit., p94.
12. T.W. Mercer, *Towards the Co-operative Commonwealth*, 1936, pp29-30.
13. See Pollard, op. cit.; and Peter Gurney and John Walton, *History of the Co-operative Movement*.
14. See Phil Gardner, *The Lost Elementary Schools of Victorian England*, 1984. Gardner argues that the 'dame schools' have had an unfairly bad press.
15. Newbigging, op. cit., pp255-6.

16. See, for example, Alan Brooke, *The Handloom Fancy Weavers 1820-1914*, 1993; and Bamford, *Walks in South Lancashire*, op. cit.

17. Cyril Pearce *Centenary History*, op. cit.

18. J.T. Taylor, *Stories and Poems*, 1928 (published posthumously), p368. David Lawton, *Webs from Fancy's Loom*, 1918, is another example of a Liberal co-operator from the Oldham area (Greenfield) who wrote extensively in dialect.

19. Allen Clarke, 'Amongst the Agitators', in *Teddy Ashton's Northern Weekly*, 3 June 1905.

20. Newbigging, op. cit., p24.

21. Allen Clarke's novel *Black Slaves and White*, published in serial form in *Teddy Ashton's Northern Weekly* during 1897 is a useful literary source. Clarke returned to the cotton famine in *The Cotton Panic*, again serialised in *Teddy Ashton's Northern Weekly*, in 1900/1, but never published in book form. Jimmy McGovern's play *King Cotton*, performed in Salford during 2010, was a creative interpretation of the relationship between Lancashire workers and black slaves during the American Civil War.

22. William Billington, 'Aw Wod This War Were Ended', in *Lancashire Songs With Other Poems and Sketches*, 1883, p27.

23. Harrison, op. cit.

24. Ibid, p66.

25. Croft, op. cit.

26. Allen Clarke probably wrote this around 1890. It was published in *Teddy Ashton's Lancashire Annual* in 1926.

27. See Keith Laybourn, 'The Trade Unions and the ILP: The Manningham Experience', in Jowitt and Taylor (eds.), *Bradford 1890-1914: The Cradle of the I.L.P.*, 1980.

28. David Clark, *Colne Valley: radicalism to socialism*, 1981, gives a thorough account of the emergence of the Colne Valley Labour Union. E.P. Thompson's 'Homage to Tom Maguire' (op. cit.) provides an overview of the growth of the socialist movement in the West Riding in this period.

3. The New Party in the North

At present the people of the North have not only ceased to possess their own country, they have ceased to know it. They never see England. They see only brick walls, chimneys, smoke, and cinder heaps ... they are strangers and aliens in their own land.

Robert Blatchford, 'The New Party in the North', 1895

The North was the birthplace of a specifically 'British' socialism as well as Co-operation. The Independent Labour Party was founded in Bradford in January 1893 and was preceded by the emergence of many grass-roots socialist groups in the industrial areas of Lancashire and Yorkshire during the 1880s and early 1890s. It was predated by the Social Democratic Federation, but the SDF was more patchy in its coverage of the North. As with Co-operation, the growth of socialism was a bottom-up thing – locally rooted and finding inspiration from thinkers such as Ruskin, Carlyle, Morris and Whitman, but little influenced by metropolitan socialists such as the Webbs.[1] It was conscious of its Chartist and Owenite inheritance, and built on the secularist and republican movements that followed the end of Chartism.

The growing dissatisfaction with the Liberal Party's treatment of capable working-class party activists – who were denied the opportunity to stand as candidates in favour of middle and upper class politicians – combined with economic depression to provide fertile ground for a new politics in the North. It began to emerge in the late 1880s and early 1890s, with the growth of small, localised, socialist groups. For example in Slaithwaite, a textile village four miles outside Huddersfield, the 'Colne Valley Labour Union' was formed in 1891 at a meeting in the Social Democratic Club, an informal social club in the cellar of a terraced house. The club itself had been in existence for some months already as an informal meeting place for local socialists

63

and trades unionists. Indeed grass-roots informal action often preceded the institutions in early socialist history.

The first national quasi-socialist organisation was the Democratic Federation, founded in 1881 as the brainchild of the eccentric London gent, cricketer and admirer of Marx, Henry Myers Hyndman, who became its de facto leader. It became the 'the Social Democratic Federation' in 1884. Hyndman's popularisation of Marx's ideas, *England's Ideal*, won a few converts for the Federation, and it developed a base in parts of London and Lancashire. Although Hyndman was an autocrat, he had difficulty controlling each branch, many of which trod their own path, particularly in some of the Lancashire mill towns. Burnley and North East Lancashire became a stronghold of the SDF, and Hyndman stood as parliamentary candidate there, gaining a respectable vote. Jeff Hill comments that by the early 1890s Burnley branch had become the most dynamic in the North West; Blackburn also had a strong organisation, and the SDF and won some local council seats.[2] What may have helped the SDF in North-East Lancashire was the relatively weak state of trade union organisation. In the spinning towns of the South East of the county, such as Bolton, Oldham and Rochdale, the cotton unions had a strong ideological hold and were often Conservative in their political inclinations.

By the late 1880s most towns in the North had some form of local socialist organisation, often but not always linked to the SDF. Nationally, the SDF's brand of socialism was arid and dogmatic; and Hyndman, a man of many contradictions, was anti-trade union. But this did not stop many local SDF activists playing a strong part in union campaigns.[3] In fact many radicalised young men and women joined but then left shortly afterwards in disillusionment. In 1886 William Morris and a few of his comrades decided they had had enough of the SDF and formed the Socialist League.[4] The SDF remained a small organisation, with perhaps less influence than it has been credited with – though the Leeds branch gave an important grounding in socialism to young working-class activists like Ben Turner and Tom Maguire. Branches were formed in Bradford, Manchester and a handful of other Northern towns. By the late 1880s other socialist groups were taking shape. In many towns and villages of the North 'labour unions' began to be formed, leading to the estab-lishment of the Independent Labour Party in 1893. In some towns

'Fabian Societies' were formed, but most owed little loyalty to the London Fabians and functioned as local debating groups.

Bolton had a thriving branch of the SDF from 1886, which dramatically increased in size following the 1887 engineers' strike. After the strike several 'labour' candidates were subsequently elected to Bolton Council, including the old Chartist James Kirkman, 'a fine old fellow, with a spirit full of zeal and fire for progress', and Robert Tootill, 'a powerful speaker, though at times carried to rashness by his own eloquence'.[5] The famous socialist agitator Tom Mann lived in Bolton in the late 1880s, working as an SDF propagandist but supplementing his meagre income from the party by running a tobacconist's shop. Mann played a leading role in the Lancashire executive, but according to Dona Torr's biography Mann had virtually no contact with the national 'centre', and little if any confidence in Hyndman's abilities as a leader.[6] Allen Clarke recalls Mann speaking on the town hall steps as well as singing at SDF socials in Bolton's Coffee Tavern. Clarke was himself recruited into the SDF by its dynamic Bolton secretary, Joe Shufflebotham, who ran his own shoe-making business in the town.[7] Shufflebotham was elected onto the School Board, and went on to play a high-profile role in local politics, demonstrating that many local SDF activists were not afraid of getting involved in 'reformist' politics. His autobiography *Something Attempted, Something Done* provides a fascinating glimpse into the potential of municipal socialism at the turn of the last century.[8] It was also Shufflebotham who chaired the first meeting of Bolton ILP, in May 1892. Robert Blatchford was the main speaker.

The SDF had only a limited impact in most Northern towns and cities. It was weak in Manchester, though it developed a strong base in neighbouring Salford. Its Lancashire stronghold was undoubtedly Burnley, which Hyndman cultivated for several years, despite disliking the place intensely.[9] The West Riding and the North East were largely deaf to the appeals of the SDF's form of socialism. In part this may have been due to the ILP having become well established by the early 1890s.

THE EMERGENCE OF SOCIALISM 'WITH A NORTHERN ACCENT' – THE ILP

The Independent Labour Party came into being well over a decade after Hyndman's organisation was formed. Its founding conference was held in Bradford in January 1893. Of the 115 delegates, nearly half, 49 in all, were from the West Riding, with a further large contingent from Lancashire.[10] By 1895, out of 305 ILP branches across the country, 102 were in Yorkshire and 73 were in Lancashire. Most of the activists attending the Bradford conference were delegates from local 'labour unions' and socialist societies.

Bradford was an appropriate and significant choice for the founding conference. One of the strongest early socialist organisations in the North was the Bradford Labour Union, formed in 1891 in the wake of Bradford's Manningham Mills strike a few months earlier (see previous chapter). The city was becoming the heart and soul of the socialist movement in England.

Within the next couple of years most towns in the Lancashire and West Riding 'textile belt' would have had some form of socialist organisation. The Independent Labour Party brought many of these diverse strands together.

The ILP was very different in shape and substance from the SDF, though the two co-operated at a local level in many Northern towns. Its socialism was primarily about values. Its leader, James Keir Hardie, rejected ideas of 'class struggle' and stressed the importance of 'community' and spirituality. His approach was shared by another dynamic young Scot of working-class origins, Ramsay Macdonald, who argued that 'The watchword of socialism is not class consciousness but community consciousness'.[11]

The politics of the ILP have been described as 'ethical socialism', with a much greater emphasis on socialist morality than the austere Marxism of the SDF. Many of its leaders, particularly Philip Snowden, who was brought up in the Yorkshire village of Cowling, and Scotsman John Bruce Glasier, adopted a quasi-religious style that was popular with working-class audiences used to the trappings of nonconformist religion.[12] The socialist movement of the 1880s and 1890s is often described as a quasi-religious movement, with mass meetings at which people suddenly converted to the cause. Though many socialists were secularists (see next chapter), Keir Hardie also shared this semi-religious view of socialism.

Keir Hardie's role in shaping the ILP was fundamental. As well as being its undisputed figurehead, he also edited and owned its newspaper *The Labour Leader*. Hardie was not a localist, however, and he saw the state, under the control of the populace, as ushering in a better

JOWETT OF BRADFORD

Many towns and cities have their pioneers who were elected to councils in the early years of the ILP. Perhaps the most outstanding of these was Fred Jowett of Bradford, who won a council seat standing for the 'Bradford Labour Union' in 1892, shortly before the ILP was formed.

Born in 1864, Jowett started work at the age of eight as a half-timer in the Bradford mills, as his mother had done before him. In 1886, he joined the Bradford Socialist League, though this organisation had only a short existence. The Bradford Labour Union was formed after the Manningham Mills Strike of 1891, during which Jowett was active in support of the strikers. He remained for many years an official of the Power Loom Overlookers' Union, ensuring a strong link between the trade union movement in the West Riding and the ILP after it was formed.[i] Jowett's parents were both co-operators and Liberals, and Jowett too was an active co-operator, holding senior positions in the Bradford Co-operative Society.

Jowett's contribution to local, regional and national politics was vast; he pioneered many important initiatives, including slum clearance and council housing. He was a strong advocate of municipal enterprise, one of his first projects being to establish a municipal milk supply to ensure working people got unadulterated milk. He worked closely with another pioneering socialist, Margaret McMillan, to introduce school meals into the city schools – and Bradford was the first local authority in the country to do so.

Jowett's main achievements were to build a solid base for Labour in local government and to use this foundation to make real and tangible changes. He was a very practical 'ethical socialist'. He was on Bradford Council for fifteen years, and led the creation of a strong socialist group of councillors, which eventually wrested power from the Liberals. He stood for parliament in Bradford West in 1900 and narrowly lost, probably because of his anti-war stance in the Boer war, which was then at its height. He was easily elected in 1906 however. Once again, in 1918, his anti-war principles cost him victory, but he was elected for Bradford East in 1922 for a two year period, during which time he served in Macdonald's first Labour cabinet, as Minister for Public Works. He was once again elected in 1929 and served until the rout of

1931, when Tories and Liberals combined to field a single candidate for the National government.

A wise and humane politician, Jowett went on to become the elder statesman of the ILP, serving on the National Administrative Council for several decades, with two spells as national chairman, and a brief period, from 1921-2, as chairman of the Labour Party. A symbol of the esteem in which the labour movement held Jowett was the naming of the new ILP assembly rooms in Bradford 'Jowett Hall'.

Jowett had a strong democratic 'instinct' and during his time as an MP (and cabinet minister) he developed ideas to give MPs greater control over civil service departments, based on his experience of the committee structures in local government. Like many socialists of his generation he was interested in Douglas's 'social credit' theories, which he saw as a way of undermining the power of the banks.

Jowett had been a friend of Philip Snowden, and his friendship survived even after 1931, when Snowden deserted Labour to join the National government. A further major challenge to Jowett's achievements came the following year, when the ILP voted to secede from the Labour Party. The fundamental issue was the Labour Party's standing orders, which tied all its MPs to vote with the party on every issue. Encouraged by Jowett, the ILP worked hard to come to a compromise agreement with the Labour Party, but to no avail.

Jowett embodied Bradford's tradition of non-conformity and dignified support for working men and women. J.B. Priestley said of him:

> if he was not a 'spectacular' figure then so much the worse for spectacular figures and the foolish crowds who applaud their antics! Lord send us more Jowetts! ... Was he a great man? Yes, I think he was a great man of a new kind, which history books have not caught up with yet.[ii]

i. Fenner Brockway, *Socialism Over Sixty Years: The Life of Jowett of Bradford*, 1946.
ii. JB Priestley, Preface to *Socialism Over Sixty Years*, p12.

world. Socialists could make significant gains at the local level by influencing, and ultimately controlling, local authorities, but the real political advances would come when Labour had a Commons majority. There was to be a long wait for this. In the meantime, the achievements of scores of ILP councillors at the municipal level were considerable – free school milk, improved sanitation, municipal lighting, council-run tramways, 'fair wages' clauses in council contracts and council housing. While the SDF, at least nationally, disdained 'palliatives', the ILP grassroots was busy improving the lives of thousands of working-class families.

THE LARGER SOCIALISM

The 1890s and 1900s were the heroic years of British socialism. A distinctive socialist culture, explored in more detail in the following chapter, developed in the North, and was particularly strong in the industrial heartlands of Lancashire and the West Riding, and the North East. Edward Carpenter, one of the leading figures in the Northern socialist movement, lectured on 'The Larger Socialism', which was more than an economic doctrine and formed a whole way of life, at both individual and collective levels. His hymn *England, Arise!* Became the anthem of the socialist movement (see Appendix 2).

This movement encompassed the ILP and the SDF branches, local socialist discussion groups (sometimes calling themselves 'Fabian Societies'), Clarion choirs, cycling and rambling clubs, and relatively short-lived but locally important organisations such as the Labour Church. Most if not all of these groups co-operated on local issues and attended each other's meetings, and many activists had shared membership. Many branches of the SDF co-operated with their ILP comrades, including in Salford, Accrington, Rochdale, Blackburn and Nelson. In Blackburn the ILP and SDF produced a joint newspaper, *The Blackburn Labour Journal*. In Rochdale, where the two organisations produced *Rochdale Labour News*, the 1900 general election was fought by Allen Clarke as the joint ILP-SDF candidate. In Bolton, the ILP and SDF merged in 1898 to form a single 'Bolton Socialist Party'. Relations between the ILP and SDF were less cordial in the West Riding, however, and here the ILP strongly opposed moves towards merger.

It was the ILP and its wider periphery that became the embodiment of 'Northern Socialism'; by the outbreak of the First World War it had sunk some deep roots in Northern towns and cities, and had marginalised the SDF and its successor the British Socialist Party in most (though not all) Northern towns and cities. It scored some stunning electoral victories in its initial years, though these were followed by temporary setbacks in the mid-1890s. It won control of Nelson Town Council in 1905, and established sizeable minorities on several major local authorities around the turn of the century, including Manchester and Bradford. Even in Northern towns well beyond 'the textile belt', such as Barrow-in-Furness, the ILP established a strong base with a wide range of political and cultural activities.[13]

Some of the biggest campaigns in the early years of the socialist movement were around 'public spaces' and freedom of speech. (These included the Winter Hill mass trespass of 1896, which is outlined in the next chapter.) One of the great battles of Northern socialism in the 1890s happened at a place called 'Boggart Ho' Clough'. (Boggarts are Lancashire 'hobgoblins' who love 'upsetting apple carts', literally and metaphorically, and there is a rich folklore about their playful tricks.) Legend had it that this particular part of North Manchester had its own resident boggart, who lived where any self-respecting boggart would choose – in a hole, and Boggart Ho' Clough had become a popular open space, owned by Manchester City Council and long used for public meetings. But in 1896 the Council banned an ILP meeting there. The ILP'ers, perhaps inspired by the resident boggart, went ahead with the meeting, and battles with the police followed. Some of the leaders were imprisoned, including the redoubtable Emmeline Pankhurst. In the end the city fathers realised they had bitten off more than they could chew; charges against the imprisoned socialists were dropped and they were released.[14]

Yorkshire boggarts may well have been at work in the Colne Valley during 1907, when Victor Grayson, an iconic figure for northern socialists, swept to victory at a parliamentary by-election on a programme of uncompromising socialism, and without the endorsement of the ILP leadership (see p75-6). This was one of the greatest victories in the history of northern socialism, and Grayson's campaign was supported not only by ILP'ers but also by suffragists, anarchists and even a few Liberals. In the textile villages of the Colne Valley, the memory of 'Our Victor' lasted well into the 1960s.[15]

The early years of the twentieth century saw both the ILP and Labour Party take off as a political force. Nowhere was the growth stronger than in the industrial areas of the North of England. The ILP was fighting on three fronts: to 'make socialists' as part of their desire to fundamentally change society; to win electoral support in key constituencies and wards; and to shift the trades unions from their traditional liberalism towards independent labour representation and socialism. This was no mean task, and the three did not always complement each other.

FORMATION OF THE LABOUR PARTY

By the end of the nineteenth century there was strong union backing in some industries, particularly the railways, for independent 'labour' representation. This eventually led to the formation of the Labour Party in 1900. It was originally called the Labour Representation Committee, but became 'The Labour Party' after the general election of 1906. The TUC Congress, meeting in Plymouth in 1899, had carried a resolution calling for the establishment of a 'party of Labour'; and it was Thomas Steels, a signalman on the Great Northern Railway and an ILP activist, who proposed the motion, which had been formulated by the Amalgamated Society of Railway Servants meeting at 'The Good Woman' pub in Doncaster:

> ... this congress, having regard to its decisions of former years, and with a view to securing a better representation of the interests of labour in the House of Commons, hereby instructs the Parliamentary Committee to invite the cooperation of all the cooperative, socialistic, trade union and other working class organisations to jointly cooperate on the lines mutually agreed upon, in convening a special congress of representatives from such of the above-named organisations as may be willing to take part to devise ways and means for securing the return of an increased number of Labour members in the next parliament.[16]

The resolution was adopted by 546,000 to 434,000 votes. The federal structure of the Labour Party, partly a result of the astute political brains of Ramsay Macdonald and Keir Hardie, but also reflecting the careful crafting of the motion by ASRS Doncaster activists, provided

MARGARET AND RACHEL MCMILLAN

Margaret McMillan was born in New York on 20 July 1860, but following her father's death she returned to Inverness with her mother and sister Rachel, with whom she was always very close. She became a socialist in Edinburgh after hearing a sermon by Christian Socialist John Glasse. She was also introduced to John Gilray, another recent convert to this religious group, and he gave Rachel copies of *Justice*, the SDF newspaper, and Peter Kropotkin's *Advice to the Young*. Rachel was impressed by what she read, and particularly liked the articles by William Morris and William Stead. During the following week she went with Gilray to several socialist meetings in Edinburgh, and when she arrived home in Inverness she wrote to a friend about her new beliefs: 'I think that, very soon, when these teachings and ideas are better known, people generally will declare themselves Socialists'.[i]

Rachel soon converted her sister Margaret to socialism too, and together they attended political meetings in London, where they met William Morris, Hyndman, Peter Kropotkin, William Stead and Ben Tillet. They also began contributing to the magazine *Christian Socialist*, and gave free evening lessons to working-class girls in London. In October 1889 Rachel and Margaret helped the workers during the famous London dock strike. They continued to be involved in spreading the socialist gospel, and in 1892 moved to Bradford, by then a hotbed of radicalism. Margaret commented in her *Life of Rachel McMillan* how comfortable they immediately felt amongst the Bradford socialists: 'They were a new order of people to us from the first. It seemed as though we had been looking for them all the years. And here they were! This was home! These were as kindred, not as friends only.'

Margaret was elected on to the School Board in 1894 as the ILP candidate, having previously worked with Dr James Kerr, Bradford's school medical officer, to carry out what was the first medical inspection of elementary school children in Britain, in 1892. Kerr and McMillan published a report on the medical problems that they found, and began a campaign to improve the health of children. Margaret campaigned for local authorities to install bathrooms, improve ventilation and supply free school meals. Like her Lancashire comrade Sarah Reddish, she campaigned against the half-time system in the mills. One of her greatest contributions was the open-air school movement, which she helped introduce into the UK. She wrote extensively on the schools and helped set up several across the North of England.

For the next few years the two sisters were based in Bradford, though they both toured the North, speaking at socialist meetings. They joined everything that was on offer: Fabian Society, Labour Church, SDF and the newly established ILP. Fred Jowett was particularly fond of Margaret, describing her as 'an eloquent and attractive speaker in great demand not only for Bradford meetings, but for meetings in other towns'.[ii] Rachel now returned to London to earn a salary that would pay for both sisters' living expenses: all of Margaret's socialist campaigning was unpaid.

After Margaret McMillan was elected to the Bradford School Board she worked closely with Fred Jowett and was now able to exert direct influence over what went on in Bradford schools. She also wrote several books and pamphlets on the subject, including *Child Labour and the Half Time System* (1896) and *Early Childhood* (1900). This combination of theory and practice led Fenner Brockway to refer to Margaret as 'almost the perfect harmony of idealist and practical reformer'.

In 1902 Margaret left Bradford to join Rachel in London. The sisters joined the recently formed Labour Party, and worked closely with Keir Hardie and George Lansbury. Margaret continued to write books on health and education. In 1904 she published her most important book, *Education Through the Imagination* (1904), and she followed this with *The Economic Aspects of Child Labour and Education* (1905). The sisters were good friends of Louise Michel, the former Paris Communard, who was exiled in London.

The sisters also joined with their old friend Katharine Bruce Glasier to lead the campaign for school meals, and eventually the House of Commons was persuaded that hungry children could not learn, and passed the 1906 Provision of School Meals Act. The legislation accepted the argument put forward by the McMillan sisters, that if the state insisted on compulsory education it should take responsibility for the proper nourishment of school children.

In 1908 Margaret and Rachel McMillan opened the country's first school clinic in Bow. This was followed by the Deptford Clinic in 1910, which served a number of schools in the area. The clinic provided dental help, surgical aid and lessons in breathing and posture. The sisters also established a Night Camp, where slum children could wash and wear clean nightclothes. In 1911 Margaret McMillan published *The Child and the State*, in which she criticised the tendency of schools in working-class areas to concentrate on preparing children for unskilled and monotonous jobs. She argued that schools should instead be offering a broad and humane education.

In 1914 the sisters started an Open-Air Nursery School & Training Centre in Peckham. Within a few weeks there were thirty children at the school ranging in age from eighteen months to seven years. Rachel, who was mainly responsible for the kindergarten, proudly pointed out that in the first six months there was only one case of illness, and, because of the precautions that she took, this case of measles did not spread to the other children.

Rachel McMillan died on 25 March 1917, a devastating blow to her devoted sister.

In her later years Margaret became interested in the subject of nursing, and with the financial help of Lloyds of London she established a new college to train nurses and teachers. Named after her sister, the Rachel McMillan College was opened in Deptford on 8 May 1930.

Margaret died on 29 March 1931. Fred Jowett wrote in 1938 that he wished there was something 'to show that Bradford recognised and honoured her service'.[iii] There now is – and what better memorial than a school named in her memory. The Margaret McMillan Primary School in Bradford celebrates her contribution on its website:

> Margaret McMillan is well known as a reformer for the care and education of children. She realised through her work that many children were unable to concentrate at school because they were tired and hungry. Her first campaign was to make sure that children were clean and changed their clothes. The first school baths were opened in Bradford in 1897. With her sister, she also set up clinics so that children had regular medical inspections at school. Margaret's main aim was to persuade the government to provide food for children at school. In 1906 an Education Act was passed to provide school meals. The first school canteen was opened at Green Lane School and was for all children in the area. Breakfast was oatmeal porridge and bread and dripping; lunch would be stew and pudding and in the afternoon they had tea and some bread. We are lucky to have our school named after such an important person in the history of children's care and education and try hard to live up to her memory through our work in school.

The Margaret McMillan College of Education opened in 1952 and in addition the city has a Margaret McMillan Community Education Centre.

i. Margaret McMillan, *The Life of Rachel McMillan*, 1927, quoted in Fenner Brockway's *Socialism Over Sixty Years: The Life of Jowett of Bradford*, p61.
ii. Quoted in *Socialism Over Sixty Years*, p61.
iii. *Bradford ILP News*, 3 June 1938.

'OUR VICTOR' – SOCIALISM SWEEPS THE COLNE VALLEY

The first few years of the twentieth century saw a growing number of Labour MPs, particularly after the 1906 general election. However, this by and large did not have the effect of inspiring socialist advance. The performance of most Labour MPs in the Commons was weak, and the Labour Party had an informal 'arrangement' with the Liberals, which included an agreement not to contest winnable Liberal seats. But the Colne Valley Labour Party drove a coach and horses through this deal when they decided to contest a parliamentary by-election in 1907. Against the wishes of Hardie and the ILP executive, they chose as their candidate a young socialist firebrand called Victor Grayson.[i]

Grayson was brought up in Liverpool, in a 'respectable' working-class family. He trained to become a Unitarian minister in Manchester, but was bitten by the socialist 'bug' and left the college to become a socialist propagandist. He was a commanding speaker and by all accounts a handsome chap – he 'cut a dash', and was popular with women. He was in demand as a speaker throughout the North of England, and became a regular visitor to Huddersfield and the Colne Valley.

The opportunity to 'turn the world upside down' arose when the sitting Liberal MP for Colne Valley, James Kitson, was elevated to the peerage. Grayson was then selected to fight the seat, on an 'undiluted' socialist platform, despite the misgivings of Hardie and Philip Snowden. The campaign soon took on the characteristics of a religious crusade, as socialists and feminists flocked to the Colne Valley to help in Grayson's campaign. On the morning of the election result, Mrs Pankhurst and her daughters were seen in the streets of Slaithwaite, rubbing shoulders with anarcho-syndicalists like Fred Bower, who had travelled over from Liverpool to help. The Liberals had assumed they would walk the election. But when the announcement of the result was made – by showing a tiny red flag from an upper window of the town hall – the crowd outside became delirious. Grayson had won, with a majority of 153. His speech, from outside The Dartmouth Arms, pulled no punches:

> ... this epoch-making victory has been won for pure revolutionary socialism. We have not trimmed our sails to get a half-hearted vote. We have proclaimed our socialism on every platform ... I have been returned through the work, devotion, the love, the idealism of the people of the Colne Valley and being returned I shall feel that my

duty is to be the old men and women's member, the young men and women's member, the starving child's member, the one who will stand above all things for human legislation first ... You have voted, you have worked for socialism. We stand for equality, human equality, sexual equality – for the abolition of the sex ties ... It is a splendid victory, comrades.[ii]

Grayson was isolated within parliament, but he used his position to campaign for 'socialist unity' between the ILP, SDF and the Clarion movement. He remained a popular speaker at local ILP branches – despite a ban by the ILP Executive. To make a living he wrote for several socialist newspapers, including Blatchford's *Clarion*; and he also contributed a regular feature for *The Woman Worker*, which was for a while edited by Ethel Carnie (and owned by Blatchford).

Yet somehow the momentum of the 1907 victory was lost, and Grayson was defeated in the 1910 general election. From then on his career went into decline, and he finally disappeared in mysterious circumstances in 1920. But the Colne Valley didn't forget 'Our Victor', and his photograph still hangs in Marsden Socialist Club, at the head of the valley. In 1941 the Colne Valley Labour Party celebrated its Silver Jubilee. Let them have the final word:

With all his faults, he brought hope to the hearts of thousands of men and women and did as much as any to plant the cause of socialism securely in the Colne Valley. It is this knowledge that still keeps his memory green and the gratitude of those who followed him undimmed.[iii]

i. See David Clark, *Victor Grayson, Labour's Lost Leader*, 1985, for the machinations around his selection.
ii *Victor Grayson, Labour's Lost Leader*, p41.
iii. *Colne Valley Labour Party Jubilee Souvenir*, 1941.

a comfortable home for both Liberal-inclined trades unionists and the socialist activists of the ILP – which immediately affiliated to the new party. And once again it was the North which dominated the new organisation.

The Labour leadership agreed a pact with Gladstone's Liberal Party that ensured that many candidates would get a free run against the Conservatives in the 1906 general election. The LRC ran fifty candidates, thirty of whom were in constituencies in the North of England. A total of thirty Labour representatives were elected, whilst the Liberals won a staggering 397 seats. The Labour successes brought a strong influx of working-class men into parliament. A total of twenty-three of the new MPs were active trades unionists, and eighteen described themselves as 'socialists'. There was still a lot of common ground between Labour and radical Liberalism. On issues like municipal reform, Home Rule for Ireland, pensions, 'fair wages' and even state ownership, they shared much in common.

MUNICIPAL SOCIALISM

Most political histories tend to focus on the national scene and parliamentary elections, often ignoring the huge importance of local government politics. And it was at the local level that socialists, particularly in the ILP, began to make a difference in the early 1900s, though their real achievements became more obvious in the inter-war years – in housing; sanitation; public transport; public health; and education.

Local politics before the First World War were often riddled with petty corruption and favouritism; and many of the smaller northern towns had only limited forms of local government, in the form of school boards, and 'local boards of guardians' who administered poor relief. Towards the end of the century, however, the pace of incorporation – by which towns formed their own councils, or 'corporations' – accelerated, and this provided great opportunities for the rapidly growing socialist movement.

The Independent Labour Party began making headway in local elections, and opportunities opened up to improve local government accountability, with an emphasis on extending municipal ownership to major utilities such as gas and water, and taking over ownership of tramways. 'Fair wages' for council work was another major plank in the reform manifesto. It was perhaps not as exciting as revolutionary action; but the work of often quite small councils such as Nelson and Farnworth could transform local communities. This was practical local socialism.

Many other towns had their 'Jowett' – outstanding individuals who played a leading role in local government. Farnworth, a small urban district near Bolton, had a powerful leader during the inter-war years by the name of John Wilcockson, a Church of England vicar and scourge of the Communists, whom he saw as being 'fake lefts'. He once told them, 'I am the dictatorship of the proletariat – not you!'.[17] Perhaps Wilcockson lacked an inclusive style of politics, but he certainly got Farnworth people hundreds of good council houses, as well as a magnificent library and town hall.

Nelson Council became the first Lancashire local authority to be Labour-controlled, in 1905. The influence of the Weavers' Union was particularly strong in this part of North East Lancashire, and the union had thrown its weight behind the ILP campaign to capture the council. Nelson remained a progressive Labour-controlled council throughout the inter-war years. St Helens Council became Labour-controlled shortly after Nelson, whilst Barrow's Poor Law Guardians had a Labour majority from 1904. On the other hand, Oldham elected its first single Labour councillor as late as 1910, and he remained a lone voice until 1914, reflecting the strength of both the Conservative and Liberal working-class traditions in the town. Manchester City Council had fifteen Labour councillors by 1901, mostly ILP members. Liverpool was more difficult territory, and had only two Labour councillors before 1911, but in the aftermath of the violent 1911 transport strike several more Labour men were elected.

After the First World War Labour gradually broke the vice-like grip of Liberalism in many towns in the North East. However it was Gateshead rather than Newcastle that was to become the largest bastion of municipal socialism in the North East. It was the attitude of the Durham Miners' Association that was crucial in turning working-class opinion towards Labour. In 1919, Labour took control of Durham County Council, a crucial breakthrough for the party in the North East, and it also won power in Bradford City Council.

Both the SDF and the ILP contested local elections. Initially these were for the school boards and local boards of guardians. As we have seen, Bolton SDF organiser Joe Shufflebotham served on the local school board for many years (see p65.

It was not unusual for radical Liberals to co-operate with socialists in the cause of municipal reform. Allen Clarke was strongly influenced by Solomon Partington, the radical Bolton journalist who played a key role in the 1896 Winter Hill mass trespass. Partington was a Liberal, but became increasingly sympathetic to the ILP cause. The two friends were closely involved in producing the monthly *Municipal Reformer*, which was printed and published in Bolton. The inspiration for this came initially from the socialist and Unitarian Reverend H. Bodell Smith, another friend of Clarke's, who lived in Blackpool. In 1898 Bodell Smith established a Municipal Reform Society and the newspaper was established shortly after, with Bodell Smith as editor and Clarke a contributor. The *Municipal Reformer* developed a national circulation and carried features on a wide range of local political issues. Several local 'municipal reform associations' were established, including one in Bolton. However, the paper was not a great commercial success, and after four years was handed over to the northern branch of the Land Nationalisation Society. Nevertheless, the impetus for municipal reform developed a new momentum in 1904, when a major national conference in Manchester attracted several hundred delegates and established the Local Government Reform League, with Bodell Smith as secretary.

Bolton's Municipal Reform Society appears to have flourished in the mid-1900s following Partington's election. Partington became president of the society and played an active part in its activities. During 1905 it advertised a series of lectures on 'Citizenship and Town Council Work', with speakers including Sarah Reddish on 'Women and Citizenship' and Partington himself on 'Rights of Way'.[18]

Bolton was not on its own in this. Neighbouring towns such as Oldham had strong civic associations – though the town council remained impervious to Labour's challenge until after the First World War. It was Manchester, as we shall see in the next chapter, which was furthest ahead in translating into reality people's aspirations about the kinds of communities that they wanted to live in.

Many towns and cities had grown up rapidly, and suffered from pollution, poor sanitation and consequent ill health. Workers' housing was in general thrown up, mostly very cheaply, with little thought to even basic amenities. The infrastructure of Northern towns and cities simply could not cope with the demands being placed upon them, and by the late nineteenth century there was awareness amongst many socialists that something must be done to improve the basic fabric of towns and cities. Town planning was a key response, and this became part of the radical municipal socialism of the ILP, emerging from the work of planners such Raymond Unwin and Ebenezer Howard. Tow planning was also influenced by Whitman, Edward Carpenter and Patrick Geddes. Carpenter in particular wrote some pioneering essays on themes such as 'Beauty in Civic Life', which have much to tell us today.

'ENGLAND ARISE!' – THE LARGER SOCIALISM OF EDWARD CARPENTER

Carpenter was hugely popular as a platform speaker and writer, from the early 1890s through to the First World War and after. Although he was born in Brighton, into a well-to-do family, and died in Guildford, he spent much of his life in Sheffield, touring the North of England night after night to give lectures on 'Love's Coming of Age', 'The Larger Socialism', 'Beauty in Civic Life' and – wonderful title – 'Civilisation: its cause and cure'. The North is totally justified in claiming him as our own.

Carpenter was not a party animal. Although a member of the Sheffield Socialist League for a short time, he preferred to advocate a 'larger socialism' that could include membership of any socialist party – or none. He had an unusual lifestyle. He lived with his lover, George Merrill, on a farm at Dore, near Sheffield, and made a living through lecturing, selling his books and making sandals. He was a mystic and a poet, and made – none-too-successful – attempts to become 'the English Whitman'. He did not fit with the ascetic, earnest working class nonconformism of Hardie, or the serious intellectualism of Bruce Glasier. And he and Sidney Webb were on different planets. It is no wonder that he fell into obscurity after the First World War. His politics did not fit with Labour or Communist orthodoxy, and were, if anything, closer to the non-violent anarchism of Kropotkin. He was our greatest libertarian socialist, and it is wonderful that Sheila Rowbotham has restored his reputation through her superb biography, published in 2009.[i]

Sheila Rowbotham sums up the breadth of Carpenter's appeal.

> A host of working class and lower middle class socialists – especially in the North of England ... respected the commitment that led Carpenter to tour the country addressing meetings in shabby halls, and loyally came to hear him holding forth on small-holdings, allotments, pollution, anti-vaccination, the conditions of work, non-governmental society, sex, science and eastern religion. Razor-grinders, labourers, engineers, quarry-men, gardeners, clerks and school teachers tucked his books into their pockets and walked out into the countryside to dream of better days (p306).

It's difficult to pin down a distinct model of socialism in Carpenter's work, but what is very clear is that he distrusted statist models. His writings on 'non-governmental society' stress the potential of voluntary co-operation, building on existing models of 'mutual aid' such as he had found in the modern co-operative movement. Sheila Rowbotham highlights the subtlety of Carpenter's politics, which included a recognition that some degree of state ownership was desirable:

> Carpenter accepted that land should be publicly owned, both nationally and by local authorities. He wanted state ownership to be combined with co-operative ventures and private small-holdings. This was partly because of his dislike of state intervention and also because he was convinced, like Kropotkin, that small-holdings encouraged enterprise, attention to detail and all-round skills (p317).

Rowbotham brings out so many of Carpenter's ideas which have a twenty-first century ring to them. He advocated 'community pubs' serving organic fruit juice and beer. He espoused a vegetarian diet and was a strong supporter of animal welfare. He proposed publicly-owned swimming pools and running tracks accessible to everyone. One of his greatest passions was the emancipation of women; he wrote and spoke on 'the subjugation of women' throughout his political life. One of his most popular books was *Love's Coming of Age*, in which he argued for a radical change from the hypocritical sexual morals of Victorian middle-class men. Carpenter made little secret of his homosexuality, but surprisingly few problems arose from this openness. Being part of the Victorian upper class must have helped – though it didn't do Oscar Wilde much good. Carpenter's main antagonist was a local bigot who tried to have him prosecuted, but he was unsuccessful in this endeavour.

Carpenter was a great admirer of Walt Whitman and was on close terms with the Bolton Whitmanites (see below). He was a regular visitor to the annual 'Whitman Day' celebrations in Bolton, and shared the Bolton group's fascination with Eastern religion and the importance of spirituality to the socialist movement.

By 1910 he had packaged his varied ideas about the future society into the concept of 'the Larger Socialism'. Sheila Rowbotham quotes him as saying that socialism must make all aspects of life 'sacred and beautiful', bringing 'loving companionship and mutual helpfulness' (p315). It must 'clear our skies and purify our streams, and secure for us great tracts of public land in which the life of the people may develop. It must teach us to sing once more at our work, and to rejoice in it; to make our workshops healthful and bright, and cheery'. During 1910 he spoke on 'The Larger Socialism' in several towns and cities across England – but note how many are in the North: Chesterfield, Sheffield, Liverpool, Bristol, Manchester, Stockport, Blackburn and Glasgow.

His poem 'England Arise' (reproduced in full as Appendix 2) became the anthem of the socialist movement:

> England arise! The long long night is over,
> Faint in the east behold the dawn appear;
> Out of your evil dream of toil and sorrow
> Arise, O England, for the day is here.
> From your fields and hills
> Hark! The answer swells
> Arise O England for the day is here.[ii]

The anthem retained its popularity through the 1920s and 1930s, and it enjoyed a revival following the 1945 Labour election victory. But it has now sunk back into obscurity, which is a shame – it is a far better tune than 'The Red Flag'. And it's interesting to note that it is 'England' – not 'Britain' – that is called on to arise. Carpenter was very much an Englishman, southern English by upbringing, northern English by adult choice.

Although Carpenter did not join the ILP – which would have been closest to his kind of ethical socialism – he was on good terms with many of its members, at leadership as well as local level. He was also on good terms with syndicalists such as Tom Mann, and supported workers' control of industry. On one occasion he was invited by the Sheffield railway workers to speak at a rally that attracted 3000 of their members.

One of the very special things about Carpenter's radicalism was his way of making links between the now and the future. He saw community allotments, small-scale co-operatives – even parish councils – as harbingers of a future non-governmental society. He saw workers' control as a gradual movement by which workers would encroach on the power of capital over decades. He was willing to get his hands dirty – literally, on his smallholding at Millthorpe. He stood for election to the local parish council. He was a truly amazing figure, and so much of what he had to say resonates with us in the twenty-first century, in a way that the writings of the Webbs, even Hardie, simply don't. But his song has yet to be clearly heard.

i. Sheila Rowbotham, *Edward Carpenter – a life of liberty and love*, 2008. Her earlier work, *Socialism and the New Life: the personal and sexual politics of Edward Carpenter and Havelock Ellis*, 1977, gives a good summary of Carpenter's philosophy.
ii. 'England Arise' was printed in countless Labour Church and Socialist Sunday School song books, and the text and music is available online. For the full lyrics see Appendix 2. See also *The Labour Church Hymn Book*, 3rd edition, 1915, p9.

KATHARINE BRUCE GLASIER

In 1889, when Katharine St John Conway (later Bruce Glasier), a clergymen's daughter from Dorset, was a young teacher in Bristol, the city's active Socialist Society helped organise a series of strikes by low-paid women workers, and to highlight their cause the strikers organised a series of 'visits' to Bristol churches that were attended by the middle and upper classes. The sight of dozens of young cotton workers filing into the fashionable All Saints Church, soaking wet after a heavy downpour, gave Katharine her Damascene conversion. The following morning she presented herself at the headquarters of Bristol Socialist Society. She was given a copy of Carpenter's *England's Ideal*. Reading him:

> awoke a new power of love and worship within me ... It was as if in that smoke-laden room a great window had been flung open wide and the vision of a new world had been shown to me: of the earth reborn to beauty and joy, the home, to use Edward Carpenter's own words 'of a free people, proud in the mastery of their own lives'...as I went back to my lodgings I vaguely realized that every value life had previously held for me had been changed by some mysterious spiritual alchemy.[i]

In the next few years she delivered lectures on socialism across the North, including one at Manchester Labour Church on 'Socialism – the Light of the World'. She was undoubtedly an inspirational speaker. Hannah Mitchell (see p130) was just one of the young working-class women who signed up for the socialist cause after hearing her speak.

Bruce Glasier was actively involved in preparations for the founding conference of the ILP in January 1893, writing that the new party, 'a child of the spirit of Liberty' ...

> claims every song that she has sung – in whatever land – as a glorious heritage. Life, love, liberty and labour make liquid music. The Labour Party is in league with life, and works for liberty that man may live.
> ... The smoke that robs even Spring of her vivid power, the foul pollutions that make our rivers sources of danger rather than delight, the hideous hoardings that deface our few green fields and lanes, these each blaspheme against our faith.[ii]

As Thompson comments, it was the combination of the 'breathless idealism' of people like Katharine with the 'sturdy trade union boots' of its working-class members that gave the ILP its uniqueness. Katharine was courted by a rising star of the ILP, the earnest young Scot John Bruce Glasier, but she was also an intimate friend of Bolton Whitmanite J.W. Wallace (see below), and according to her diary almost chose a platonic relationship with Wallace instead of her marriage. The friendship survived the marriage, and the three became leading influences within the ILP. The Bruce Glasiers moved to Chapel-en-le-Frith, and embarked on an itinerant lifestyle, travelling from one socialist meeting to another. John became editor of the *Labour Leader* in 1904, following the ILP's purchase of the title from Keir Hardie, but during the war he became increasingly ill and Katharine took over the editorship, continuing the paper's anti-war editorial stance. John died on 7 May 1920. Katharine was now more vulnerable to the political sniping of some ILP figures, particularly Snowden, who was highly critical of her pro-Bolshevik approach in the paper. Matters came to a head when she refused to publish an article by Snowden that attacked the new Soviet government. In March 1921 she was relieved of the editorship, and probably experienced some kind of breakdown.

After John's death in 1920 her friendship with Wallace had intensified, and she became a frequent visitor to his Lancashire home. She became increasingly influenced by Wallace's mysticism, and her diary mentions her achieving a 'cosmic consciousness of my own' as she meditated by the waters of Rivington on a summer's evening in 1926.[iii]

Despite her treatment by the ILP leadership, Bruce Glasier remained enormously popular amongst the rank and file membership. She returned to her early work as a 'tramping propagandist', spending much of the next eighteen years on the road. She contributed a regular feature to *Labour's Northern Voice* and frequently wove Whitmanite themes into her articles. By the late 1920s she had become the ILP's elder stateswoman, a much-loved figure who had kept her youthful radicalism to the end. She was actively involved in a range of campaigns, including the fight for pit-head baths, and continuing Margaret McMillan's work for deprived children.

On her eightieth birthday in 1947, over a thousand friends and comrades attended a party in her honour at Bradford's Co-operative Assembly Hall. She addressed them for three quarters of an hour on 'The Religion of Socialism', one of her favourite lecture themes. She died peacefully in June 1950.

i. Laurence Thompson, *The Enthusiasts*, 1971, p66.
ii. *The Enthusiasts*, p75.
iii. See Paul Salveson, *With Walt Whitman in Bolton: spirituality, sex and socialism in a Northern mill* town, p34.

At a local level many voluntary associations emerged which promoted radical town planning – such as the 'Beautiful Oldham Society' and the Bolton Town Planning Association.

One option, pursued by Ebenezer Howard and others, was to create entirely new communities. The example of Letchworth is well known, but there were similar schemes in Manchester, promoted by the City Council – in Burnage, Blackley and Fairfield. Several enlightened industrialists had also created their own communities as far back as the 1820s, and some survive today. Barrowbridge, near Bolton, Calder Vale, between Preston and Lancaster, and of course Saltaire, near Bradford, are all excellent examples of good quality housing provided by employers. A bigger challenge was to restructure and rebuild existing towns and cities.[19]

WOMEN IN NORTHERN SOCIALISM

The early socialist organisations in the North had many prominent women members and the ILP had some extremely popular women lecturers, including Enid Stacy, Sarah Reddish (see p52-3), and Katherine Bruce Glasier – who lived to a grand old age and was described by the ILP in its Jubilee Souvenir as a 'vigorous propagandist for socialism' and 'the grandmother of the Labour Movement' (see p83-4). The ILP members' predisposition towards a more ethical politics was inspiring to many women. As June Hannam writes, writers such as Edward Carpenter and Walt Whitman influenced the ILP in the view that socialism would bring a 'moral transformation of all areas of people's lives and would lead to a society based on the principles of justice, love and beauty'. This vision of socialism, with its emphasis 'on comradeship, the development of an alternative socialist culture, on personal change and the creation of new forms of everyday life, including a change in the relationship between the sexes', was particularly attractive to women.[20]

Caroline Martyn was one of the ILP's most outstanding orators and an enormously popular figure on the North of England socialist lecturing circuit. Allen Clarke describes in enthusiastic terms hearing her speak on the Blackpool sands:

Carrie Martyn's voice by the blue sea – in the sunshine of a golden day – I hear it now as a I write, eloquent, pathetic, pleading for the fallen and forsaken and oppressed; pleading for justice to labour, and brotherhood among all men (sic).[21]

Many of the women lecturers – including Bruce Glasier – used the semi-religious style of 'come to Jesus' oratory as practised by Snowden. A contemporary observer describes Carrie Martyn speaking at an open air meeting in Eagley, a mill village on the outskirts of Bolton, in 1894:

> I knew nothing of the subject of Socialism, and did not care much about it, but for curiosity's sake I took my seat on a tree stump that Friday evening … In company with two or three hundred people I listened to an exposition of Socialistic principles, illustrated and interspersed with the sayings and doings of the Carpenter of Nazareth. My wonder at what seemed to me the intrepidity and courage of a young defenceless woman grew and changed to amazement at myself that I had never seen things in this light before. She had spoken as no woman had ever spoken in my hearing. Scales fell from my eyes and ere long I was a Socialist.[22]

A feature of the early socialist movement was 'The Clarion Van', a horse-drawn caravan which toured the North distributing socialist literature and providing a ready-made platform for speakers. Several women activists took part in the Clarion Van campaigns, particularly *Clarion* women's columnist 'Julia Dawson' (Mrs Myddleton-Worrall), and in 1896 she had the idea for a Clarion Women's Van. The first van was named in memory of Caroline Martyn, and Myddleton-Worrall accompanied it on its tours around England. Ada Neild Chew, of Crewe, was another regular speaker from the back of the van on its tours of the North, as was Sarah Reddish, as we have seen.

The number of popular women speakers in the ILP was reflected in the substantial presence of women who were active at branch level. Many of these women were working-class, and many were also trade union members. Even within organisations like the ILP, however, it seems that there was greater radicalism among working-class women in the North as compared with their sisters in London. One woman complained in a letter in *Labour Leader* that the 'advanced women in the North would not be able to understand the servile place given to women in the London ILP'.[23]

The overall picture that emerges, though, is of a more women-friendly culture within the ILP, especially in the North, compared to within the SDF, whose leaders – Hyndman and Bax in particular – veered towards misogyny. Katharine Bruce Glasier found an atmosphere of 'swift and eager welcome for every woman comrade and of settled conviction as to the women's equal rights of citizenship with men' – though again this was contrasted with Glasgow and London, where 'there were, alas, a few hostile forces, even within the pale of the socialist movement itself'.[24] The SDF made some attempts to reach out to women, and encouraged the formation of women's sections in 1908-9. However, its ideological rigidity on class as the ultimate political yardstick militated against whole-hearted support for women's suffrage, which it often dismissed as a diversion. Hannah Mitchell describes her experience of speaking on a women's suffrage platform in Ashton-under-Lyne when it was attacked by groups of both right-wing Christians and SDF men![25] This was certainly the exception to the norm, but reflected *in extremis* the attitudes of many men within the SDF towards 'middle class feminists'.

The Women's Social and Political Union (WSPU), formed by Emmeline Pankhurst, was a cross-coalition of women and had strong support within the ILP, of which Emmeline Pankhurst was a member. Northern working-class women played a key role in the campaign for women's suffrage, brilliantly described by Jill Norris and Jill Norrington.[26] The Lancashire and Cheshire Textile and Other Workers' Labour Representation Committee was formed in 1903 to unite working-class women in the North West behind the demands of women's suffrage; many ILP members were active within it, including Selina Cooper, Sarah Reddish, Esther Roper and Sarah Dickenson. Mass meetings were held in Manchester, Blackburn and Liverpool during the winter of 1903-4, and were addressed by male supporters including Keir Hardie and Philip Snowden as well as Sarah Reddish, Selina Cooper and Eva Gore-Booth.

A major campaign was fought within the recently formed Labour Party, and both female and male ILP activists (including Yorkshire textile union leaders Ben Turner and Allen Gee) attempted to get the party to support women's suffrage, on the same terms as the then current male franchise. Some opponents within the party tabled amendments in favour of total 'adult suffrage', which would extend the suffrage to all men and all women – a worthy, but at the time unrealistic, aim.

Two election campaigns highlighted the issue of women's suffrage in the early 1900s: the Wigan contest in the 1906 general election and the Colne Valley by-election of 1907. In the first, a local working-class ILP socialist, Thorley Smith, fought his campaign around the demand for women's suffrage, and was strongly backed by Esther Roper and other socialist feminists from the North West. Thorley Smith polled a very respectable 2000 votes, and pushed the Liberal into third place. Victor Grayson's Colne Valley campaign, as we have seen, was even more sensational, pulling off a stunning victory on a platform of 'revolutionary socialism' and 'votes for women'.[27]

The North produced many outstanding working-class women leaders who played an important part in the suffrage campaigns of the early twentieth century, including Selina Cooper, Annie Kenny, Teresa Billington, Sarah Reddish, Hannah Mitchell, and Ellen Wilkinson. Some male socialists supported them, most notably Keir Hardie. Allen Clarke, in his *Northern Weekly*, ran pro-suffrage articles by men like John Tamlyn as well as writing editorials himself, including the provocative 'Are Women More Fit to Vote Than Men?'.[28] The comic character Bet Spriggs, of the Tum Fowt dialect sketches, was recruited to the cause to place the blame for unemployment and low pay squarely on male politicians:

> That comes o' men havin' a vote an aw t'power an' electin' th'Government. Why, they'n noan sense to put up an umbrella when it rains; they hannot gumption to look even after theirsels, let alone their wives an' kids.[29]

Other leading ILP men were vehemently opposed to the women's suffrage campaign, which they tried to dismiss as 'middle-class'. Yet the formation of the Lancashire Women Textile Workers' Representation Committee was one organisation that gave the lie to that view. During 1906 a delegation to London met Prime Minister Campbell Bannerman and walked down the Thames Embankment with banners proclaiming that 'Women Produce the Wealth of Lancashire' and '306,000 Women in the Cotton Trade Want Votes'.[30]

Disappointed in the lack of official Labour Party support, and with its own internal divisions, the Women's Social and Political Union distanced itself from the ILP, and at the same time moved its headquarters from Manchester to London. Some socialist women, such as

Selina Cooper, now also became disillusioned by the increasingly violent tactics of parts of the movement, which included arson attacks on public buildings. Male socialist supporters of women's emancipation, particularly Keir Hardie and northern comrades such as Gee and Turner, to a certain extent became isolated within the Labour Party, and even within the ILP.

Women had been almost entirely excluded from trades unions until the emergence of the 'new unionism' in the 1880s, and had virtually no involvement in formal politics. Following the end of Chartism there are very few examples of working-class women being politically active until the 1880s. Women textile workers were amongst the first that did start to become organised, notably the weavers in East Lancashire, many of whom joined their local associations as early as the 1870s. (Margaret Lahee's novel *Sybil West* (1891) has excellent descriptions of life in Rochdale's mills from a woman weaver's perspective.) By 1888 women workers were taking strike action in parts of Yorkshire, including the blanket weavers. The following year women weavers marched through Wakefield in protest against wage reductions. Whilst some of the male-dominated unions reluctantly agreed to admit women into membership, getting women elected as officials was to be a much longer battle. Alice Foley, a Bolton weaver and socialist of the 'Clarion' generation, was one of the first to 'make it'. She was appointed to the staff of the powerful Bolton Weavers' Association in 1930. From 1949 until 1961 she was Secretary of the Association, one of the most powerful jobs in the textile unions.[31]

Robert Blatchford established a paper aimed specifically at women – *The Woman Worker* – which lasted a few years before the First World War, ending in 1910. For a brief period Lancashire mill worker Ethel Carnie edited the paper, and contributed poems and short stories about the lives of working-class women in the North.[32]

THE CLARION AND MERRIE ENGLAND

Robert Blatchford did more than anyone in the early socialist movement to win supporters, and was fundamental in creating the broad socialist culture that is explored in the next chapter. Through his newspaper *The Clarion*, established in Manchester in 1891, and his best-selling book *Merrie England*, he won tens of thousands of converts to the socialist cause.

ROBERT BLATCHFORD: THE CONTRADICTIONS OF ENGLISHNESS

As a boy Blatchford lived an itinerant life style. His father had died when he was just two years old, and he and his elder brother spent nine years travelling around with his mother, who was an actress, before the family eventually settled in Halifax. As a young man he spent six years in the army, which probably contributed to his mixture of down-to-earth jocularity and concern for 'the common man' – combined with a yen for militarism. He left the army in 1878 and started writing.

His break into professional journalism came through a meeting with A.M. Thompson, a journalist on *The Sunday Chronicle*, a paper based in Manchester that hovered between Liberalism and socialism. Blatchford found he had a knack for writing, and his articles, signed 'Nunquam Dormio' ('I never sleep') quickly became popular. His 'conversion' to socialism came in the mid-1880s, largely through his direct experience of working-class poverty in the Manchester slums. His socialist influences were diffuse. He had read *A Summary of the Principles of Socialism*, written by that unlikely combination of H.M. Hyndman and William Morris; and he had been influenced by the now forgotten but extremely important work of its time, Henry George's *Progress and Poverty*. Blatchford's socialism owed nothing to Marx, a bit to Morris and Hyndman, and much to his own direct experience, sense of 'fairness', and outrage at the conditions that many working-class people had to endure.

In August 1889 he began a series of articles which came to form the basis of *Merrie England*. These were written as a series of letters to a 'typical' working man – John Smith of Oldham – and were published in book form in 1892. Thompson estimates the total sales of the book approached two million, and countless working-class autobiographies tell of how the book 'made them into socialists': it put across a clear, simple message based on people's own experience.

By 1891 Blatchford was ready to take charge of a clearly socialist newspaper, and he became editor of *The Clarion*. The first issue appeared on 12 December 1891 and sold 40,000 copies; and within the first few months circulation settled down to a creditable 30,000. He had taken A.M. Thompson and Edward Fay with him, and they created a newspaper which was lively, popular and socialist. In one incident they managed to see off an attempted libel case brought by a railway company that was aggrieved at Blatchford's exposure of how it had cheated employees out of overtime pay.

Young working-class men and women devoured what had soon become known as 'The Perisher', and they flocked to join the growing number of cycling, walking and cultural groups being set up in *The Clarion*'s name. Whilst these groups owed complete loyalty to the paper and to Blatchford, it is important to stress that Blatchford did not 'control' them. The cycling club, formed in 1894, had an energetic executive led for many years by Tom Groom. News of their rides, 'annual meets' and other doings was extensively reported in the paper, but each group had its own organisation.[i]

There was another side to Blatchford's populist socialism, which was to lose him many friends. He never shook off his youthful militarism and 'jingoism'. Whilst many socialists opposed Britain's role in the Boer war, Blatchford supported it. In the early years of the twentieth century became increasingly anti-German, and when war broke out in 1914 he was stridently pro-war. Hardie and many other socialists opposed the war, or in some cases gave it half-hearted support. Not so Blatchford, who used his paper to rally support for the war and against Germany. In an echo of some of the debates on the left today, he berated socialists who seemed to be ashamed of 'their own country' and argued for a 'progressive patriotism'.

By 1924 Blatchford was supporting the Conservative Party, and was an increasingly isolated figure. Yet his failings should not blind us to his remarkable achievements – the man who did more than anyone to 'make socialists' and make socialism fun.

Andrew Davies, in *To Build a New Jerusalem*, makes the observation that today Blatchford is a 'largely forgotten figure' – 'No plaques or statues commemorate the man who was probably the most successful British socialist propagandist of all time'; and he quotes *The Manchester Guardian*: 'for every convert made by *Das Kapital*, there were a hundred made by *Merrie England*'.[ii]

i. See Laurence Thompson's *Robert Blatchford: portrait of an Englishman*, 1951, pp164-5.
ii. A.J. Davies, *To Build a New Jerusalem: The Labour Movement from the 1880s to the 1890s*, 1992, p65.

Like other socialists, including Katharine Bruce Glasier, Macdonald, and Philip Snowden, Blatchford's socialism was above all about values, not economics. His politics were light years away from those of Hyndman, or for that matter of Keir Hardie: he was undogmatic and very conscious of the different political landscapes in the North and the South. He had perhaps more in common with the 'Beer and Britannia' Toryism that was a feature of many Lancashire towns than with the more austere socialism of Hardie and Glasier.[33] Perhaps more than any other individual Blatchford was responsible for 'making socialists' – and he made them by the thousand.

Blatchford joined the ILP on its formation but was never a 'party' animal. He had a difficult relationship with Keir Hardie, who owned his own newspaper, the *Labour Leader*, which he later sold to the ILP. Stodgy and worthy, the *Labour Leader* was the opposite of *The Clarion* in everything except its socialism. Blatchford's biographer Laurence Thompson said that 'those who read it, loved it, not as a weekly paper, but as a friend'.[34]

Keir Hardie did not like it. In 1903 he wrote:

> for a time in England, the fibre of the Socialist Movement was almost totally destroyed by a spirit of irresponsible levity … Socialism is a serious task, demanding serious work at the hands of its advocates, and anything which introduces levity or frivolity into the movement is hindering, not helping, its progress.[35]

Blatchford used his paper to promote greater unity between the ILP and the SDF. Though the two parties had different policies in some areas, and perhaps most importantly a different culture, at local level, especially in the North, the two often worked very closely, and frequently ran joint candidates in elections. Along with Grayson he was to be largely instrumental in the establishment of the British Socialist Party in 1911, which was based on the SDF and a small number of ILP branches. Numerous efforts had been made before this to unite the ILP and SDF, with lukewarm support from the ILP leadership and outright hostility from many parts of the North, particularly Yorkshire. Hardie was right to exercise caution on this issue – too close a relationship with the SDF would have alienated the Northern trades unions, whose support was essential to create a mass working-class party.

Despite their mutual dislike, Blatchford and Hardie had much in common in their vision of socialism, though Blatchford's politics certainly had a greater element of sheer fun and pleasure than the rather stern, puritanical socialism of Hardie. He and Allen Clarke (see p99-100) were temperamentally more akin, and for a while shared a house

BEN TURNER – A RADICAL YORKSHIRE UNION VOICE

Ben Turner was born in Holmfirth and brought up in the hand-loom weaving culture that remained strong in the West Riding in the 1860s and 1870s. His first job was in a local weaving shed. His socialism was nurtured in the Leeds Socialist Party in the late 1880s, where he met many of the great socialists of the time, including Edward Carpenter and Michael Davitt. As a boy he had attended the Huddersfield Secular Society Sunday School, along with Owen Balmforth (see Chapter 2). In his autobiography *About Myself* he writes of his interest in Irish politics '[I] took up as a young fellow the side of the Home Rulers ... I read the life of James Stephens, knew about Michael Davitt, read the poems of Davis and other songsters for Irish freedom, and was generally steeped in the atmosphere of the advanced or revolutionary period'.[i]

Turner had a meteoric rise within the labour movement, becoming a cabinet minister in the 1921 Labour government and a member of the TUC General Council when it was formed in 1920. Perhaps more than any leading national politician, he kept his 'northern' roots, being intensely proud of his Yorkshire cultural heritage, a feeling he shared with his friend Philip Snowden, who occasionally wrote in dialect to Turner.

In his autobiography he recounts the ferocious but good-natured arguments between the Yorkshire and Lancashire delegates to the International Textile Workers' Federation. On one occasion in Berlin, the arguments between the rival shires' delegates became so heated that the conference chair, Wilhelm Liebknecht, asked the security guards to close the proceedings down. Liebknecht was later surprised when he found the two warring factions in an adjoining room calmly sat down smoking their pipes and chatting, and wondering why the conference had terminated early. Turner commented: 'these "bobbies" couldn't understand how keenly we could argue and interject and yet be personally, as we were, on the best of terms'.[ii] The episode tells us much about the relationship between Lancashire and Yorkshire.

The talented Lancashire poet and cartoonist Sam Fitton was a good friend of Turner's, and his poem 'Turner and Gee' was an appeal in (Lancashire) dialect for readers to support the efforts of his Yorkshire friend.[iii]

i. Ben Turner, *About Myself*, 1930, p10.

ii. *About Myself*, p155.

iii. 'Turner and Gee' was published in *The Cotton Factory Times*, c 1923 (undated cutting, Stalybridge Library).

in Blackpool, though the two friends fell out over Blatchford's support for the Boer War and re-armament.

UNION AFFILIATIONS – BEGINNING OF A SEISMIC SHIFT

Throughout the second half of the nineteenth century the relationship of unions to politics was complex. Some unions were firmly 'non-political'. Many, particularly in mining, supported the Liberal cause. The Durham Miners' Association was solidly Liberal throughout its existence in the nineteenth century. Some individual union leaders, like James Mawdsley of the Lancashire cotton spinners, were Tories. However, by the 1880s a growing number of trades unionists were of the view that working people needed independent representation in parliament. That did not necessarily mean they were advocating socialism: some union leaders were strongly Liberal in their views but were increasingly disenchanted with the Party's failure to support working men candidates. In turn, Hyndman's SDF was – at least nationally – anti-trades union, seeing them as a barrier to achieving full socialism.

It was the Independent Labour Party that provided a bridge between the unions and the emerging socialist movement. The ethical socialism of Keir Hardie and Ramsay Macdonald was less of a threat to the cautious trades unionists than the full-blooded marxism of the SDF, which in any case was ambivalent towards trades unionism. ILP influence became well established in certain unions in the North, generally those representing semi- and unskilled workers that began to spring up in the 1880s. The weavers' unions in North East Lancashire had strong ILP involvement, as did the Amalgamated Society of Railway Servants in the North-West and Yorkshire.[36]

However, the stranglehold of the Liberal Party on the miners' unions in Lancashire, Yorkshire and the North-East took a long time to break. The ILP used its influence to encourage the unions to support the formation of an independent 'Labour' political organisation. As we have seen above, it was a Yorkshire ILP delegate, Tom Steels of the Amalgamated Society of Railway Servants, who moved the resolution at the 1899 TUC Conference that led to the formation of the 'Labour Representation Committee'.

The early Labour Party was not so much a 'socialist' organisation as the political expression of some of the trades unions, with vestigial

Liberal views, and a socialist minority represented largely by the ILP. The party was very much the creature of the unions, bringing the benefits of a mass working-class base of support along with the reality of a very cautious stance on political change. Its federal structure permitted 'socialist organisations' like the ILP, and even the SDF for a time, to be members. But there was no doubt as to where the real power lay.

However, many of the unions remained distrustful of the new party, and of 'socialism' in general. Writers such as Allen Clarke saw one of the biggest obstacles to socialism being the conservative cotton unions. The leader of the Bolton cotton spinners for many years was James Mawdsley, an active Conservative supporter. Clarke was most critical of the 'narrow' trade unionism practised by the skilled textile workers, who combined very powerful trade unionism for themselves with being deaf to the plight of underpaid workers. In March 1897 Clarke wrote that 'the factory folk of Lancashire are in the main antagonistic or apathetic to the Socialist movement', suggesting that the reasons for this were strong trade unionism combined with high wages for the skilled workers.[37] Clarke was particularly outraged by the spinners' support for the half-time system of child labour, and poured scorn on their support for child labour during the campaigns against half-time working in 1899. That battle was not won until after the First World War.[38]

The growth of trades unions in the North, and Britain as a whole, was an uneven process, marked by great surges forward that were often followed by major defeats, such as that suffered by the Lancashire miners after their strike in 1844.[39] The skilled unions were able to consolidate their position during the second half of the nineteenth century and many were recognised by the employers. But this was seldom the case for unskilled workers, many of whom had no union representation well into the twentieth century, despite earlier attempts at organisation.

The early twentieth century saw a period of increased militancy that has been linked to the rise of 'syndicalism' as a political philosophy, though in reality the strikes were primarily about basic issues of pay and conditions and union recognition. A handful of syndicalists like Tom Mann (who had previously stood for election in 1895 as a socialist in Yorkshire's Colne Valley) were prominent in the strikes, but they were vastly outnumbered by ILP and other socialist activists.

Discontent was particularly strong amongst the dock workers and railwaymen. In the words of Sidney Webb, in the summer of 1911 'the pot boiled over'. Liverpool was the epicentre of the struggle, with dockers coming out in June and July. This was followed by the railwaymen in August. A range of simmering grievances suddenly exploded into a strike wave that left the union leaderships completely unprepared. Many of the strikers were not even union members. By mid-August Liverpool was virtually at a standstill, and 7000 troops were drafted in to 'maintain order'. The railway strike became a national stoppage – the first in British railway history. The leadership eventually caught up with the Liverpool men and issued the instruction to stop work. A telegram was sent to 2000 branches and railway centres across Britain: 'Your liberty is at stake. All railwaymen must strike at once. The loyalty of each means victory for all'.[40] The telegram was signed by the leaders of the four railway unions representing non-clerical staff. The Railway Clerks Association had a no-strike policy, but instructed its members not to do anything to help break the strike.

Many workers who were not on strike joined in mass demonstrations in cities like Liverpool, Manchester and Hull. In some places, including Liverpool and Llanelli, the military intervened and strikers were shot dead, further inflaming the situation. After a few days the rail strike was settled, but on terms which left many activists outraged. The core demand for union recognition was fudged, and a commission of enquiry was established to look into the railway workers' claims. But something big had happened. The railway workers had discovered their strength, and the old attitude of 'defence not defiance' amongst the railway unions was dead.

The small syndicalist current in the labour movement before the First World War sought a revolutionary seizure of power by industrial workers, with workers' control of each industry. It was hostile to parliamentary methods and saw 'the general strike' as having an almost mystical significance. There is no doubt that syndicalist ideas were current amongst a small number of working-class activists in Liverpool and Manchester, but their political influence can be exaggerated; and for many activists, such as Tom Mann and J.T. Murphy, it was a staging post on the road to joining the Communist Party after the First World War.

Tom Mann, by 1910 a convinced syndicalist, was active in Liverpool in the run-up to the docks and rail strikes, and was elected chair of the Liverpool Strike Committee in August 1911. Liverpool had become a crucible for revolutionary ideas because of its role as a world port. Radicalised seamen from around the world met comrades from other industries at the 'International Club', which flourished in the city before the First World War. This was an informal drinking and debating club, with a strong Spanish element, led by Lorenzo Portet, an anarcho-syndicalist who had fled Spain in the early 1900s. The club also attracted Jewish exiles from eastern Europe. Lee Foo, secretary of the Liverpool branch of the Chinese Seamen's Union, was also involved in the club's activities.[41]

Merseyside also had a 'Communist Club', a very active Clarion movement and a small but influential group of union revolutionaries who were sympathetic to the libertarian ideas of syndicalism. Yet syndicalists didn't 'cause' the 1911 strike, though people like Mann certainly helped to give it direction and leadership. For a short time syndicalism was popular on wider sections of the left, and some of its adherents were strong supporters of 'industrial unionism' – one union for each industry. The most obvious example of the success of the idea of industrial unionism was the formation of the National Union of Railwaymen, in 1913 – less than two years after the 1911 strike. This brought together four of the six main unions, though the locomen and the railway clerks remained aloof. The NUR wasn't, however, a 'syndicalist' union. From the start it was committed to nationalisation through parliamentary means, and it was strong supporter of the Labour Party. However there were a number of syndicalists active in it, as there were in the miners' union (mainly in South Wales) and in the engineering industry. Many of the syndicalists, Tom Mann included, joined the Communist Party of Great Britain when it was established in 1920.

The Great Dublin Lock-out of 1913 mobilised huge support in Britain. Strike leader James Larkin spoke at packed meetings in Manchester's Free Trade Hall, and thousands of pounds were collected to support the workers and their families. The large Co-operative Society factory at Pelaw, Gateshead, chartered and stocked a ship to take food to help the families. Larkin declared that this had been a decisive factor in bolstering workers' resistance.[42]

ALTERNATIVE PATHS

Some socialists – including, as we have seen, Victor Grayson and Robert Blatchford – lobbied strongly in the early 1900s for 'socialist unity' rather than the 'labour alliance' between the Labour Party and the Liberal-inclined unions. And when the British Socialist Party was created, from the SDF, local socialist groups and some disgruntled branches of the ILP joined, unhappy about the party's growing parliamentarism. Yet rather than creating a united socialist party the BSP only succeeded in antagonising the ILP at both national and local level, and took only a minority of the party with it. Whilst maintaining its own idea of a pure and unadulterated socialism, it presented little in the way of popular appeal, and was not much more than a revamped SDF. The bulk of the BSP subsequently merged with other small leftist groups to form the Communist Party of Great Britain in 1920.[43]

It's easy to argue that Blatchford and Grayson were the heroes and Hardie and Macdonald the villains in the 'socialist unity' project. The reality was more complex. The Northern activists in the ILP, especially in the West Riding, had little sympathy for the SDF's style of socialism. It was seen as mechanistic and dogmatic, and as emphasising economic solutions rather than the spirit of comradeship and fellowship which the ILP espoused. Many ILP socialists believed in greater municipal and state control of services, but as the means to a wider end. For most of the SDF, state ownership was 'the end'.[44]

The 'labour alliance' project of Hardie and Macdonald aimed to create a mass party with the support of the trades unions and the 'liberal' middle class. The implications were unquestionably a watered-down form of socialism, but it was one that would carry much wider popular appeal. If they had lost to the purists of 'socialist unity', the Labour Party as it emerged in the twentieth century, based on deep roots in the working class, might not have happened. And the Liberal Party could have continued as the alternative to Conservatism, with a much smaller 'Socialist Party' on the political fringes.

ALLEN CLARKE: BOLTON'S 'TEDDY ASHTON'

Allen Clarke was one of the most important figures in the growth of socialism in Lancashire. Though he is virtually forgotten today, he was the doyen of late nineteenth-century Lancashire dialect writers,

Clarke was the son of cotton workers, born in Bolton in 1863 into a highly political family. As we have seen, he was strongly influenced by the 1887 Bolton engineers' strike, which formed the backdrop to his novel *The Knobstick*. However, his early political writings, in papers such as his own *Labour Light*, can hardly be said to be original. It was when he used the Lancashire vernacular to put over a socialist message that he really came to life as a greater writer, as we see in the novels, the early poetry and many of the 'Tum Fowt' sketches.

In Clarke's invention of 'Teddy Ashton' as the archetypal Lancastrian, he was following a well-established literary convention. His fellow Boltonian J.T. Staton was one of several dialect writers in the 1860s and 1870s who created a 'typical' character – in his case 'Bobby Shuttle' – who could be used as a commentator on issues of the day. The character was usually superficially slightly daft, but with plenty of common sense and homely wisdom. (In later years George Formby (father and son) became such a stage creation – the seemingly thick Lancashire lad who always managed to turn the tables on the 'toffs'.) Clarke created a character with whom his working-class readership could identify – Bill Spriggs – and also his wife Bet. His supporting characters, Joe Lung, Patsy Filligan, Ben Roke and other denizens of 'The Dug an' Kennel' were used to poke fun at authority and affirm a strong sense of pride in being part of the Lancashire working class. 'Teddy Ashton' featured as a character in some of the sketches, occasionally acting as secretary to 'The Tum Fowt Debatin' Menociation'.

Clarke became a strong supporter of the 'Labour Church' movement, which had a solid base in Bolton from the early 1890s, and was a congenial home to socialists and radical Liberals. It was led by James Sims – 'a sturdy old veteran in the cause of labour' – who became a good friend. He was a regular attender at Labour Church meetings, and was advertised as speaking on 'The Riddle of the Universe' on Sunday 19 April 1903.[i]

Clarke supported the broad socialist cause, and in 1900 was selected as the joint ILP and SDF candidate to fight the Rochdale seat in the general election. This was during the Boer War, which Clarke, and most socialists, had strongly opposed. His election manifesto – 'My Say to the

People of Rochdale' – emphasised his moral beliefs and his understanding of working-class life. He opposed colonialism, child labour and unemployment, with a wish to 'make the world brighter for everybody'. 'My Say to the People of Rochdale' was written in Lancashire dialect, and appeared in *Rochdale Labour News*.

Clarke's politics evolved in a more radical direction after 1900, and he had a growing interest in Tolstoyan anarchism. Tolstoy was a leading proponent of non-violent anarchism, advocating rural communes to alleviate unemployment in the industrial cities, which would ultimately become the way of life for everyone.[ii]

Clarke's socialism was similar to the libertarian 'larger socialism' of his fellow Whitmanite Edward Carpenter (see p80-2), with whom he shared many friends. Clarke spoke glowingly of *Love's Coming of Age* in a *Northern Weekly* editorial on 20 January 1906, and the same edition also carried a review of Ernest Crosby's pamphlet *Edward Carpenter: Poet and Prophet*. There were more major features on Carpenter by Crosby in the *Northern Weekly* on 7 and 14 February 1903, as well as an article by Carpenter himself, on 'The Unrest of Civilization'. And on 20 January 1906, Clarke wrote of 'this wise and good man', and urged readers to get a copy of Tom Swan's book *Edward Carpenter – The Man and His Message*.

Clarke's poem 'A Gradely Prayer' (printed in full as Appendix 3), written in 1903, was enormously popular, and reflects Clarke's basic philosophy of comradeship, the open air, and spirituality in a 'gradely' Lancashire context. It is still recited in Lancashire pubs today.

Clarke's peak of popularity was between the years 1896 and 1908, when he was producing his weekly newspaper, alongside *The Clarion*, *Cotton Factory Times* and *Yorkshire Factory Times* (all of which he wrote for). Perhaps not quite as influential as Blatchford, he nonetheless had a huge impact, converting thousands of people to socialism through laughter and the open air, coupled with a strong sense of regional identity. Not a bad combination.

---

i. *Teddy Ashton's Northern Weekly*, 17 April 1903.

ii. Clarke's writings in *Northern Weekly* between 1905 and 1907 are saturated with references to Tolstoy and include some short stories by him. The two men corresponded and Tolstoy planned to translate some of Clarke's writings into Russian. See Paul Salveson, *Lancashire's Romantic Radical: the life and writings of Allen Clarke/Teddy Ashton*, 2009

NOTES

1. See E.P. Thompson, 'Homage to Tom Maguire', op. cit.; and Jowitt and Taylor, op. cit.
2. 'Social Democracy in the Labour Movement: The SDF in Lancashire', *North West Labour History Society Bulletin*, 1982-3. Martin Crick's *The History of the Social Democratic Federation*, 1994, is a well-balanced study which emphasises the local and regional differences within the SDF.
3. See Crick, op. cit.
4. E.P. Thompson, *William Morris: Romantic to Revolutionary*, 1955 (and revised second edition 1976) gives a thorough account of the split.
5. 'Amongst the Agitators', *Teddy Ashton's Northern Weekly*, 1 July 1905.
6. See Dona Torr, *Tom Mann and His Times*, 1956, p253.
7. *Teddy Ashton's Northern Weekly*, 8 July 1905.
8. Joseph Shufflebotham, *Something Attempted – Something Done*, n.d., c 1898.
9. For Hyndman's scathing comments on Burnley see Crick, op. cit.
10. See Jowitt and Taylor, op. cit; and Keith Laybourn, *The Rise of Socialism in Britain, 1881-1951*, 1997, p31.
11. Ramsay Macdonald, *Socialism and Society*, 1905, p144.
12. For Philip Snowden see Colin Cross, *Philip Snowden*, and the more recent biography by Keith Laybourn, *Philip Snowden: a biography*, 1988. Stephen Yeo's 'The Religion of Socialism' in *History Workshop*, 1977, casts much light on this aspect of ethical socialism, and on Snowden's 'come to Jesus' style.
13. See Jack Power and A. Mowat, *Our Fifty years Struggle for Socialism in Barrow*, 1946.
14. See Peter Gurney, 'Politics of Place', *Manchester Region History Review*, 1997, for an account of the 1896 events.
15. David Clark's biography of Grayson (op. cit.) quotes people's stories about Grayson, based on personal interviews with those who could remember him.
16. See Andrew Thorpe, *A History of the British Labour Party*, 1998, p8; the full text of the motion is on Rosie Winterton MP's website at www.ros-iewintertonmp/doncaster/history.
17. A story passed down within Farnworth Labour Party.
18. *Teddy Ashton's Northern Weekly*, 20 August 1905.
19. See Tristram Hunt, *Building Jerusalem: the rise and fall of the Victorian city*, 2004, as a general introduction, particularly the chapter on 'Garden Cities and the Triumph of Suburbia'. Also Anthony Sutcliffe (ed.), *British Town Planning: the formative years*, 1981, especially Michael Harrison, 'Housing and town planning in Manchester before 1914'.
20. June Hannam, 'Women and the ILP 1890-1914', in *Centennial History of the Independent Labour Party*, 1992, p207.

21. *Teddy Ashton's Northern Weekly*, 30 September 1905.

22. Lena Wallis, *The Life and Letters of Caroline Martyn*, 1898 (republished 2011), p44.

23. June Hannam and Karen Hunt, *Socialist Women: Britain 1880s to 1920s*, 2002.

24. Ibid, p81.

25. Hannah Mitchell, *The Hard Way Up*, 1968, p156.

26. Jill Liddington and Jill Norris, *One Hand Tied Behind Us – the rise of the women's suffrage movement*, 1976.

27. See Clark, op. cit.; and also Fred Bower, *Rolling Stonemason*, 1928. Bower was a Liverpool anarchist who helped in the campaign and describes meeting the Pankhursts in Colne Valley.

28. *Fellowship* (formerly *Teddy Ashton's Northern Weekly*), 8 October 1907.

29. Ibid.

30. Jill Liddington, *The Life and Times of a Respectable Rebel: Selina Cooper*, op. cit., p170.

31. Alice Foley, *A Bolton Childhood*, 1973.

32. Ethel Carnie's *Songs of a Factory Girl* was published in book form some years later, in 1911.

33. See Laurence Thompson's lively *Robert Blatchford: portrait of an Englishman*, 1951.

34. Ibid., p130.

35. Ibid., p117.

36. See David Howell, *British Workers and the Independent Labour Party 1888-1906*, 1983.

37. *The Labour Prophet*, March 1897.

38. See Allen Clarke, *The Effects of the Factory System*, 1899, for his denunciation of child labour. The book had a major impact nationally and was translated into Russian by Tolstoy. Edmund and Ruth Frow's *The Half-Time System in Education*, 1970, is an account of the system, and of the role of the ILP and the NUT in opposing it.

39. Challinor, op. cit.

40. See Philip Bagwell, *The Railwaymen* (vol. 1) for a detailed account of the strike.

41. Bob Holton, 'Syndicalism and Labour on Merseyside 1906-14', in H. Hikins (ed.) *Building the Union*, 1973.

42. See Denis Smyth, *The Onward March of Labour, the story of the great 1913 Dublin Lockout*, no date c. 1972.

43. For a good general introduction see Willie Thompson, *The Good Old Cause: British Communism 1920-1991*, 1992.

44. See Crick op. cit. (note 2 above) for a full discussion of the SDF's ideology.

4. A Northern Socialist Culture

The ILP'er was involved in a movement which was far broader than
a purely political one. Through the Labour clubs they created their
own culture; a distinctly new life-style. At the centre of this culture
was the desire for a higher form of social relationship which they
maintained with each other ... the 'camaraderie' was the factor
which encouraged the flowering of Labour clubs ...[1]

Northern working-class culture has long been stereotyped by
images of brass bands, marching triumphantly ahead of union
banners carried by determined-looking, usually overweight, men.
There's no doubt that events like the Durham Miners' Gala remain a
fabulous celebration of a particular Northern working-class culture
that has almost, but not quite, disappeared. But there's a lot more to it
than that, and always has been. It was during the 1890s and 1900s
that 'culture' was fully exploited as part of the socialist movement. The
ILP, supported by *The Clarion* and local socialist newspapers encouraged a plethora of cultural groups to get established, and the socialist
club movement resulted in local bases in every town and often reached
down to local village communities. This was not, it should be stressed,
mass working-class culture. It appealed to a narrow but important
layer of working-class men and women who valued education, 'community' and individual 'advancement'. Some, but not all, would be
from religious backgrounds, both Nonconformity and Anglicanism,
and there was a smattering of Catholics and a larger number of
Spiritualists. These people formed the leadership of many working
class organisations, including the emerging ILP, but also trades unions,
the co-operative movement and other cultural and religious
organisations.

The socialist culture which emerged in Lancashire and Yorkshire
during the 1890s and 1900s had comradely echoes in other parts of
the UK. The South Wales valleys developed a similarly vibrant culture

and there was an exchange of 'big name' speakers. In Aberdare for example, the ILP offered an example of an alternative society:

> With its own institute, the party offered weekly meetings, regular concerts, an ILP Band of Hope, its own football team, annual teas, a children's Christmas Party, education classes, numerous committee meetings and the chance to see famous figures such as Victor Grayson, the 'victor of the Colne Valley' at the Market hall. The ILP in Merthyr even had its own tobacconist and newsagent, whilst the Swansea Socialist Society ran a shop and boot club.[2]

A similar pattern of an all-embracing local socialist culture developed in the Fife coalfields, ultimately leading to the election of Willie Gallacher as Communist MP for West Fife in 1935. 'Red Clydeside' became legendary, with its origins in Glasgow's factories, shipyards and railway depots, personified by ILP activists such as James Maxton and David Kirkwood. There were many more parts of Britain that each had its own distinctive socialist culture, often developed from earlier radical traditions, above all Chartism.

In areas like the Colne Valley of Yorkshire, larger towns including Halifax, Bradford and Huddersfield, and the East Lancashire cotton towns, a particularly vibrant culture emerged in the 1890s. Jeffrey Hill, in his history of Nelson describes the 'alternative culture' which developed in the north-east Lancashire town:

> The ILP ... was more than a political organisation. Since its inception in the early 1890s the ILP had always contained an influential body of opinion which argued that the party existed as much to make socialists as contest elections. Educational and recreational activity was therefore an essential part of its operation. Nelson ILP held fast to this principle. In addition to a regular programme of classes and discussion groups on the leading political and economic issues of the day, it laid on more mundane activities such as weekly whist drives and classes in 'physical culture', which included boxing, weight-lifting and wrestling. Associated with the ILP was the Socialist Sunday School.[3]

Hill goes on to describe the range of recreational and cultural activities of the local socialist movement 'which presented a challenge to the ethic of capitalism prevalent in society at large' and which helped to underpin labour solidarity in the town, leading to its description as 'Little Moscow' during the inter-war years. A similar culture grew up in Bolton around the Socialist Club, the headquarters of 'The Bolton Socialist Party', a result of a merger of the local ILP and SDF and still in existence today.[4]

David Clark describes the role of the socialist clubs as providing the bases for 'a counter-culture' which included 'Clarion cycling clubs, a socialist brass band, even more choirs, a handbell group and Socialist Sunday schools'.[5]

The socialist culture of the period between the 1890s and the First World War provided an alternative life for working-class activists, literally from the cradle to the grave. Children were given socialist 'baptisms', with middle names based on socialist and radical heroes, a tradition which stretched back to Owenite and Chartist times. They would attend the socialist Sunday school and join their parents in the socialist club, most of which offered a teetotal atmosphere with an emphasis on education and 'healthy' recreation; and the Clarion cycling and rambling provided a way out from town to countryside. The culture was bolstered by a socialist press, with national papers such as *The Clarion* and *Labour Leader*, as well as a plethora of local publications and more regional papers such as *Teddy Ashton's Northern Weekly*, *Cotton Factory Times* and *Yorkshire Factory Times*. More spiritual needs were met by the Labour Church. Its 'northern-ness' was underpinned by poetry and prose written in dialect by working-class socialists such as Allen Clarke, Ben Turner, Tommy Armstrong and Hannah Mitchell.

A LOCAL SOCIALIST PRESS

The spread of locally-rooted socialist organisations in the North was encouraged by local socialist newspapers and the socialist club. There was a great blossoming of local socialist journalism between the early 1890s and the First World War. Papers like *The Rochdale Labour News*, *Bradford Pioneer*, *Halifax Labour News*, *The Bolton Socialist* and *Huddersfield Worker* had substantial circulations within a small catchment area. Some, like *The Leeds Citizen*, survived long after the First World War, well into the 1930s. The *Citizen* itself finally closed in the 1960s. These were essential tools in building a popular base for the ILP and Labour Party, ensuring Labour's electoral advances before and after the Great War.

Joseph Burgess was one of the most important figures in Northern socialist journalism in the 1880s and 1890s. He started his working life at the age of nine as a 'little piecer' in the Failsworth mills and knew the hardships of factory life. He began writing poetry, some written dialect and very good quality, whilst still working in the mill and got a paid job on the *Oldham Express* in 1881.[6] He published *The Oldham Operative* from 1884, and shortly after its demise got an editorial job on *The Cotton Factory Times*, which had become a popular pro-union paper in the Lancashire cotton districts. He later went on to edit *The Workman's Times*. Soon after *The Cotton Factory Times* appeared its publisher, J. Andrew of Ashton-under-Lyne, established a Yorkshire stable-mate *The Yorkshire Factory Times*. Both were immensely popular and introduced thousands of textile workers to the new Labour politics.[7] They combined detailed reports of labour disputes, pay rates and meetings, leavened with poetry and short stories, often in dialect.

Among the most important, and historically most neglected, of working-class newspapers were the creations of Allen Clarke (see p99-100). After working in a mill as a half-timer Clarke had progressed to being a pupil-teacher in a Bolton school, and then succeeded in getting an administrative job with *The Bolton Evening News*. But in 1890, when the hoped-for entry into journalism hadn't happened, he left in disgust and started his own newspaper *The Labour Light*. This only lasted a few months but gave Clarke valuable writing experience. He joined the staff of *The Cotton Factory Times*, fell out with Burgess, and set up his *Teddy Ashton's Northern Weekly* in 1896. The paper was an immediate hit, and built up sales of around 30,000 a week – mostly within a twenty-mile radius of Bolton. It was a perplexing mix of socialist politics, eastern philosophy, Lancashire dialect and whatever entered Clarke's mind that week.[8]

CLUB LIFE AND NORTHERN SOCIALISM

David Clark notes the fundamental importance of the network of socialist clubs which grew up in the Colne Valley in forming a solid base for the achievements of the Colne Valley Labour Union, which ultimately led to Victor Grayson's victory in 1907, and supported a socialist culture which survived the First World War. He says:

It was the Labour clubs which were to be crucial factors in the successful development of the new political party in the Colne Valley and elsewhere. Not only did they provide the permanency upon which the activities of the party could be based but they also symbolised the emancipation of the members from the existing political parties. In turn, they were instrumental in persuading the new movement to adopt a Socialist outlook.[9]

The emergence of labour or socialist clubs provided the base which allowed a wide range of activities to flourish, and found obvious inspiration from the many Liberal and Conservative clubs which flourished in the Northern industrial towns. At the same time, the separate socialist club formed a haven where like-minded working-class socialists could meet in a friendly and supportive atmosphere. Clark notes that they provided an opportunity for working-class men and women to participate in dances, teas, socials and rambles, as well as political discussions. In addition, they provided a means of developing members' skills in running complex, democratic organisations.

Colne Valley was not unique, though the extent of club life was remarkable for a semi-rural area. Stephen Yeo quotes an account of club activity in Lancashire in the 1890s:

> ... at Barrow-in-Furness a group of unaffiliated working men managed to pay the rent of a large building, and to bring speakers from a distance, greatly helped by their letting of the big hall for a Saturday night dance at £1 a week. Besides this hall they had in the building a reading room, billiards room, and trading department of which the mainstay seemed to be tea and boots! Wigan also ran a Saturday night dance. At Burnley the big St James Hall, leased by the branch, was used for meetings ... The portrait of Karl Marx would look down from the wall ...[10]

In the early 1900s the local ILP, which published *The Barrow Pioneer*, had its own rooms in the town. There was a Clarion Vocal Union which supported local socialist events, and in 1908 Barrow Socialist Society, affiliated to the ILP, organised 'The Great Labour Bazaar and Fancy Fair'![11] Bolton Socialist Club was founded in 1896 and quickly outgrew its modest accommodation in a town-centre back street. It moved into a substantial Georgian terraced building on Wood Street in 1905, and has stayed there ever since. It remains a 'political' socialist club owned by Bolton Socialist Hall Ltd. 'The Socialist Ten Commandments' are displayed on the club walls.

Many clubs that were simply rented were given up during political downturns. However, many club buildings were purchased outright following intense fundraising activities. Areas of strong socialist activity had large networks of local socialist clubs, owned by their members. Three such clubs survive to this day in Colne Valley and are still used as Labour Party meeting venues.

Alan Brooke has written a fascinating history of just one of the Colne Valley clubs – Honley – subtitled 'popular socialism in a Yorkshire textile village'. The club moved into new premises in 1907, and the event epitomised the thriving socialist culture of the day:

> At 2.30 in the afternoon the procession left the tram terminus at Honley Bridge, headed by about 40 Clarion cyclists, followed by Honley Brass Band and then 300 children wearing red rosettes and ribbons and the girls with red sashes over their white frocks.[12]

In the years that followed the club developed a range of social and educational activities. Like many socialist clubs, it had a 'Socialist Sunday School' modelled on nonconformist practice but with a strong socialist content. The 'Socialist Ten Commandments' were learnt by earnest young socialists.

The socialist movement took the political club idea a step further from the established Liberal and Tory examples, providing club houses which offered affordable holiday accommodation for working class socialists. From the mid-1890s Clarion club houses mushroomed in the North (based on the successful cycling club that was inspired by Blatchford's Clarion newspaper (see p120-1)); these provided accommodation for day and weekend visitors, or for tired socialists needing rest and recuperation for longer vacations. Many old-time Clarion cyclists can still remember the Clarion Houses that dotted the countryside in the North of England. These were usually residential centres where supporters could spend a weekend – or longer – amongst friends and comrades, being well looked after with suitably uplifting socialist literature on hand to study. The first was at Bucklow Hill in Cheshire. It opened in 1897 after a successful fundraising appeal by 'The Clarion Cyclists Club House Co. Ltd'.

One old Clarionette described 'the utter absence of Sabbatarianism, class distinction and moth-eaten convention' at the club house.[13] Unfortunately the landowner, Lord Egerton of Tatton Hall, disapproved of the use to which his property was being put and refused to renew the lease in 1903. However, alternative accommodation was secured in an old farmhouse at Handforth, near Wilmslow. This was designed for mass catering, with a dining room that could seat two hundred. It had fifty beds in four dormitories, with space for at least a dozen tents in the adjacent field. Its brochure stressed its appeal, based on 'co-operation for pleasure, intellectual recreation and interchange of opinions and ideals'. The clientele was eclectic, described thus by Manchester Clarion cyclists Mabel and Collin Coates: 'Artists, lawyers, doctors rubbed shoulders with miners and little piecers, all linked by the common ideal and their faith in socialism'.[14]

Other club houses followed, with Menston Clarion Clubhouse, near Bradford, opening in 1908. A further Clarion House opened near Ribchester, in the Ribble Valley, in 1913. Others came and went but Ribble Valley Club House survived until the early 1950s, and Menston is still in existence. One other 'Clarion House' deserves a mention, though it was originally set up as an ILP club house – that at Roughlee, near Burnley. It was established in 1912 and is still going strong today as 'Nelson ILP Clarion House'. On any Sunday throughout the year you will find cyclists and walkers sitting down with huge steaming mugs of tea, beneath pictures of Keir Hardie, swapping tales of walks and rides and talking politics.

THE MUSIC OF SOCIALISM

Choirs were particularly popular in the pre-war socialist movement, in regular demand for fund-raising concerts as well as open air events. In Colne Valley, the ILP established a Clarion Choir in 1897. It grew into several sections, covering villages such as Mossley, Slaithwaite and Golcar. By 1905 Mossley had both a Clarion mixed and a male voice choir. The choirs were federated in the Clarion Vocal Union, which organised annual gatherings of massed choirs. Halifax was the venue in 1897, with choirs from Keighley, Bradford, Leeds, Sheffield, Oldham, Manchester, Rochdale, Preston and Halifax itself being represented. The Halifax ILP's *Record* noted that 'the total number of singers present was 397, and the singing was all that could be desired'.[15]

When Keir Hardie contested the East Bradford by-election in 1896 a mass meeting was held at St George's Hall, chaired by the venerable Alderman Jowett. As well as a litany of ILP star speakers, the united choirs of Halifax, Keighley and Bradford Clarion Vocal Unions sang. The choirs were evidently highly mobile. Philip Snowden's *Autobiography* tells of a 'politics inspired by idealism and religious fervour ... Vocal unions were formed which accompanied cycling corps into the countryside at weekends, and audiences were gathered on village greens by the singing of the choirs; then short and simple addresses on Socialism were given'.[16]

When Jim Larkin visited Manchester in 1913, at the height of the Dublin Lock-Out, a mass meeting in The Free Trade Hall heard not only Larkin but also the Manchester Clarion Choir. The brass band movement was established during the early nineteenth century and owed much to employer paternalism. The cost of instruments was prohibitive without some external help, and many employers, particularly in textiles, saw the advantage in supporting 'their' band. Some of this was undoubtedly disinterested, but, consciously or unconsciously, they thereby helped to instil a degree of working-class respect and subservience to 'the masters'. There was also an independent band tradition, sometimes community based, but by the 1890s also linked to the socialist movement. The ILP, SDF and many trades unions held regular demonstrations during elections and in support of major strikes. Having a brass band at the head of the march was calculated to raise the spirits and attract public attention.

The Colne Valley had its own Milnsbridge Socialist Band, formed in 1908, who performed in full uniform; in nearby Golcar the ILP had a string quartet. Liverpool even had its own socialist orchestra. Many towns had 'glee clubs' associated with the ILP, or 'Pleasant Sunday Afternoon' societies, which organised country rambles during the summer months and musical activities during winter.

A key part of socialist art was of course the banner. No self-respecting trade union or ILP branch would, by the late 1890s, have been without one. The artistic form was based on religious banners, though by 1900 the political message had become clear. Heroes of the labour movement – Keir Hardie being a favourite but occasionally Karl Marx and even Lenin in the 1920s – were emblazoned across banners proclaiming messages ranging from the subservient to the seditious. Many survive in local museums, with a superb display in

Manchester's People's History Museum. But to see them in action, the annual Durham Miners' Gala is the place to be.

SOCIALIST EDUCATION

The ILP and SDF had comprehensive programmes of education along-side their more propagandist activities. These extended well beyond adult members, with the establishment of 'Socialist Sunday Schools', formed by the ILP and the associated Labour Churches, to cultivate a new generation of socialist boys and girls. The Socialist Sunday School movement had a long history, surviving well into the 1940s.[17] The North can't claim the movement entirely as its own: the first 'Socialist Sunday School' was formed in Battersea in 1892. But the idea was quickly copied in the socialist heartlands of Lancashire and Yorkshire, with groups set up in Huddersfield, Halifax, Leeds and Liverpool during 1897. The movement was able to run its own magazine for many years – *The Young Socialist*, edited by Edith Pearce, wife of Fred Pearce, the Lancashire writer and friend of Allen Clarke's.

Jeffrey Hill's description of Nelson's Socialist Sunday School would have been fairly typical of others in the North:

> It offered a secular alternative to the many chapel and church-based Sunday schools. Children would sing 'hymns' from the Socialist Sunday School Hymn book, play games to musical accompaniment and have lessons … the School was also well known for its football team.[18]

The School also had secular 'baptisms', with children being given middle names after well-known figures of the socialist movement.

The early socialist organisations placed great stress on education and 'making socialists'. Bradford-born Barbara Castle recalled the early ILP as being a veritable 'workers' university'. Hannah Mitchell's introduction to socialism was through a fellow-lodger lending her a copy of some of Blatchford's articles from *The Sunday Chronicle*. This inspired her to go to educational sessions run by Bolton Socialist Club, where she heard Katherine St John Conway speak. She then became a regular attender of the club and reader of *The Clarion* when it began publication in 1894. When she moved to Ashton-under-Lyne she became a supporter of the local Labour Church, which provided a non-sectarian debating forum for socialists. She wrote that 'ministers of religion, politicians, artists, feminists, all who felt they had a message to benefit humanity, were welcome ...'.[19]

Formal adult working-class education developed alongside, and sometimes in conflict with, the socialist and trade union movement. The WEA – Workers Educational Association – was formed in 1896, with the intention of offering 'liberal' adult education to workers. It eschewed any political direction and won support from paternalistic employers. A new generation of radical socialists increasingly found much of the WEA's approach to be inadequate for their needs. The Plebs League was formed as a spin-off from Ruskin College in 1909, and built up strong support amongst the miners' and railway workers' unions. By the 1920s it had been heavily influenced by the newly founded Communist Party of Great Britain, though many Labour and ILP members also remained active. It had branches in some very small industrial communities where there was a strong radical tradition, particularly the South Wales valleys, but also in towns and villages in the West Riding and Lancashire. In the North East it built up strong support amongst the left wing of the Durham Miners Association, and by 1917 fifty branches had affiliated. The Durham coalfield had a relatively strong anarchist undercurrent, and Will Lawther, a future leader of the NUM, set up the Chopwell Anarchist Club in 1912, in the small West Durham pit village that was later to become famous as one of the many 'Little Moscows' dotted around the coalfields. Lawther organised informal classes on economics at the Chopwell club and also at the neighbouring steel town of Consett during 1915. The Plebs League continued until 1926 when it was absorbed by the National Central Labour College, which ultimately became part of the TUC.

Trade union education developed very much according to the political inclinations of individual unions. The North never had anything approaching the depth of educational resources created by the South Wales Miners, with their extensive network of libraries. Many unions, however, made use of NCLC and WEA courses. The Durham Miners Association was an early supporter of the WEA in the North East and a principal funder when the Association was formed in 1909. Other unions, including boilermakers, pattern makers, postal workers and engineering trades, joined the WEA in the North-East soon after its formation.[20]

THE RELIGION OF SOCIALISM

There was a close but highly complex relationship between religion and socialism, stretching back to Owenism in the 1820s. Many of the early radical handloom weavers were 'free thinkers' who espoused varying degrees of atheism, pantheism or agnosticism. At the same time, the influence of the Quakers and Unitarians on radical politics in the North in the early nineteenth century should not be underestimated. The mass Irish influx during and after the famine of the 1840s led to the re-establishment of Roman Catholicism in the North, with a particularly strong presence in Lancashire (where it had never completely died out, particularly in the west of the county), and much of the West Riding textile districts. The 'Catholic Interest' was especially strong in Liverpool Labour politics for decades, though Merseyside is, in so very many ways, a special case in terms of its political development. The role of secularism amongst working-class radicals needs more research; it clearly helped to shape left-wing politics in the transitional period between Chartism and socialism.[21]

It has been argued that the 'ethical socialism' of the ILP which developed in the North during the 1890s owed much to Methodism.[22] This can be challenged to an extent. Certainly some leading figures in the ILP, such as Philip Snowden, were brought up in the Methodist faith, but the new socialism of the 1890s marked a turn away not only from Liberalism, but also from its stable-mate, nonconformist religion.

In his study of socialism in the Colne Valley David Clark notes that nonconformity was actually weaker there than in other parts of Yorkshire.[23] This is an important point since Grayson's famous victory of 1907 is often ascribed to the 'nonconformist tradition of independence' in the Valley. Furthermore, many if not most of the socialist activists had little or no involvement in organised religion. There were several clergymen active in Colne Valley socialism, but some were Anglican rather than Methodist, including the Rector of Kirkheaton, the Curate of Thongsbridge and the Vicar of New Mill, all in small weaving communities in the Colne Valley. These men espoused a form of 'Social Christianity' which sat easily with the ILP's ethical socialism. Clark writes: 'As the Colne Valley Labour Union developed, the hold of ethical socialism grew there. With its basic ethical appeal it proved equally attractive to the non-Christian radical and the social Christian alike'.[24]

Some nonconformist lay preachers, such as Thomas Enoch Thorpe of Golcar, ran into trouble with their fellow chapel-goers because of their left-wing views. The Congregational minister of Marsden, the Reverend F.R. Swan, was the most important figure in nonconformist socialism; he actually left the ministry to become a full-time organiser for the Colne Valley Labour League in 1907. Overall, many socialists across Yorkshire and parts of Lancashire kept well away from any form of organised religion, though their socialist appeal was frequently couched in broadly 'Christian' terms. The two most popular socialist journalists, Blatchford and Clarke, were antagonistic towards the established church, and Blatchford was an atheist for much of his life. Clarke adopted a broader semi-mystical view, dabbling in spiritualism and eastern religion (see below).

Many of the socialist propagandists adopted the trappings of religion, with speakers using a rousing 'come to Jesus' style of oratory, as we have seen with Snowden. One of Snowden's most famous speeches was 'The Christ That Is To Be'. Katharine St John Conway, Caroline Martyn and Victor Grayson are all described as having the same effect on mass audiences as religious revivalists. But we should not confuse form and content. The Labour Church movement, founded by John Trevor in Manchester in 1891, was not so much a theological movement as an attempt to wean working-class men and women away from the embrace of Methodism and Anglicanism, and provide a non-sectarian and non-denominational meeting point for local socialists who had an allegiance, however broadly-defined, to Christianity.[25]

Similarly, the 'Socialist Sunday Schools' used the trappings of religious Sunday schools, but with a programme of songs, stories and discussions that were largely secular and socialist in character. 'The Socialist Ten Commandments' are a good example of early socialism's use of the form of popular religion to put over a socialist message.

A more sophisticated attempt to reconcile Christian theology and socialism emerged in the 1900s, with the Reverend R.J. Campbell's 'New Theology' movement. Campbell was brought up a Methodist but trained in the Church of England, with whom he subsequently fell out. He took up a ministry at a congregational chapel in Brighton, before eventually moving to Stockport. He joined the ILP in 1907, and in March of that year delivered a lecture in Liverpool in which he announced the 'New Theology' movement. Keir Hardie and John Bruce Glasier were both present at the meeting, with Hardie taking the chair; Ramsay Macdonald sent warm greetings. Higher endorsement from the ILP leadership would be impossible to get. Campbell and Colne Valley's Reverend Swan set up 'The Progressive League' to promote the 'New Theology'. Its first object was 'to provide a common meeting ground and fellowship for all who are in sympathy with progressive Christian thought'.[26] Interest in 'New Theology' had waned by the outbreak of the First World War. Campbell converted back to Anglicanism in 1916, but kept his progressive socialist views.

If Methodism's contribution to socialism has been exaggerated, the role of Quakers in socialism has, if anything, been under-rated. Many of the Quakers who went to prison rather than fight in the First World War were also members of the ILP.[27] Will Hall, the Labour MP for Colne Valley for many years, was from an ILP and Quaker background, and was far from being untypical. However, it was not until 1977 that there was a formal 'Quaker Socialist Society'.

The links between the early socialist movement and spiritualism have been well documented by Logie Barrow.[28] Both movements enjoyed strong support in the industrial North, with links going back to Owenism, Chartism and secularism in the 1860s. Even the Marxist SDF had a strong body of spiritualists amongst its ranks, though it was stronger within the ILP. J.T. Ward, an ILP councillor in Blackburn for twelve years, was a spiritualist 'healer' and director of the spiritualist magazine *The Two Worlds*, which Allen Clarke wrote for and Rochdale ILP'er Peter Lee edited for a short time. Clarke wrote a popular account of his own experiences following the death of his first wife and two of his children.[29] During her time in Bradford Margaret McMillan became an attender of the local spiritualist Lyceum, and Montague Blatchford, brother of Robert, adjudicated the choirs of the North-East Lancashire Lyceums. *The Bolton and District ILP Pioneer* had contributions from at least three spiritualists within its seven issues.[30] Barrow points out the close links between the Labour Church movement and spiritualism in East Lancashire, with several members of Blackburn Labour Church being involved with the local spiritualist church. In the West Riding, future Colne Valley MP Ernest Marklew was a life-long spiritualist and socialist and edited *The Medium*. In a Commons speech he declared that, 'All I am … and all I hope for, I owe to spiritualism'.[31]

James Swindlehurst, a 'moral socialist' of Bolton, was involved in the Chartist movement in his youth, and wrote an account of old

Owenite and Chartist handloom weavers whom he met and chatted with in a Bolton park, *Summer Evenings with Old Weavers*. This is a fascinating account of a way of life which was rapidly becoming extinct but whose political echoes still reverberated in the North.[32] Swindlehurst believed that 'individual effort is required before man can work out his own salvation'.[33] He was victimised for his radical beliefs and his family suffered eviction; his wife had to give birth in the street.

SOCIALISM AND SPIRITUALITY

Alongside the strong religious residues within the Northern socialist movement, there was something else which deserves a section of its own – a degree of what for want of a better term is 'spirituality'. This was personified in the figure of Edward Carpenter and also Allen Clarke, both of whom took a strong interest in eastern religions. Carpenter visited India on several occasions and wrote extensively on Hinduism. In *A Visit to a Gnani*, Carpenter comments on the similarities between socialism and eastern philosophy.[34]

Clarke was similarly inspired by eastern religions, both Hinduism and Buddhism, whilst being caustic about organised conventional western religion. In *The Eternal Question* he argues: 'How blind and foolish men have been to take all their religion from one Book, when God is giving every generation the Bible (that is, Books) fit for its special needs and dreams ...'. He concludes in saying that spiritual truth lies in many theologies, and 'its lessons include lofty and beautiful extracts from the Bible, Talmud, Buddha, The Koran, Swedenborg, Marcus Aurelius, Wordsworth etc. – all the great souls of history'.[35]

Clarke's philosophical inclinations were nothing if not diverse. Whilst promoting spiritualism in *The Eternal Question*, he also advocates the Buddhism outlined by the late nineteenth-century British writer and Theosophist A.P. Sinnett, whose *Esoteric Buddhism* is seen as a revelation: 'Intuitively I felt that here was the truth; the broad outlines were correct, whatever errors there might be in the details'.[36]

As we have seen, Carpenter and Clarke shared a love of Walt Whitman, whose poetry has strong echoes of eastern mysticism. The story of the links between Lancashire and Walt Whitman (see below) is one of the most fascinating (and bizarre) chapters of Northern socialist history – when a coterie of mainly ILP activists formed a sort of early 'men's group' to discuss Whitman's poetry and philosophy.

THE INFLUENCE OF WALT WHITMAN

The great poet of American democracy, Walt Whitman, had a huge influence on the early British socialist movement, particularly in the North of England. The man whom many acclaim as the United States' greatest-ever poet had very close ties with a group of friends, many of whom were socialists, in Lancashire. They included Dr John Johnston, a native of Annan but long-time resident of Bolton and a key figure in the town's progressive movement as well as a highly respected doctor, and J.W. Wallace, an architect's assistant, ILP activist and mystic.

These were the central figures in the Bolton group which referred, only half-jokingly, to Wallace as 'The Master'. Wallace was a close friend of both the Glasiers and Keir Hardie, and a member of the ILP's National Administrative Council. He used this position to promote his almost fanatical devotion to the prophet of comradeship and the open air, and in this had some measure of success. Most socialist publications in the 1890s carried adverts for *Leaves of Grass*, Whitman's ever-changing collection of his writings, and his poetry featured in most collections of socialist verse. *Labour's Garland – Poems for Socialists*, published by *The Huddersfield Worker* and edited by James Leatham, included an excerpt from Whitman's prose on the cover and part of 'Song of the Redwood Tree' and 'To a Foil'd European Revolutionaire' amongst the poetry.[37]

What made Whitman so popular in the North of England? He cut a striking figure, with a shock of white hair and beard, wearing a cap perched at a jaunty angle. Allen Clarke, a good friend of Wallace and Johnston, wrote in 1919 that:

> it is fitting that Bolton should be distinguished above all towns in England by having a group of Whitman enthusiasts, for many years in close touch, by letter and visit, with 'the Master', for I am sure Walt Whitman, the singer of out-door life, would have loved to ramble our Lancashire moorlands.[38]

The correspondence with Whitman started with a birthday greeting sent in 1887, signed by Wallace and Johnston, both members of Bolton

ILP. Whitman was touched, and there began an exchange of letters which cast fascinating light both on Whitman himself and on life in Lancashire in the late nineteenth century. Wallace and Johnston both visited Whitman in America, and detailed accounts of the two visits were published as *Visits to Walt Whitman in 1890-1891 by Two Lancashire Friends*, in 1917. Johnston was a skilled photographer, and the book is well illustrated with photographs taken during Johnston's visit in 1890.[39]

Whitman died in 1892, but by then a firm friendship with other American 'Whitmanites' had been established by this small group of enthusiasts in the town which was then at the heart of the Lancashire cotton industry. They called themselves 'The Eagle Street College', after the modest two-up two-down terraced house where Wallace lived with his parents in the mid-1880s. They used to meet at Wallace's home each week to discuss Whitman and other great thinkers and poets of the time. Wallace moved to Adlington, a small village on the edge of the Bolton moors, in the mid-1890s, and this encouraged the group to come to visit and explore the magnificent scenery around Rivington and Anglezarke.

The highpoint of the group's social calendar was the celebration of Whitman's birthday on 31 May. The day included a brisk walk up to Rivington, wearing sprigs of lilac, Whitman's emblematic flower. In the vicarage garden they would be entertained by the Unitarian minister Samuel Thompson. There would be readings from 'Leaves of Grass' and the passing round of a 'loving cup' containing spiced claret. More often than not Wallace would deliver an 'address' on the political and spiritual significance of Whitman. A good time was had by all, and they were able to work off the claret on the walk back down to the railway station at Adlington.

The group were, at least initially, mainly lower middle-class men, who included among their number clerks, a journalist, clergymen and one or two skilled workers. They were not a metropolitan intelligentsia, but neither could they be described as representative of Bolton's industrial working class. They were probably typical of the sort of person drawn to the young Independent Labour Party, with its message of ethical, rather than Marxian, socialism. As Fred Wild, an early member of the group commented, 'these young men were all from the Parish Church and for the most part were engaged as clerks or minor gaffers and were attracted to Wallace by his personality and intellectual powers'.[40]

Wallace had a wider circle of friends who were infected by his love for Whitman, including Keir Hardie, who frequently visited him in Adlington. Edward Carpenter, Robert Blatchford and the Irish co-operator Horace Plunkett were also amongst his friends and correspondents. Whitman and Carpenter were particularly close friends and Carpenter visited the poet in America. Whilst Carpenter was overtly gay, Whitman kept his sexuality something of a mystery, though America's modern gay community has claimed him as their own. Much of his poetry is a powerful celebration of love between men, with some strongly erotic themes and imagery. Equally, he was the poet of spirituality and comradeship, and love of the open air.

Johnston was a close friend, and possibly lover, of Edward Carpenter, and served as his informal GP, enjoying the periodic train ride from Bolton to Dore, through the heart of the Peak District. He had at least one holiday with Carpenter in North Africa, and there is a photograph of the two of them standing alongside a camel. Johnston was a key figure in several of Bolton's radical causes, including 'The Progressive League', which brought together the town's middle-class socialists and liberals to discuss issues around town planning and philosophy. He was a good friend of Bolton's redoubtable co-operator and feminist Sarah Reddish, and shared her concern about the welfare of children. His book, *The Realisation of the Child*, argued that children could only develop mentally and physically if they were well clothed, fed and housed.

As we have seen (see p83-4), Wallace's close friend Katharine Bruce Glasier (who in her later years often referred to him as 'Uncle Wallace') shared his spiritual – as opposed to spiritualist – philosophy; her writings and speeches are saturated with Whitmanite mysticism. Like many other socialists of her time, including Carpenter, she was also an admirer of the writing of Rabindranath Tagore, the Bengali poet and philosopher.[41] Katharine's drift into a highly spiritual form of socialism, which included becoming a Quaker, accelerated following the death of her husband John in 1920 and her son Glen in 1928. Her tribute to her son, *The Glen Book*, first serialised in *Labour's Northern Voice*, is also a strong celebration of Whitman and his philosophy, with numerous excerpts from *Leaves of Grass*. She quotes extensively from Whitman about a coming new age 'rounding forward to another springtime of the Spirit of the Whole ... an age of reason and faith with far more wonderful works than man has yet seen is drawing near'.[42] In a more cynical age it's easy to see Katharine Bruce Glasier's blending of socialism and spirituality as naive and even comic. But we are foolish to ignore the ageless wisdom of Whitman, Tagore and Carpenter. Katharine made a brave attempt to harness their work to her political practice.

SOCIALISM ARRIVES BY BIKE

The Clarion created the most successful socialist leisure network Britain has yet seen. Its main strength was the cycling club, but it also included several other activities, among them rambling, field studies, choral singing and drama groups. The cycling club was formed in 1894, at a time when cycles were becoming affordable to most working-class people. The Clarion Cycling Club combined recreation – getting out of the industrial towns for a Sunday ride with your mates – with an evangelical attempt to spread the socialist gospel. One London-based journalist wrote:

> Many quiet nooks in the Midlands and North of England have been invaded during the last few days by a band of cycling socialists who call themselves 'The Clarion Club'. They have been endeavouring, with scant measure of success, to propagate their views in the country districts and to advertise the socialist organ after which their club is named.[43]

The cycling club became immensely popular, and its annual 'meets', often in Peak District towns like Ashbourne or Bakewell, attracted several hundred delegates. The Skipton 'meet' of 1899 attracted four hundred attendees, and the organisers ran out of beds. The emphasis was on having a good time, promoting fellowship – and spreading the socialist message. The Chester Meet of 1898 attracted the attention of the Cheshire Constabulary, concerned about possible threats to public safety. The report of one of the plain clothes officers sent to the observe the meeting included the observation that 'if these chaps kill anybody, it will be from laughing'.[44]

The cycling club and the associated sporting and cultural bodies spawned by *The Clarion* attracted women as well as men. Alice Foley mentions saving up to buy her first bike, despite being on 'short time' at the mill – and then learning ride it:

Stolid perseverance won in the end, I shortly joined the Clarion Cycling Club and a new era of fun and comradeship opened out. In merry company we slogged up hills and freewheeled joyously down them thrilling to the beauty and excitement of a countryside as yet unspoiled by the advent of motor transport.[45]

RADICAL RAMBLERS

Alongside cycling, the early socialist movement encouraged walking groups and 'field naturalists'. A network of Clarion, ILP and Labour Church rambling groups developed in the 1890s. There was a political edge to this activity. The ethical socialism of the 1890s, strongly influenced by Whitman, had a deep attachment to the open air and countryside. This chimed with an inherited attachment to the countryside, which was far from having been eradicated by industrialisation. Many thousands of rural working-class families had been forced into overcrowded towns and cities at the beginning of the nineteenth century. But if they were lucky enough to live in towns like Bolton, Rochdale, Burnley, Huddersfield and Halifax they were within a walk – or a tram ride – of open countryside. Rights of way over the moors were jealously guarded, and encroachments on these rights were violently resisted.[46]

The popular narrative runs that 'Kinder Scout' in 1932 was the first major rights of way battle in which working people claimed their rights of access. But that's not so. Kinder Scout was certainly important, but major rights of way battles had been fought as far back as the 1820s, notably in Flixton, now a Manchester suburb, where attempts to close a right of way enjoyed by generations of local people resulted in pitched battles. Throughout the nineteenth century working-class people contested attempts to close public rights of way. One of the most well-documented fights was over access to Darwen Moors, which was won in 1897. The victory was celebrated by the erection of the 'Jubilee Tower' to celebrate Victoria's Golden Jubilee the following year. It looks like a rocket about to take off.

The biggest rights of way struggle in the nineteenth century was at Winter Hill, a tract of moorland north of Bolton.[47] On three successive weekends in September 1896 thousands of Bolton workers attempted to reclaim a right of way which had been blocked by the local Tory landowner. It was a highly political – and personal – dispute.

The squire, Richard Ainsworth, was widely disliked, and his opponents were a mixture of local socialists and radical liberals. Joseph Shufflebotham, secretary of the Bolton branch of the SDF, was the key figure from the socialist side, supported by Solomon Partington, radical Liberal, journalist and future councillor.

Ainsworth closed the main path over Winter Hill – Coal Pit Lane – to allow his grouse-shooting to be unimpeded, and positioned gamekeepers across his land to turn people away. In response, Bolton SDF appealed to local people to join them 'for a walk' to reclaim their right of way, on Sunday 5 September 1896. They assembled on the outskirts of the town centre, mustering a respectable crowd of a few hundred. As the demonstrators marched up Halliwell Road, through a densely-populated working-class area of town, many more joined in. By the time they reached the outskirts of town, around 10,000 people were on the march.

When they reached the barricade erected by Ainsworth a minor scuffle ensued, and some gamekeepers found themselves thrown over a wall. The gate was torn down and the crowd marched on, over Winter Hill and down into the small village of Belmont, where the local pubs were besieged by the hungry and thirsty walkers. A further walk was organised for the following Sunday, and the SDF and their supporters held nightly demonstrations on the Town Hall steps to raise support. The second march attracted even more support than the first, estimated at around 12,000 people, nearly all of whom were local. The final march took place on the following Saturday, with a smaller march, numbering around 6000. But by then Ainsworth had taken the initiative and started issuing writs against any identifiable marchers.

Eventually, a small group of the 'ring leaders', including Shufflebotham and Partington, were taken to court. There they were defended by Richard Pankhurst – husband of Emmeline, the women's suffrage leader, and a leading figure in the Manchester ILP. Despite a strong defence, the case went in favour of Ainsworth. Although the defendants were not sent to prison – unlike the later Kinder Scout campaigners – they were heavily fined. The case caused shockwaves across Lancashire, and may have influenced people in Darwen to take similar action to claim a right of way over the Darwen Moors – which proved more successful. The Winter Hill campaign helped strengthen Bolton's SDF branch, and even led to the composition of a song by

Allen Clarke, which was sold as a broadsheet to raise money to help pay the fines:

Will yo' come o'Sunday mornin'
For a walk o'er Winter Hill
Ten thousand went last Sunday
But there's room for thousands still!
Oh the moors are rare and bonny
And the heather's sweet and fine
And the road across the hilltops is the people's – yours and mine![48]

The memory of the struggle, and the treatment meted out to the leaders of the campaign, rankled with Bolton people and helped Partington ensure a stunning victory when he stood for election on a radical platform in Bolton's 1904 local elections.

PICNICS, GARDEN PARTIES AND SOIRÉES

The ILP and its sister group the Labour Church often combined countryside walks with picnics. Allen Clarke recalls Bolton Labour Church outings to the local moors when they had 'gypsy teas' and sang 'England Arise!'. It was normal for the usual cycle of evening meetings to be replaced by weekend outdoor activities during the summer months, and these invariably included socialist songs and, often, a short homily from a local speaker. A love of botany was often a feature of the ILP outdoor enthusiasts, and Clarke mentions Fletcher, 'the clever collier botanist' from Westhoughton, who often accompanied Labour Church and ILP walks. James Sims, who was one of the central figures of the Labour Church movement and president of the Bolton branch, was a skilled botanist, with a particular knowledge of ferns and mosses.[49]

The Clarion Cycling Club rides usually included either a roadside picnic or a stop off at a friendly café, or Clarion club house. Allen Clarke perhaps did more than anyone to develop the socialist picnic, based on his *Northern Weekly* readership. The first 'Teddy Ashton Picnic' was held at the local beauty spot of Barrow Bridge, on the outskirts of Bolton. It attracted a massive crowd totalling around 10,000.[50] The picnics became annual events, attracting large crowds, often entertained by Clarion Choirs.

As well as the outdoor picnics, Northern socialists loved to organise garden parties and soirees. In Colne Valley, socialist mill-owner France Littlewood opened up his large house for an annual garden party which attracted hundreds of local socialists.[51] During the winter months, as well as the more formal political discussions, soirees and tea parties were held.

ALTERNATIVE WAYS OF LIVING: CO-OPERATIVE COLONIES

The 'community building' experiments of the Owenite and Chartist periods had fizzled out during the 1840s. However, the movement to create co-operative or 'communist' colonies revived in the 1890s, partly as a result of the influence of Tolstoy and his brand of non-violent 'Christian Anarchism'. The influence of Tolstoy on English socialism is virtually ignored by socialist historians, but for a few years before the First World War his influence was considerable. Sales of his publications in Britain were boosted by the establishment of the 'Free Age Press', managed by Tolstoy's agent Vladimir Tchertkoff, who was based initially in Purleigh, Essex, and later in Christchurch, Hampshire. Both Allen Clarke, through his *Northern Weekly*, and Blatchford in *The Clarion* promoted the writings of Tolstoy. His novel *Resurrection* was serialised in *The Clarion* during 1899 and 1900.[52]

Libertarian socialists in the North East established the Clousden Hill commune in 1896, which survived until 1902. It had a direct link to the wider co-operative movement, with many co-operative shops in the North East buying its produce. Its history is recounted in Nigel Todd's *Roses and Revolutionists*.[53] In Blackburn, a group of Tolstoyans tried to create a cash-free community, based on barter and donations, but it had a short life. Starnthwaite, near Kendal, was the location for another community, which, though again shortlived, was much used as a base for 'rest and recreation' by itinerant ILP propagandists. Percy Redfern, later to play an important role in the Co-operative movement, was secretary of a 'Tolstoy Society' in Manchester in the 1890s.[54]

Allen Clarke, writing in *Effects of the Factory System* (first serialised in *The Clarion* in 1895/6 then published in book form in 1899), called for a future society based on mutual aid and co-operation, saying he 'would like to see Lancashire a cluster of small villages and towns, each fixed solid on its own industrial base, doing its own spinning and weaving; with its theatre, gymnasium, schools, libraries, baths and all things necessary for body and soul'.[55]

Clarke became one of the most devoted apostles of alternative living. His paper carried regular advertisements for The Free Age Press and carried regular features on Tolstoy and his work. Clarke corresponded with Tolstoy, who translated *Effects of the Factory System* into Russian. He summed up the challenge in a pamphlet published in 1904:

> Certain circumstances have created an anti-natural, absurd and ailing state of things and today we are confronted with two great problems, insisting on a solution – the unemployed question and the physical (which also means mental) deterioration of the nation. Both these problems can be resolved by getting back to the land, and returning to that labour which nature meant should be the fundamental of every man's occupation.[56]

He tried to put his Tolstoyan vision into practice with the 'Daisy Colony' Scheme ('Daisy', as he explained to Tolstoy, because the daisy is the most communistic of flowers!). It is a story which has echoes of the experience of most attempts to build 'communist colonies' at the time. It was fairly common for a group of enthusiastic socialists to get together to create a socialist utopia, but the realities of human nature and economics often conspired to wreck the hopes of the idealists.

Clarke launched the appeal in his *Northern Weekly* on 4 July 1903. A meeting took place at Bolton's Vegetarian Restaurant, Newport Street, in September, and attracted some 30 people from all over Lancashire. Branches of the 'Daisy Colony' scheme were formed in Bolton, Blackburn, Stockport, Manchester, Reddish, Tottington, Heywood, Burnley and Rawtenstall. Eventually they totalled thirty-one, with outposts in Marsden, Bradford and even Glasgow. The agreed objects were: 'To form a communistic colony and natural holiday resort, as soon as enough money is raised to purchase land, in the north of England (near Blackpool if possible) to start market gardening etc. and then develop hand industries and a college of agriculture'.[57]

The 'Teddy Ashton Picnics' helped bolster support for the plans, and numerous fund-raising concerts were held. In February 1905 Clarke announced that some land and a house had been rented at Carleton, near Blackpool. William Addison, Vice-President of Bolton Labour Church and a former activist in the agricultural workers' union in East Anglia, was appointed manager, a move which caused some jealousy among some of the scheme's members. However, some people moved into the house and the colony attracted a lot of visitors who purchased produce from the colony. But by July 1906 problems were mounting up and there were reports of squabbles among the colonists. Clarke admitted that 'brotherhood, so sweet in the mouth, proves very bitter in practice'.[58] Clarke concluded that the scheme could not work on 'communist' lines, and suggested a co-operative allotments scheme, similar to that run by Blackpool Clarion. By 1907 the scheme was declared a failure and the colonists had departed. The lease was surrendered to the landlord, leaving Clarke with substantial debts.

NORTHERN SOCIALIST LITERATURE

It's a pity that mainstream social history seems to have heard of only one 'working-class' novel – Tressell's *Ragged Trousered Philanthropists*. This captured the imagination of thousands of working-class readers, though its political message was ambivalent, tending to portray 'typical' working-class figures as fools.[59] But there was so much more. Allen Clarke wrote twenty-three novels, most of which were overtly political. *The Red Flag* – subtitled '*a tale of the people's woe*' – is essentially the novel of the socialist movement in North-East Lancashire. It was published by the SDF's printing house, Twentieth Century Press, in 1908. Literally dozens of novels and hundreds of poems with a socialist theme were serialised in *The Cotton Factory Times*, and in many of the local journals.

The early 1900s saw a flowering of regional working-class literature, encouraged by the two 'Factory Times' newspapers on either side of the Pennines, and Clarke's *Northern Weekly*, which lasted until 1908. Many local socialist newspapers encouraged working-class writers, some – though by no means all – in dialect. Clarke encouraged a circle of writers which included Fred Plant of Stockport, Arthur Laycock of Blackpool (son of the famous Samuel), the cartoonist, cotton worker and poet Sam Fitton of Shaw, Ethel Carnie, the weaver, poet and novelist from Great Harwood, and Sarah Robinson, poet and short-story writer, from Padiham. In 1908 Clarke initiated moves to form an association of Lancashire writers, which finally took shape as the

Lancashire Authors' Association, founded in Rochdale in 1909. Clarke was elected chairman, a role to which he proved spectacularly unsuited. He was ultimately deposed because of his high-handed disregard for protocol. The first secretary was Robert Brodie, a young ILP member and dialect poet from Bolton, who wrote as 'Billy Button'.

Both Fred Plant and Arthur Laycock, the first socialist councillors to be elected for Stockport and Blackpool respectively, were accomplished novelists. Many of Plant's novels and short stories, several about life in Lancashire mills and mines, were only published in serial form in Allen Clarke's newspaper, *Teddy Ashton's Northern Weekly*. His novel *The Conductor's Sweetheart* is set during a strike on the local tramways, in which police mounted a series of baton charges against the tramway workers. W.E. Tirebuck, born in Liverpool in 1854, wrote several novels and short stories, including *Miss Grace of All Souls*, set during the 1893 Miners' Lock-Out in Lancashire.[60]

Not all socialist writers during this period were men. Ethel Carnie, a mill worker in East Lancashire, was a talented poet who had work published in both local newspapers such as *The Blackburn Mail* and labour publications such as *Cotton Factory Times*. She became editor of *The Woman Worker*, an off-shoot of *The Clarion*, moving to London at the behest of Robert Blatchford in 1909. The move was not a success, however, and she appears to have fallen out with Blatchford. By the following year she was back home in Great Harwood, working as a warper and beamer in a local mill. This did not put an end to her writing, and her first novel *Miss Nobody* was published in 1913. Her most overtly socialist novel, *This Slavery*, was published in 1925.[61] Her novel *Helen of Four Gates* was made into a film in the 1930s, and was shown at the 2011 Bradford Film Festival. Sarah Robinson of Padiham, whose father had been active in the Chartist movement, contributed poetry to *Teddy Ashton's Northern Weekly*.

Socialist art proved less accessible to working-class socialists. Walter Crane, head of Manchester School of Art, epitomised the romantic style of socialist art that developed in the 1890s, strongly influenced by art nouveau. Woman are bounteous goddesses, men are fustian-clad peasants, earthy of the soil. They are invariably gazing towards the rising sun of socialism. Crane's romanticised imagery of the workers was fairly quickly superseded by the equally unrealistic Bolshevik images of heroic industrial workers toiling over anvils, hammers in hand. However in the early 1900s Sam Fitton, a mill worker in Shaw, near Oldham, emerged not only as a talented dialect poet but a highly skilled cartoonist, illustrating many of Allen Clarke's sketches about mill life.[62]

THE REVOLT OF BILL AND BET SPRIGGS: DIALECT IN THE SERVICE OF SOCIALISM

> I daresay Teddy Ashton's droll sketches have done more to help reforms than far more pretentious and direct articles. For 'Teddy' even in his comic (dialect) sketches, pokes sly fun and undermining sarcasm at the iniquities and social injustices of the day'
>
> Allen Clarke writing in *Teddy Ashton's Northern Weekly*[63]

Several Northern working-class writers used dialect to get over a socialist message. Dialect was used in many local socialist papers from the 1890s, on both sides of the Pennines. The Lancashire-based *Cotton Factory Times* and its sister *The Yorkshire Factory Times* carried regular poems, short stories and even novels which made much use of dialect. Across the Pennines Ben Turner also wrote dialect poetry that supported the socialist cause, and several of his poems in Yorkshire dialect were published in local newspapers before the First World War, as well as in *The Yorkshire Factory Times*. In the North East, miner Tommy Armstrong wrote songs and poetry in the dialect of the Durham Coalfield to support his fellow miners, be they strike ballads or laments about pit disasters.[64] What all each had in common were deep roots in their respective communities and a desire to use their literary skills to promote the cause of labour. Writing in dialect sent a strong message that they were part of a very distinctive community, based on shared values and experiences.

Most of the radical dialect writers tended to be on the west side of the Pennines (Clarke, Burgess and later Mitchell and Fitton), though Yorkshire produced some socialist politicians, like Turner, who used dialect to further Labour's cause. The huge popularity of dialect literature during this time is remarkable, and grew out of an established tradition. The form really took off in the 1850s with Edwin Waugh, soon followed by Ben Brierley and Samuel Laycock. By 1900 it had achieved enormous popularity.

Clarke's initial 'Tum Fowt Sketches' (see p99) were written as light entertainment, to soften the harder political material in his publications. But then he began using the sketches to poke that 'sly fun and undermining sarcasm' against social ills of the time. By the early 1900s he had published sketches such as 'Bill Spriggs at the Labour Church', 'Bill Spriggs as a Vegetarian' and even 'Bill Spriggs and the New Theology'.[65] During a major strike in one of the Bolton weaving sheds in 1906 over the introduction of modern looms which would be managed by fewer weavers, he wrote a series of letters in dialect from 'Billy Pickinpeg', and also a sketch called 'Th'Patent Automatic Cemetery Looms' which helped win support for the strikers.[66]

Clarke's 'Teddy Ashton' sketches were claimed (by himself!) to have sold over a million copies. Whatever the exact figures may have been, there is no doubt he built up a mass readership. Working-class readers of the local press eagerly lapped up 'homely' dialect sketches and poems, or heard them recited at tea parties and soirees, often organised by local co-operative societies. The attempt, and a highly successful one it was, by writers like Clarke to use dialect to get across a simple socialist message was very much a product of its time, and its popularity began to wane in the 1930s. But for a time, socialism was able to speak in a pronounced Lancashire or Yorkshire dialect, and further deepen the hold that socialism, and particularly the ILP brand, had on the industrial working class of the North.

Walter Hampson, a locomotive driver from Normanton, near Wakefield, was an important figure in Yorkshire dialect circles. He was a member of the ILP and active in the National Union of Railwaymen, which published his poems (in standard English) as *Songs of the Line* in 1905. His most popular work was, however, in dialect. For many years he edited – and wrote the bulk of – *John Hartley's Yorkshire Clock Almanack*, which circulated widely in the West Riding. Ben Turner was a frequent contributor, as late as the 1930s – by which time he had received a knighthood and served in Labour cabinets. Viscount Snowden, as he was by 1931, was another occasional contributor to the publication. Unlike Clarke, Hampson did not use dialect as a vehicle for political comment, and most of his sketches are of the classic 'homely' subject themes.[67]

The appeal of dialect had weakened after the First World War, but interest remained significant. Hannah Mitchell was a regular contributor of dialect sketches to *Labour's Northern Voice* throughout the 1920s, writing as 'Daisy Nook' – a reference to Ben Brierley, dialect writer and radical Liberal, who wrote his *Daisy Nook Sketches* in the

HANNAH MITCHELL – 'DAISY NOOK'

Hannah Mitchell, a talented working-class woman who played an active role in the women's suffrage campaign, became one of Manchester's most effective local politicians. But despite – or because of – her prominent role in the women's suffrage movement, it took many years for her to be accepted by the Labour Party as a suitable candidate for the local elections. Though she was elected to the Ashton Board of Guardians in 1906 it was to take another seventeen years before she became a councillor in Manchester. Her local ILP branch nominated her in 1921, only for the nomination to be rejected by the City party; and when she was nominated by the ILP in 1923 she was turned down in favour of a rather disreputable businessman. Shortly afterwards he became bankrupt, and it was only then, in her words, that 'my opponents in the Labour Party swallowed their scruples and accepted me'.[i]

In Mitchell's view many of her Labour colleagues on the Council were less interested in city governance than in 'exciting debates', and generally making political gestures such as defying the Lord Mayor. She herself was a real innovator, suggesting radical but achievable initiatives, such as 'electors' councils' in each ward, who would advise their elected members on important local issues. She was a community activist, arguing for cafés in parks so that tired mothers could have a cup of tea whilst taking the kids out for a walk; and she worked tirelessly on the Public Assistance (formerly Poor Law) Committee. But most of all she loved her time on the Libraries Committee. Another of her innovations was the 'travelling library' which toured areas without a branch facility, an idea she picked up from a visit to the United States. For some historians getting travelling libraries, public baths or park cafés organised may not count as being worth a mention – but they made a huge difference to the working-class people they served.

As Mitchell pointed out, many male colleagues dressed up anti-women arguments in 'Marxist' terminology: 'One of the first things I sensed in public life was the strong under-current of anti-feminism which pervades most public bodies. The Labour Party itself was only lukewarm on such matters as "equal pay", while on the employment of married women most of them were definitely reactionary'. Sometimes, she continues, 'they went all Marxian and stressed the bad economics of two incomes going into one home, while men with a capital "M" were unemployed'.[ii]

i. Hannah Mitchell, *The Hard Way Up*, 1968, p195.
ii. Hannah Mitchell, *Hard Way Up*, p217.

1880s about a local beauty spot in North Manchester. Mitchell too wanted to put across a simple socialist message to an audience who might not be totally convinced of Labour's alternative. Many of her sketches also express a strong working-class feminism, unsparing in its criticism of working-class male attitudes towards women.

A DISTINCTIVE TRADITION TAKES SHAPE

By the start of the twentieth century, that distinctive 'Northern' socialism which Blatchford identified was firmly rooted in the textile districts of Lancashire and Yorkshire, and in the mining communities of the North East. It was strongly 'values' based, with a stress on fellowship, community and co-operation. The ILP's 'ethical socialism' has been derided by some as woolly, and too susceptible to losing its radical cutting edge. But much the same could be said of the SDF despite its marxist rigidity: some of the early SDF recruits – such as Bevin – ended up as cabinet ministers in the Labour governments of the inter-war years, pursuing laissez-faire economic policies indistinguishable from those of right-wing Liberals. In contrast, some of the foremost 'ethical socialists' remained true to their ideals throughout their lives, notably Katharine Bruce Glasier, Selina Cooper, Allen Clarke, Fred Jowett and Edward Carpenter.

The 'values' of the ILP stressed community and fairness; opposition to child labour; a hatred of war; gender equality; socialisation of industry; and a love and respect for the countryside. For many there was a strong element of religiosity, not necessarily in the sense of organised religion, but sometimes in the form of a more spiritual faith. It had a strong streak of working-class 'cultural' individualism, nurtured in the weaving communities of the Pennines with their strong tradition of independence and self-help. It was rooted in community, but was at the same time internationalist. One side was highly practical: the work of the ILP's municipal pioneers had nothing 'woolly' about it and led to very direct improvements to local health, child care and education. And it also had a poetry to it; the locally-rooted dialect of Allen Clarke, Ben Turner, Hannah Mitchell and Joseph Burgess, but also the mysticism and earthy, sensual joy of Whitman and Carpenter. The 'Clarionettes' would add: 'and having a good time!'

NOTES

1. Clark, op. cit., p184.
2. Eddie May, 'The Mosaic of Labour Politics 1900-1918', in D. Tanner et al (eds), *The Labour Party in Wales 1900-2000*, p66, citing research by Deian Hopkin.
3. Jeff Hill, *Nelson: Politics, Economy, Community*, 1997, p110.
4. Neil Duffield, *Bolton Socialist Club*, 1986, is a good short history of the club.
5. Clark, op. cit., p184.
6. Joseph Burgess, *A Potential Poet?*, 1927.
7. See Eddie Cass, 'The Cotton Factory Times 1885-1937', in *Manchester Region History Review*, 2006.
8. See Salveson, *Lancashire's Romantic Radical*, op. cit. for a full outline of Clarke's journalism.
9. Clark, op. cit., p182.
10. James Leatham, quoted in Stephen Yeo, 'The Religion of Socialism', in *History Workshop* 1977, p40.
11. See Jack Mowat and Albert Power, *Our Struggle for Socialism in Barrow*, 1949.
12. Alan Brooke, *Honley Socialist Club*, 1992, p11.
13. Denis Pye, *Fellowship is Life: the National Clarion Cycling Club 1885-1995*, 1995, p44.
14. Ibid., p45.
15. *The Record* (Halifax), July 1897.
16. Philip Snowden, *Autobiography*, 1934, p71.
17. See Fred Reid, 'Socialist Sunday Schools in Britain 1892-1939', in *International Review of Social History*, 1966. Edith Pearce was also editor of the Lancashire Authors' Association magazine, *Red Rose Leaves*.
18. Hill, op. cit., p110.
19. Mitchell, op. cit., p116.
20. Nigel Todd, *The Right to Learn: The WEA in the North-East of England 1910-2010*, 2010.
21. See Sam Davies, *Liverpool Labour*, 1996.
22. Leonard Smith, 'Religion and the ILP', in James, Jowitt and Laybourn (eds), *The Centennial History of the Independent Labour Party*. For Merseyside see Davies, op. cit., and for Colne Valley, Clarke, op. cit.
23. Clark op. cit., pp50-2.
24. Ibid., p187.
25. Hannah Mitchell, op. cit., pp114-20, has some good descriptions of practical activities in the Labour Church around Ashton and Oldham.
26. Clarke wrote a send-up of the pretensions of 'New Theology' in one of his *Tum Fowt Sketches*. Stephen Yeo, in his article on 'The Religion of Socialism', looks at Campbell's theology in the context of early socialism.

Sheila Rowbotham's *Edward Carpenter*, op. cit., p312, includes a useful discussion on 'New Theology'.

27. See Cyril Pearce, *Comrades in Conscience*, 2001, for the role of Quakers in the anti-war movement in Huddersfield.

28. See Logie Barrow, *Independent Spirits: Spiritualism and English Plebeians 1850-1910*, 1986.

29. Allen Clarke, *The Eternal Question*, 1901.

30. See Barrow, op. cit., pp117-8, for a fascinating account of socialist involvement in 'the after life' movement.

31. Ibid., p121.

32. James Swindlehurst (as 'JS'), *Summer Evenings with Old Weavers*, n.d. but c 1890.

33. See short biography in Barrow, op. cit., p123.

34. Edward Carpenter, *A Visit to a Gnani*, 1911.

35. Allen Clarke, *The Eternal Question*, op. cit., p 228.

36. Ibid., p139.

37. James Leatham (ed.), *Labour's Garland – Poems for Socialists*, n.d. c 1900.

38. Allen Clarke, *Moorlands and Memories*, 1920, p62.

39. Paul Salveson, *With Walt Whitman in Bolton*, 2009; and J. Johnston and J.W. Wallace, *Visits to Walt Whitman by Two Lancashire Friends*, 1917.

40. Salveson, With Walt Whitman, op. cit., p17.

41. Tagore's influence on many English socialists, including Ramsay Macdonald, was considerable, but there is little written about it. See Krishna Dutta and Andrew Robinson, *Tagore: The Myriad-Minded Man*, 2008.

42. Katharine Bruce Glasier, *The Glen Book*, 1947.

43. Pye, op. cit., p17.

44. Ibid., p23.

45. Alice Foley, *A Bolton Childhood*, 1973, p72.

46. See Harvey Taylor, *A Claim on the Countryside*, 1997; also Tom Stephenson, *Forbidden Land*, 1989; Howard Hill *Freedom to Roam*, 1980; Colin Speakman, *Walk!*, 2011. It's significant that all the key works on the rights of way movement have been written by Northerners!

47. Paul Salveson, *'Will Yo' Come O' Sunday Mornin'? The Winter Hill Trespass of 1896*, 1982 and 1996, p20.

48. Ibid., p20 (2nd edition).

49. Allen Clarke, 'The Old Chartist and the Mosses', *Windmill Land*, 1916, for references to Sims.

50. *Teddy Ashton's Northern Weekly*, 25 May 1901, has a full account of the first picnic; see Salveson *Lancashire's Romantic Radical*, op. cit., p87, for photo of part of the group.

51. Alan Brooke, *Honley Socialist Club* op. cit.

52. Clarke corresponded with Tolstoy on many subjects, including the Daisy Colony Scheme. See Paul Salveson, 'Getting Back to the Land; The Daisy Colony Scheme', *North West Labour History*, 1985.

53. See Nigel Todd, *Roses and Revolutionists*, 1986, for an account of the Clousden Hill colony.
54. Percy Redfern, *Journey to Understanding*, 1946.
55. Allen Clarke, *Effects of the Factory System*, op. cit., p174.
56. Allen Clarke, *Can We Get Back to the Land?*, 1904.
57. *Teddy Ashton's Northern Weekly*, 21 May 1904.
58. In 'A Little Communist Experiment on a Lancashire Farm', *Liverpool Weekly Post*, 23 March 1935.
59. See F.C. Ball's uncritical *One of the Damned*, 1973; but also Chris Walker's *British Socialists and the Politics of Popular Culture*, 1990, which takes a more searching view of Tressell's politics.
60. See Ingrid von Rosenberg, 'French Naturalism and the English Socialist Novel: Margaret Harkness and William Edwards Tirebuck', in Gustav Klaus (ed.), *The Rise of Socialist Fiction 1880-1914*, 1987.
61. See Edmund and Ruth Frow, 'Ethel Carnie: writer, feminist and socialist', in Klaus, op. cit.
62. Sam Fitton, *Gradely Lancashire*, 1929. Fitton's poems are collected in *Gradely Lancashire*, 1929. His cartoons are reproduced in Terry Wyke and Alan Fowler, *Mirth in the Mill: the gradely world of Sam Fitton*, 1995.
63. Clarke (as 'Ben Adhem'), *Teddy Ashton's Northern Weekly*, 26 August 1905.
64. See Ray Tilly, *Tommy Armstrong: The Pitman Poet*, 2010.
65. Allen Clarke (as 'Teddy Ashton'), *Tum Fowt Sketches*.
66. 'Teddy Ashton' (Allen Clarke'), Th'Patent Automatic Cemetery Looms', in *Teddy Ashton's Northern Weekly*, 20 May 1905.
67. See Dave Russell, *Looking North: Northern England and the national imagination*, 2004, p120, for a brief account of Walter Hampson.

PART 2

Centralism Triumphant?

5. Between Communism and Labourism

After the First World War, Liberalism and socialism diverged. The Labour Party, based on an alliance between the trades unions and the ILP, succeeded in winning majority support within the industrial working class, reflected in electoral successes nationally in 1923 and 1929, but also in local government, with scores of northern towns and cities electing Labour administrations. Ideologically, Labour became increasingly centralist and statist in its outlook, though the 'co-opera-tive' tradition of local democracy and participation was never entirely extinguished. The 'alternative culture' which developed in many Northern towns gradually weakened as the Labour Party became more of an electoral machine.

The ILP gradually cut itself off from the mainstream, unhappy with what it saw as the rightward drift of the Labour Party. It was under-standable – but disastrous for the ILP. The Labour Party of Herbert Morrison was in the ascendant, and the loss of the left-wing irritants in the ILP after its departure from the party in 1932 was a gift to the Labour establishment. The Liberal Party entered a coalition with the Conservatives in 1931 taking Macdonald and Snowden with them. The Labour Party was reduced to a rump of 52 MPs, though this masked what was still a substantial vote. The Liberals' alliance with the Tories in an anti-Labour coalition killed any scope for co-opera-tion between Labour and Liberal Parties for generations.[1]

To the left of the Labour Party, centralism rode even more supremely. The Communist Party of Great Britain had been formed in 1920 from the merger of the British Socialist Party and a number of smaller parties, including Sylvia Pankhurst's Workers' Socialist Federation which published the splendidly-titled *Workers' Dreadnought*. A few discontented branches and individuals from the ILP also joined.

Far from creating a radical party of the left that was part of the vibrant democratic working-class tradition we've traced from Peterloo, however, the young CPGB was a rigid mouthpiece for Lenin's Communist Party in Soviet Russia. This was despite having attracted some of the most able working-class leaders in the British labour movement, above all Harry Pollitt. Pollitt was intensely proud of his Lancashire working-class roots; he trained as a boilermaker in Manchester's engineering industry and was brought up in the small town of Droylsden. His favourite 'party piece' at social events was a recitation of Samuel Laycock's dialect poem 'Tha'rt Welcome Bonny Brid'.[2] Yet this subjective local culture which Pollitt clearly treasured found little echo in the politics of the fledgling party, which idolised Soviet Russia and insisted on a rigidly centralist approach to both internal party discipline and the model of socialism the CPGB wished to impose on Britain.

A more independently-aligned CPGB – or even an enlarged British Socialist Party, in line with the visions of Blatchford and Grayson – might have won stronger support. There were major tensions within the ILP about the lack of radicalism in the mainstream Labour Party, which were what had led the ILP to leave. Clearly, if the CPGB had been able to offer a more congenial home, there could have been a modest re-alignment on the left to the benefit of both small parties. But it wasn't to be. By the early 1930s the CPGB had embarked on its most sectarian 'third period' politics, which viewed social democratic parties such as the Labour Party and even the ILP itself as 'social fascist'. This caused huge damage to the left in many countries. In Germany the results were catastrophic, with a divided left allowing Hitler to take power. The British CP was internally divided over the sectarian 'third period' with many leading party members being unhappy with the ultra-left policy turn. The return to 'mass politics' in the later 1930s, although yet again as a result of a switch in Comintern strategy, allowed the party to regain some popularity, and it played a courageous role in the fight against unemployment and fascism, particularly in London and Manchester.

At a local level, the Communist Party and the ILP co-operated. There was immense sympathy within the labour movement for the

Russian revolution, and strong opposition to early government attempts to support the anti-Soviet forces during the civil war of the early 1920s. One of the most remarkable examples of solidarity occurred in Barrow in 1924, when a German ship docked at the port. The German sailors had a long string of grievances and effectively went on strike. A Soviet vessel was docked nearby and the Russian sailors supported their German comrades, backed by local ILP'ers and Communists, who brought food and other gifts to the strike-bound ship. The German sailors won most of their demands, thanks to this remarkable show of international support.[3] There were many other instances of local co-operation between ILP and Communist Party activists, throughout the 1920s and 1930s. Joint campaigning took place around unemployment and anti-fascism, and in support of local strikes.

Whilst Labour remained heavily male-dominated in the interwar years, there was a growing number of highly effective Labour women in the Northern towns and cities, including Ellen Wilkinson, Hannah Mitchell and Selina Cooper. However, the Labour Party in general remained reluctant to get involved in some of the issues that were important to many women – what it saw as 'personal' issues, such as birth control.[4] Whilst this was partly because of the strong Catholic influence within the Labour Party, particularly in cities like Liverpool, the reluctance was not purely religious: it also reflected a traditional male politician's view of the world, and of what was deemed to be 'political' as against 'personal'.

SOCIALIST CULTURE IN THE INTERWAR YEARS

Whilst *The Clarion* declined in influence during and after the First World War, *The Daily Herald* fulfilled the need for a left-of-centre, popular, newspaper. It began life as a strike newsletter in 1911 and built up a loyal readership through to its demise in 1964, when it became *The Sun*. At its peak in the 1930s it had an audited readership of over two million. The Communist Party's sprightly *Daily Worker* never achieved those kinds of sales, but it had a readership well beyond party ranks, attracting a talented team of journalists. The Labour Party and TUC set up *The Daily Citizen*, but this never had the liveliness nor the independence of *The Daily Herald.*[5]

A major development in the early 1920s was the establishment of *Labour's Northern Voice* in 1925 by the Lancashire, Cheshire and

North Staffs ILP. This provided a platform for young socialist writers like Hannah Mitchell and helped the ILP consolidate its strength in the region. Katharine Bruce Glasier was a regular writer, and it carried in-depth features on socialist policy, as well as news from around the region. Some local papers, such as *The Leeds Citizen* and *Huddersfield Worker* (later *Citizen*), kept going throughout the interwar years and for decades after. Others were more ephemeral. The *Barrow Leader* was launched by the local Labour Party in 1924, and its circulation peaked at 5,000 before it ceased two years later.

Many of the socialist clubs which had grown up before the First World War made a gradual transition from 'universities of socialism' into more traditional working-class drinking clubs. In the West Riding, the extensive network of socialist clubs, particularly strong in the Colne Valley, had shrunk. By the 1930s much of the stuffing had been knocked out of the more political socialist clubs. The disappointments of the 1929 Labour government followed by the defection of many senior Labour figures to the National government in 1931 – including the Colne Valley's Philip Snowden – led to disillusionment. Alan Brooke notes, with regret:

> Activity moved from the realm of community life to that of a soul-less bureaucratic machine and the Socialist clubs, built up painstakingly, with so much energy, time and money invested lovingly towards the advance of humanity, declined into mainly social clubs.[6]

UNEMPLOYED STRUGGLES – BEYOND THE MYTHS

The popular view of the North in the interwar years is one of mass unemployment, with images of barefoot children on street corners and groups of unemployed miners hanging around listlessly without even the hope of a job. And that certainly was the picture for many major towns and cities from the early 1930s onwards (though the 1920s also saw temporary periods of high unemployment). The ways in which the labour movement responded to mass unemployment during this period is very relevant to modern-day politics, and a look at contrasting approaches from within the left will be useful.

Two of the most influential books on 'the unemployment question' were written by Salford's Walter Greenwood and Manchester's Ellen

Wilkinson (also known as 'Red Ellen' of Ardwick). Wilkinson became the MP for Jarrow (see p140) after an earlier stint as MP for Middlesbrough East, and wrote *The Town That was Murdered* in the mid-1930s, when it became one of the Left Book Club's best-selling titles.[7] When she was writing it male unemployment in Jarrow was over 72 per cent. Greenwood's *Love on the Dole* was a passionate and moving fictional account of how unemployment wrecked families; many of the book's incidents, such as 'The Battle of Bexley Square', when police baton-charge an unemployed demonstration, were based on real events that Greenwood had witnessed. At a time when unemployment is creeping towards three million, it's worth looking at how socialists in the 1930s responded to mass unemployment. Far from being a single 'militant' campaign, there were a range of responses across the North aimed at reducing the devastating impact of unemployment and poverty.

Ellen Wilkinson was one of the main organisers of 'The Jarrow Crusade', supported by a cross-section of the town to highlight the appalling misery of mass unemployment; and the images of the 'hunger marchers', with their capes and mouth organs, struck powerful chords not just in the North, but across the country. The march came about through the failure of humble 'deputations': the final straw was being told by a government spokesman that 'Jarrow must work out its own salvation'. The town council had recently become Labour-controlled and the Jarrow Labour Party executive, with Wilkinson, now agreed to organise a march to London. The Mayor was enthusiastic, and in Ellen Wilkinson's words 'decided that if there were to be a march it must be a town's march, with the backing of the whole citizens ... from Bishop to businessman'.[8] Whilst the initiative was a Labour Party one, supported by dozens of local Party organisations along the way, at national level neither the Labour Party nor the TUC supported the march. The Bishop of Durham wrote to *The Times* denouncing this 'revolutionary mob pressure'. But the overall reception of the marches was enormously welcoming. For example, Ellen Wilkinson describes the state of the marchers' footwear as 'coming to pieces' when they reached Leicester, but the local Co-op's boot repairers stayed up all night, working without pay to repair the boots, with leather supplied free by the Society. Her account is peppered with such examples of collective kindness along the route. The Mayor of Barnsley opened the baths specially, 'all heated and ready for the men', and even in Harrogate the local Territorial Army fed this dishevelled 'army' of the unemployed.

'RED ELLEN' OF JARROW: THE NORTH'S LA PASIONARIA

Ellen Wilkinson was elected onto Manchester City Council in 1923, the same year as Hannah Mitchell. She was from a working-class background, but her family had encouraged her education and she had won a place at Manchester University.

Wilkinson was 'converted' to socialism by hearing Katherine Bruce Glasier speak at a public meeting in 1910. Five years later, at the age of twenty-four, she was appointed women's organiser of the Co-operative Employees Union. For a brief while she joined the Communist Party on its formation in 1920. Clearly destined for great things, she was selected to fight Middlesbrough East constituency in 1924 and won it for Labour, becoming Labour's only woman MP. She was a powerful advocate of workers' rights, and her tiny stature and shock of bright red hair added to her charisma. Friends and foes knew her as 'Red Ellen'. She lost her seat in the 1931 debacle, but was selected to fight Jarrow in 1936. Having won the seat she became one of the most powerful voices for the unemployed, leading the famous 'Jarrow March' in 1936, and writing *The Town That was Murdered*.

Recognising the mortal danger to democracy posed by fascism, Wilkinson helped organise aid for Spain during the Civil War, among other things setting up the Dependents' Aid Fund to help the families of International Brigaders. Kenneth Morgan draws comparison between Wilkinson and the Spanish Republic's Dolores Ibarruri – 'La Pasionaria'. Wilkinson became a regular writer for *Tribune* and was an advocate of the Unity Front with the Communist Party in the run-up to the Second World War.[i]

She was a passionate woman, both in her politics and in her relationships. Morgan refers to her 'complicated maze of personal relations', which included a long affair with the right-wing Labour leader Herbert Morrison. Her creativity also found expression in literature; she somehow managed to find time to write several novels, as well as her great work on Jarrow.

Like Mitchell, she felt strongly about the issues of daily life that had a disproportionate impact on women. For example, her Hire Purchase Act, passed in 1938, gave some protection against the serious debt problems and resulting heart-breaking repossessions that were endured by many working-class families. She also introduced the bill for free school milk that became law in 1946. Tragically, she committed suicide a year later, apparently in despair at her failure to have been – what she thought – was a more effective socialist reformer.

i. K.O. Morgan, *Labour People – Hardie to Kinnock*, 1992.

Jarrow was not the only unemployed march from the North of England to London. Many others, organised by the National Unemployed Workers' Movement (NUWM) received a much more hostile response from the press and from much of the police. Traditional 'left' labour historians tend to argue that this is because Jarrow was an inoffensive, cross-class 'procession', rather than a class-conscious march which aimed to undermine state power. That's true. The Jarrow Crusade was organised by a coalition of Labour Party, Liberals, Conservatives, church groups and local businesses; the main backer of the NUWM was the Communist Party of Great Britain.[9]

Yet the question has to be asked: which form of protest was the most effective? The 1936 Jarrow Crusade made a stronger impact on the national conscience precisely because it was community-based. The images which have survived of dignified and peaceful protest by unemployed workers are those of Jarrow, not the more militant confrontations and occupations of the NUWM. The lessons were in fact learnt by the CPGB in the late 1970s and early 1980s, when it was the driving force behind the 'People's March for Jobs' from Liverpool to London. Class struggle had been replaced by a broad democratic alliance, and the 'People's March' of that period, now largely forgotten, was a very effective mobilisation from which lessons can be learnt today. Its approach owed more to Jarrow than the NUWM.

ORGANISING THE UNEMPLOYED

The NUWM was strong in the North of England, particularly in the main industrial and commercial centres such as Liverpool, Manchester, Sheffield and Newcastle. Whilst its backbone was the CPGB – led by the well-respected figure of Wal Hannington – many of its active members were in the ILP, or were non-aligned. Quite a few were also members of Special Branch. Relationships with the Labour Party got off to a bad start soon after it was formed in 1921 (at conferences in London and in Manchester); some contact was, however, made with the TUC, but they pulled out of dealings with the organisation in 1927, because of its links to the Communist Party.

The activities of the NUWM on Merseyside were particularly effective and determined. By 1932, 28 per cent of insured workers in Liverpool were unemployed, though the percentages in ship-building and shipping were 47 percent, and in the building trade 38 per cent. The NUWM had at least eight branches on Merseyside, with a strong CPGB element in their leadership. For two weeks in September 1932 Birkenhead and Liverpool were, in Tony Lane's words, 'in a state of near insurrection ... Demonstrations, battles with the police and looting of shops went on in Birkenhead for four days'.[10]

The testimony of some of the organisers, such as Joe Fitzgerald, points out that the NUWM did its best to maintain discipline on the demonstrations, trying to avoid police provocation:

> On our marches men would appoint themselves as stewards, put on arm-bands, and discipline the marchers. They'd tell the marchers not to go throwing bricks, or would identify prostitutes who'd been inserted into the march by police, bricks tucked under their shawls ... you see the police would deliberately try and plant people like prostitutes to stir up trouble, so that we could be presented as an undisciplined mob.[11]

The NUWM was active in 'community politics' in many parts of Liverpool, providing advice to claimants and also telling people who the more sympathetic clerks were in the Public Assistance Committee (PAC) offices. Very often, NUWM activists would represent claimants at the PAC, often shaming them into providing extra support. Evictions became commonplace, and again the local activists would intervene, as Jack Fitzgerald explained:

> Someone would rush in and tell us that Mrs So-and-so was being evicted tomorrow. We used to have a group of fellers handy and tell them that we wanted to see them at the woman's house at the time the bailiff was due. We'd ask the woman's permission to go in, and if she said yes about four of us would go inside. The other blokes would go up the street knocking on doors and telling the women that Mrs X was going to be evicted, and asking for help ...[12]

When the bailiff arrived the reception party would persuade him to leave: 'the four of us would pick him up and put him over the wall. This sort of thing didn't happen all that often. But then you only had to do it a few times and word would get round ...'.

USING THE LOCAL STATE

There was another side to the way socialists in the North met the challenge of mass unemployment. Up to 1929, the old systems of elected 'Boards of Guardians' survived in each town, with responsibility for 'poor relief' that included unemployed assistance. The Boards enabled socialists to be elected to local decision-making bodies, and helped them develop their skills in governance. Furthermore, as unemployment began to grow in the early 1920, socialists were able to ensure that unemployed families got the best possible support. In Poplar, East London, the guardians, led by the ILP's George Lansbury, refused to obey government strictures on unemployed relief, and paid what they regarded as reasonable.[13] 'Poplarism' became a by-word for militant local government, a kind of 'localism' of which few Tories would approve. But the ability of local elected bodies to provide real help to the unemployed was usurped in 1930 by the introduction of 'Public Assistance Committees' (PACs). The local boards were abolished, and the PACs were administered by more remote, and usually Conservative-controlled, county councils. However, the counties were broken down into areas which had their own boards, with local councillors nominated to sit on them. And although they now had far less flexibility, as the budgets were set by the county council, some socialists were able to influence decisions at local level.

Having a sympathetic council administering relief made a big difference. Labour controlled Leeds City Council between 1933 and 1935, and used its power to provide more generous allowances and to instigate a programme of public works. But when Labour lost control to the Conservatives, little time was lost in rolling back Labour's achievements, with a new and draconian interpretation of the Means Test. To avoid the ensuing unpopularity, responsibility for administering relief was then transferred from councillors to administrators.

Selina Cooper sat on the PAC Board for the Burnley area, and engaged in constant battles with officialdom and right-wing colleagues in the administration of relief, including over the issue of whether locked-out weavers were eligible for unemployment relief. Labour councillors, backed up by a friendly Labour minister, Arthur Greenwood, weighed in to support the weavers' claim.[14] One of the duties of the PAC members was administering the hated 'means test', and by 1932 Cooper was on the Nelson Relief Committee, which refused to administer the means test – with the support of several other Labour-controlled town councils across Lancashire. As Jill Liddington says of the Labour councillors in North-East Lancashire during the years 1928-33:

> so many ... were prepared to use every method that lay within the law to protect their own class whose living standards had become subject to such savage attack. Selina Cooper, according to the chief constable, was one of those whose protest only just kept within the rule of law.[15]

WORKING-CLASS EDUCATION DURING THE INTER-WAR YEARS

The socialist movement that erupted in the late 1880s had a similar emphasis on education to that of its Chartist and Owenite forebears, and this continued into the interwar years. Most socialist clubs and institutes had reading rooms and extensive libraries, and in South Wales a large network of miners' libraries developed which lasted well into the 1950s. Liverpool had its own 'Council for Independent Working-Class Education', which was linked to the Plebs League. Its lecture list for 1920-1 offered a wide range of topics, 'to be delivered to any industrial or political organisation'. As well as lectures on 'Marxism and Darwinism' and 'The French Revolution', it also offered talks on 'The Medieval Guilds', 'The Science of Hope' and 'Empire in India and Elsewhere'. Lantern lectures were also available on subjects such as 'The Industrial Revolution' but also 'Primitive Man' and 'The Great Sea Serpent'.[16]

The tradition of using a propaganda van for the socialist cause continued into the motorised age, and the ILP had a well-developed programme of evening lectures, weekend schools and street meetings. During 1927, for example, *Labour's Northern Voice* advertised open-air lectures from 'The ILP Van' that included 'a week's mission' in Miles Platting. In the same year, Levenshulme Labour Party was advertising an 'illustrated lantern lecture' on 'International Labour Sport' by E. Deveney. The programme of lectures and debates in the ILP at this time was eclectic, with a strong emphasis on nursery education and birth control as well as international questions.[17]

The WEA put down strong roots in many working-class communities in the North of England. In the North East, at least a third of all tutorial class students were miners, reflecting the strong backing of the Durham Miners' Association.[18] The DMA also had a controlling influence within Durham County Council, and ensured the WEA had sufficient funds to provide an extensive programme across the county. The National Council of Labour Colleges established classes in many Northern towns. In Barrow, for example, it ran series of courses between 1921 and 1924, and even persuaded the Tory-dominated Education Committee to allow free use of school premises, together with a small grant!

KINDER SCOUT AND THE OPEN AIR MOVEMENT

The tradition of working-class enjoyment of the countryside goes back well into the early nineteenth century, and found political expression, as we've seen, in the 1896 Winter Hill rights of way battle. The 1932 Kinder Scout Mass Trespass had echoes of Winter Hill, not least because it was led by working-class political activists.[19] The part of the Dark Peak around Kinder Scout had been closed to the public for generations, and the landowners' enforced their 'rights' through the employment of a tough group of gamekeepers. The initiative to challenge the closure of the moors through a mass trespass was taken by a small group of Communist Party members, who were involved in the British Workers' Sports Federation, which was to all intents and purposes a CP front organisation. About five hundred ramblers took part in the protest, and scuffles broke out with the gamekeepers. Some of the leaders, including Benny Rothman, were arrested and ultimately given jail sentences.

The significance of the Kinder Scout protest was that it highlighted the large expanses of countryside that were closed to the public. It was part of the inspiration for the 1949 Countryside and Rights of Way Act, which helped to open up more of the countryside. Rothman remained involved in countryside and rights of way issues, and he led the 1982 celebration of the Winter Hill Trespass, as well as a similar event for Kinder Scout in the same year. By then he had become the 'grand old man' of the mass trespass, a thought which would have tickled him. He was also supportive of new movements, including SCAM – Sheffield Campaign for Access to the Moorlands. Many of the demands of this group were won by the last Labour government's Countryside Act, which opened up uncultivated land to public access. Rothman died in

1996, and Northern Rail named one of its trains after him in 2006. *Benny Rothman – the Manchester Rambler* is often seen on routes through the Peak District, taking thousands of Manchester and Sheffield ramblers out into the countryside to enjoy fine moorland, walking without the fear of being attacked by gamekeepers.

The Clarion Cycling Club enjoyed a revival in the 1930s, though the newspaper after which it was named had long since disappeared. Membership reached an all-time high of 8,306 in 1936. And, despite the onset of widespread car ownership after the war, membership went up from 3,000 in 1944 to over 6,000 in 1949. But this growth was short-lived, and membership went into a rapid decline through the 1950s and 1960s; it had less than a thousand members by 1966.

ANTI-FASCISM, SPAIN AND THE INTERNATIONAL BRIGADES

The tradition of internationalism continued during this period, particularly in the movement's strong support for the republican cause in the Spanish Civil War, which was the great international cause of the first half of the twentieth century. Hundreds of men – and some women – from the North volunteered to go to Spain to fight Franco and his fascist army, which in 1936 had rebelled against the democratically elected Republican government. Most of the volunteers were young working-class men, from the mines, railways and engineering, though most were unemployed at the time. Many of them were members of the Communist Party, but a number were ILP members or supporters.[20]

Some left-wing members of the Labour Party – like Ellen Wilkinson – worked with CP and ILP comrades to support the democratic cause in Spain. Bob Edwards was a Liverpool trade unionist and ILP activist who led the ILP contingent in the independent left-socialist organisation POUM on the Aragon front between 1936 and 1937. Edwards subsequently became Labour MP for Bilston, in 1955. However, in some towns and cities the Labour Party was split, with many Catholics, though by no means all, being influenced by the official church line to support Franco.

The labour movement in Manchester and Salford strongly supported the Republic, and many socialists and communists volunteered to join the International Brigade.[21] Sam Wild, the Commander of the British Battalion, who came from Ardwick and was an activist in the National Unemployed Workers' Movement, was awarded the Spanish Medal of

Valour. Wild survived the war, but Oldham's Clem Beckett, a member of the Communist Party known as 'Dare Devil Beckett' for his feats as a speedway rider, was one of the forty-two men from the Manchester area who died in Spain. Lillian Urmston from Stalybridge joined the International Brigade as a nurse. She tended the wounded at the bloody battle for Aragon, and was still caring for the sick among the refugees as they fled over the Pyrenees to France in 1939.

Frank Graham, who subsequently established a successful commercial publishing business, organised the Sunderland contingent that joined the International Brigade, many of whom, like Graham himself, had been active in the National Unemployed Workers' Movement. Graham was a high-profile left-wing activist in the North East, and his Special Branch file described him as 'one to watch'! He died in a nursing home in Newcastle in 2006. Many Teesside workers went to fight in Spain, many never to return. There is a memorial plaque in their honour inside Middlesbrough Town Hall.

Humberside also played an important role during the Spanish Civil War, offering strong support to the 'aid for Spain' movement. The city provided homes for forty Basque children who arrived from Bilbao on the Spanish liner 'Habana', and sent eight men to join the Brigades – who are commemorated by a small plaque in Hull City Council's Guildhall. One of the four Hull men who were killed in the combat was Robert Wardle, a docker who joined in 1938, leaving behind his wife and two children. He was killed just a few weeks after arriving in Spain, gunned down by tanks at Calaceite, a village south of Barcelona, along with a hundred others. Joe Latus was more fortunate. He survived and returned to the city to open a bookshop. He later became one of the directors of Hull FC rugby league team. His daughter Dilys Porter has launched a campaign to get a more prominent memorial to the veterans erected in the city. She has a box of mementos of her late father, including his International Brigade identity card. It bears the inscription 'Better to die on your feet a free man than on your knees as a slave'.[22]

At home, there was mass resistance to fascism on the streets. Whilst Cable Street in east London has been the most well-documented example of anti-fascist resistance, the Communist Party and ILP led opposition in most of the Northern towns and cities. There was a pitched battle between the British Union of Fascists and local socialists and communists in Stockton in 1934 and regular fighting in Manchester, Bolton, Salford and Leeds.[23]

THE UNIONS BETWEEN THE WARS: REALISTS OR REACTIONARIES?

The unions' relationship with the Labour Party throughout much of the twentieth century never really deviated from their early conservatism, and was at the root of the party's inability to present a radical alternative to Liberalism. Yet the reality, however unpalatable, was probably that the mass of the working class were not too keen on 'all-out socialism', be it of the SDF, ILP or later Communist Party flavour. The first minority Labour government – elected in 1924 – made some important headway, for example on housing, in laying the foundations for a major programme of council house building. But it hardly embarked on a programme to change society.

The unions in the interwar years were increasingly engaged in fighting a defensive battle against wage cuts and unemployment. A small number of activists supported campaigns by the CPGB; and in a few unions, such as the mineworkers', they took on leadership roles. By and large, however, the unions remained dominated by cautious men – and a very few women – who arguably had more immediate things to worry about than the future socialist transformation of society.

The General Strike of 1926, if anything, confirms this cautious analysis. Far from being an embryonic revolution, the nine days' strike in support of the miners was undertaken with great reluctance by the TUC leadership, and the earliest possible settlement was grasped, thereby leaving the miners to struggle on for months on their own, increasingly isolated and ultimately defeated. There was strong support in towns and cities across the North for the miners, but even at community level there was little evidence of insurrection. In West Yorkshire, the strike was strongly supported but there were only minor clashes between strikers and police. The authors of a history of the Labour Party in West Yorkshire during the interwar years laconically note that:

> apart from a march to Leeds, organised by some Communists at Castleford, the only notable event for West Yorkshire Communists was the police raid on the headquarters of the Shipley Communists. Vic Feather, who eventually became General Secretary of the TUC, was present. An instinctive urge drove him to the toilets when he

heard a knock on the door. When he returned the Communist activists and their printing equipment were gone.[24]

In some of the mining areas things were far less placid. The derailment of 'The Flying Scotsman' at Cramlington by striking Northumberland miners is well documented – and their actions were widely condemned by the striking unions. On the other hand the placement of machine guns on Newcastle Central station had more to do with government 'PR' than defence against any imminent revolutionary surge.

Ben Turner, who had started life as a weaver in Holmfirth (see Chapter 3), and had received his political education in William Morris's Socialist League, became a key figure in the attempted 'historic compromise' between labour and capital in the late 1920s; he was on the Labour side of the 'Mond-Turner Talks', established in 1928, between a group of major employers, led by ICI's Sir Alfred Mond, and the TUC, with the aim of setting up machinery for joint consultation about the more general problems of industry. The talks were strongly opposed by the 'left' in the labour movement, but the unions were in a weak bargaining position after the defeat of the 1926 strike, the onset of mass unemployment, and the passing of the 1927 Trades Disputes and Trades Unions Act, which had outlawed secondary industrial action and required union members to contract-in to political funds. The talks potentially could have led to the sort of industrial peace which post-war Sweden experienced, but the main stumbling block proved to be the employers, who were unwilling to grant the unions any greater role in industry. With hindsight, far from being an attempt at class betrayal, the talks could have led to a modernised industrial relations landscape which would have strengthened British industry's post-war competitive position.

NORTHERN ART AND LITERATURE

Interwar Britain saw the emergence of some exceptionally talented working-class writers and artists. Scotland had its 'Lewis Grassic Gibbon', whilst Wales had Lewis Jones, author of *We Live* and *Cwmardy*. Each of these expressed a distinctly 'national' working-class perspective in their writings. In the North of England, writers like Walter Greenwood succeeded to an extent in bringing a strongly regional 'feel' to descriptions of working-class life, using dialect and place to good

effect. But the 'radical' phase of Lancashire and Yorkshire dialect literature had passed. The socialist editor of *The Yorkshire Clock Almanack*,
Walter Hampson (see previous chapter), continued to turn out entertaining but non-political stories of ordinary Yorkshire life. Allen Clarke,
in Lancashire, either re-published earlier work or reminisced about his
youthful radicalism through the pages of the *Liverpool Weekly Post*.

The work of the Ashington Group of miner-painters has recently
been celebrated by the play *The Pitman Painters*, written by Lee Hall,
who was inspired by a book of the same name by William Feaver. The
remarkable story began in 1934 in a WEA art class in Ashington,
Northumberland. A group of miners, including some ILP members,
signed up for an art appreciation class taught by Robert Lyon, a leading
art academic at Armstrong College, then part of Durham University.
Within a few years the group was staging exhibitions, and attracting
national attention.[25] The work of the group is varied, capturing social,
domestic and industrial life in Ashington – a town described by *The
Shell Guide to Northumberland Durham* for 1937 thus: 'Ashington:
Pop. 40,000. Mining town, mostly built in the early part of this
century. Dreary rows a mile long. Ashpits and mines down the middle
of still un-made streets'. Completely refuting the dismissiveness of the
Shell Guide's middle-class authors, the 'Group', as they called themselves, created great beauty out of the pitheads and slag heaps that were
all around them. Their art was not 'political', but Oliver Kilbourn, one
of the Group, created the banner for Ellington Lodge of the NUM.
The Group finally disbanded in the early 1980s, and the hut which
had been their home for nearly five decades was demolished in 1984.
Much of their work has survived and is displayed in the Woodhorn
Mining Museum in Ashington.

On Teesside, Andy Croft has charted the radical cultural activities
which took place at Ormesby Hall, near Middlesbrough. This was the
home of poet and playwright Ruth Pennyman, sometimes known as
'The Red Duchess', and it became a hub of left-wing culture; Michael
Tippett wrote his first opera *Robin Hood* whilst staying there, and it
was subsequently performed by unemployed ironstone miners.
Pennyman's play *Happy Families* was performed in venues across
Teesside during 1937 to raise money for Quaker Relief in Spain.[26]

The North East produced several talented working-class writers
during this period, notably Harold Heslop, the miner novelist from
the Durham coalfield; and the Lancashire novelist Ethel Carnie wrote

her finest work, *This Slavery*, in 1925.[27] Shortly after, Carnie became involved in the Workers' Theatre Movement in the North. Mary Agnes Hamilton, born into a middle-class Manchester family, wrote both fiction and non-fiction, and also for the ILP paper *The New Leader*. She was Labour MP for Blackburn in the short-lived 1929 Labour government. Her novel *Follow My Leader* (1922) is about the political and moral dilemmas of a young politically active woman. Jack Common, son of a loco driver at Heaton depot in Newcastle, was another major figure in interwar literature, though he left his native city for the south.

WAR

The Spanish Civil War had alerted the labour movement to the threat posed by fascism, and the increasing likelihood of all-out war with Nazi Germany inevitably caused tensions within sections of the pacifist-inclined left, which had played such an honourable role in resisting the First World War. But the war that was looming was quite different in nature from the war between rival empires that was the root cause of the 1914-18 carnage. Hitler, Mussolini and now Franco were showing that fascism meant the total destruction of working-class and democratic organisations, and that 'neutrality' was not an option. In the run-up to the war the CPGB played an outstanding role, as part of the more relaxed 'Popular Front' policy agreed in 1936, in building an alliance of the left and democratic forces to resist fascism. But then it all went wrong again. After war was declared between Britain and Germany, Stalin came to a deal with Hitler to avoid going to war. The Comintern line changed and the conflict between Britain and Nazi Germany was dubbed an 'imperialist war'. Many leading figures in the party, including Pollitt, strongly disagreed with this about turn and were removed from their posts.

There is not a specifically 'regionalist' narrative about the Second World War. The major towns and cities of the North – Manchester, Liverpool, Sheffield, Leeds, Newcastle – were pounded by German bombs, but so were London, Coventry, Glasgow, Plymouth, Birmingham and Bristol. The United Kingdom was united in a way it has never been before, or since – across classes, regions and nations. Politically, there was an electoral truce for much of the war, though sections of the Labour left did make occasional challenges to the consensus.

One such challenge was made by Common Wealth, a party formed by Richard Acland, Liberal MP for Barnstaple, and J.B. Priestley, amongst others. It advocated three core principles – 'Common Ownership, Vital Democracy and Morality in Politics'. The party favoured public ownership of land, and Acland gave away his Devon family estate of 19,000 acres to the National Trust. Priestley was chairman of the new party, but after a dispute with Acland he resigned. Common Wealth won three by-elections, of which two were in the North – Skipton and Eddisbury, in Cheshire (the third was in Chelmsford). The party was dissolved in 1945 and most members joined (or re-joined) Labour.[28]

The Communist Party's 'imperialist war' line was to change after the Soviet Union had been attacked by Hitler's forces in 1941, but considerable damage to the party's prestige had been done. However, after Pollitt was re-instated as General Secretary, the Lancashire engineer entered his most outstanding phase as a genuinely popular leader. Pollitt and the highly disciplined CPGB cadres in industry played key roles in setting up production committees to increase the war effort, and ensured that potential strikes were avoided. In big factories such as Metropolitan Vickers in Trafford Park, the CP shop stewards effectively controlled the plant and ensured efficient production. The party's popularity was also boosted by the heroic sacrifices being made by the Red Army. Many major engineering works, such as the locomotive works at Horwich, near Bolton, transferred production from locomotives to T-42 tanks for Russia. The tanks rolled off the production line with messages such as 'Good luck Uncle Joe' chalked on the sides.

It was difficult for 'normal' political activity to continue during war conditions, but the ILP maintained its programme of meetings and conferences, and *Labour's Northern Voice* continued as a monthly newspaper. Towards the end of the war, by which time a struggle for survival had shifted towards thoughts of what post-1945 Britain might look like, some socialists began to develop radical ideas which would influence a future Labour government. The Army Bureau of Current Affairs (ABCA) undoubtedly helped to stimulate political thinking. At home, some Labour Party members were starting to address the needs of post-war reconstruction in the wake of widespread destruction of homes by enemy action. C.W. Kay, the MP for Bow, is recorded in *Labour's Northern Voice* as making the case for regional planning and the need for an administrative body between local and national government: 'planning for housing should not be left to small local authorities', he argued at a meeting in Halifax. 'There ought to be a regional organisation to enforce national plans.'[29] However, the idea of 'regional government' took a long time to gestate, despite the imposition of a regional structure of governance on post-war Germany by Britain.

War often hastens tendencies already at work within society, and perhaps never more so than in the position of women. During the First World War many women had been drafted into traditional male occupations and promptly thrown out at the end of the conflict. Once again, in the Second World War, tens of thousands of women were drafted into 'war work' – in factories, railways and agriculture. But this time, it was no longer a case of grudging acceptance – by both unions and management – but of a wholehearted welcome. Many women had tasted independence for the first time, whilst others had experienced far better working conditions than they had put up with before. One Bolton mill worker I knew, who had transferred to 'war work' in a nearby engineering factory, remembered how much better working conditions had been during the war, with children's nurseries, canteens and safe working conditions. She and her workmates expected this to be the norm after the end of the war.

NOTES

1. See Matthew Worley, *Labour Inside the Gate: a history of the British Labour Party between the Wars*, 2005.
2. Verbal anecdote from Eddie Frow. See also Kevin Morgan, *Harry Pollitt*, 1993; and Pollitt's autobiography *Serving My Time*, 1941.
3. Mowat and Power, op. cit., p.29.
4. Martin Pugh, *Women and the Women's Movement in Britain 1914-1959*, 2002.
5. See Harrison op. cit.; and William Rust, *The Story of the Daily Worker*, 1949.
6. Alan Brooke, *Honley Socialist Club*, op. cit., p36.
7. Walter Greenwood, *Love on the Dole*, 1933. Ellen Wilkinson's *The Town That was Murdered* was published in 1939, though written three years earlier.
8. Wilkinson, op. cit., p198.
9. See Wal Hannington, *Unemployed Struggles*, 1936.
10. Tony Lane, 'Three Liverpool Militants', in Hikins, op. cit., p16.
11. Ibid., p165.
12. Ibid., p174.

13. Noreen Branson, *Poplarism 1919-1925: George Lansbury and the Councillors' Revolt*, 1979.
14. Liddington, op. cit.
15. Ibid., p383.
16. Programme in author's collection.
17. *Labour's Northern Voice*, 1927 (various issues).
18. See Todd, *Right to Learn*, op. cit.
19. Benny Rothman, *The Kinder Scout Trespass*, 1982.
20. See for example Greater Manchester International Brigades Committee, *Greater Manchester Men Who Fought in Spain*, 1983.
21. North West TUC members' *70th Anniversary of the Spanish Civil War*, 2006, has articles on several International Brigade volunteers, including Lilian Urmston of Stalybridge.
22. See for example 'Remembering Hull Heroes', http://static.hullcc.gov.uk/hullinprint/archive/feb2007/remembering_hulls_heroes.php.
23. A good general account of the 'Aid for Spain' movement is Jim Fyrth, *The Signal was Spain: The Spanish Aid Movement in Britain 1936-9*, 1986.
24. J. Reynolds and K. Laybourn, *Labour Heartland*, 1987, p77.
25. William Feaver, *Pitmen Painters; The Ashington Group 1934-1984*, 1993, p14.
26. Croft, op. cit., p11.
27. Gustav Klaus, *The Socialist Novel in Britain*, 1982.
28. See D.L. Prynn, 'Common Wealth: A British 3rd Way Party of the 1940s', in *Journal of Contemporary History*, Jan/April 1972.
29. *Labour's Northern Voice*, 24 November 1944.

6. The High Tide of Social Democracy

THE 'NEW DAWN' OF 1945

The war changed everything. Many soldiers returning home had been radicalised by the fight against fascism, the heroic sacrifices of the Soviet Union, and the progressive work of the forces' educational organisations such as the Army Bureau of Current Affairs. Popular pro-Labour papers like *The Daily Mirror* were of huge importance in creating a mood for change. The same spirit infected the unions, who weighed in behind Labour's programme to legislate for a better society. The Labour victory of 1945 was massive, unprecedented and pretty much unexpected. The new government brought about a better environment for pay bargaining and improved conditions in the newly nationalised industries, and vastly improved healthcare for working-class families in the new National Health Service; and there was also widened access to higher education, as well as full employment. Labour's 1945 general election victory changed Britain for the better, in lots of ways.

The British people now had a very different world to look forward to than their parents had had in 1918. But how 'socialist' was the Attlee government? It depends on your definition of 'socialism'. There was plenty of nationalisation – railways, mines, shipbuilding, road transport – and there was state provision of universal services. The post-war years seemed to confirm the 'Webb model' of socialism, with a very much top- down approach to reform. What was missing was that vision of Keir Hardie, of 'community' and empowerment. This wasn't a totally foreign concept to post-war Labour. As at least one historian has argued, the incoming Labour government wanted to encourage a new 'socialist man and woman'.[1] But the traditional 'left' version of history – that there was a huge tidal wave of support for radical measures – is at least open to challenge. People certainly wanted change, but whether they wanted a full-blown social revolution was another thing altogether.

There were different political forces at work within government, ranging from the dominant statist approach through to a distrust of the state and state ownership and an emphasis on co-operative structures. It would be wrong to assume that the flow was 100 per cent towards a centralised state socialism. Many socialists influenced by the old ILP form of politics were lukewarm towards state ownership in itself; and in the immediate post-war years there were attempts by Labour local authorities to take on a more interventionist role. But a heavily centralised approach was undoubtedly the strongest current, and it had come to complete dominance by the late 1940s; arguably, it was what the scale of the tasks of post-war reconstruction required. The great hero of the Labour left, Nye Bevan, was perhaps the biggest centraliser of all. But whilst basking in the warmth of post-war reconstruction, Labour was laying the seeds of its ultimate failure.

In the North, Labour had become 'the natural party of government' in many major towns and cities, though its leadership was often lacking in imagination and drive. With the awkward squad of the ILP dispatched into the wilderness after 1932, and the CP providing little in the way of a challenge in local politics, traditional Labour could rule much as it wanted, with virtually no opposition. There were exceptions to this. Nelson kept its image as 'Little Moscow', and streets on council houses in Chopwell (Durham) still had names like 'Lenin Avenue'; but this kind of politics was becoming less convincing by the 1950s.[2]

Most unions welcomed the nationalisation of the mines, railways and road transport. But it didn't bring them much in the way of employee participation, which had long been an article of theme amongst many socialists and trades unionists. Reliable time-servers, like Bill Allen of the locomen's union, were brought onto the Railways Board, but their presence had hardly any impact on how the industries were actually run. This was a period when the Labour Party, by and large, embraced a centralising version of modernism. Local variation and idiosyncrasy were of little importance in this brave new world.

DIFFERENT MODELS OF STATE OWNERSHIP

There were minority voices which questioned the model of state ownership chosen by Labour. T.E. Nixon of the National Union of Railwaymen produced a pamphlet arguing for 'workers' control of the railways', noting that 'it is a remarkable fact that the foster-parent of modern democracy – The Labour Party – should have made no attempt to reconcile progressive democratic tendencies with its policy of the socialisation of industry'.[3] Nixon suggested an elaborate structure of area, regional and national machinery, which would give railway workers a real say in the running of their industry, backed up by a 'National Transport College', which would give railway workers the necessary management skills to run the industry.

Francis Andrews, a leading figure in the Union of Post Office Workers, and an ILP activists, argued strongly that nationalisation without worker's control had little to do with socialism.[4] At a conference in Manchester in January 1949, a 'North-West League for Workers' Control' was formed, to complement a similar body established earlier in London. Price Jones, a Lancashire NUM activist from Gin Pit, near Leigh, proposed an elaborate scheme of workers' control for the mines, with pit, area, regional and national decision-making bodies.[5] But these voices gained little hearing within government. The state-owned industries gave token recognition to employee participation, but the reality was one of top-down management. The Attlee government did lots of good things *for* working class people, but they were expected to be grateful, and passive, recipients of Labour's largesse.

The dramatic narrowing of Labour's parliamentary majority in the 1950 general election came as a shock. Ironically, Labour actually won more votes in 1950 than in 1945, but there was shift in geographical patterns which favoured the Tories. Labour continued to do well in the North of England, Wales and Scotland, but lost support in the South East of England. Defeat came a year later, with women voters in particular deserting Labour. The Tories came to power with the advantage of a strong economy emerging from post-war austerity, and were able to capitalise on the boom years of the 1950s. Labour was to be out of power until 1964.

EMERGING REGIONAL CONSCIOUSNESS

The 1950s saw a cautious emergence of a 'Northern' regional consciousness, reflected in the BBC's northern programmes broadcast from Manchester. This consciousness found a focus in arguments over the siting of the National Theatre during 1953. The Conservative government, almost unthinkingly, proposed to locate it in London. However, Ellis Smith, MP for Stoke-on-Trent South, argued differently. He argued that 'the North has a culture of its own and it should find expression in a national theatre', and noted that 'the Northern accent [is] not popular in the South, indeed among people of all political parties'; it was his belief that too many people had forgotten where the labour movement had started.[6]

Hannah Mitchell continued to write on northern culture in the early 1950s. Her last piece in *Labour's Northern Voice* was a review of the Yorkshire Dialect Society's collection of dialect poetry, *A Northern Broadsheet*, in September 1956. But it was the emergence of a new generation of writers, Northern-based and in some cases working-class, which did most to stimulate an awareness of 'The North'. The late 1950s saw a string of successful novels, many made into films, with 'Northern' and 'working-class' themes. Dismissed by some conservative critics as kitchen-sink drama, works such as *A Taste of Honey* by Salford's Shelagh Delaney, Stan Barstow's *A Kind of Loving*, John Braine's *Room at the Top*, and Sillitoe's *Saturday Night and Sunday Morning* (admittedly set in Nottingham), changed the way 'the North' was perceived – internally and externally. In the North East, the work of Alan Plater and Alex Glasgow, particularly his *Close the Coalhouse Door*, were immensely popular.

Most of these were not overtly political works of the sort encouraged by the inter-war Communist Party. To an extent they were 'anti-political', verging on nihilistic in the case of some, such as *Saturday Night and Sunday Morning*. But what they did do was to create a sense of pride in region and class.

Within the Labour Party, the 1950s and early 1960s saw a new flowering of local activity that has been little documented. There was a plethora of Labour Party local newspapers, perhaps foremost being *Labour's Northern Voice*, which spawned many more local editions, initially in the Northern towns and cities but later extending south. The papers were highly conscious of Labour traditions, and frequently ran articles celebrating ILP heroes and heroines of the early years.

NEVER HAD IT SO GOOD?

The 1950s and early to mid-1960s were periods of relative industrial calm, though the cosy relationship between union leaders and employers – both public and private – was slowly being undermined by the re-emergence of a powerful movement at the grassroots, led by factory shop stewards. The post-war industrial truce came to a gradual end as sporadic strikes broke out in many different sectors, typically over pay. Engineering, docks and car-making were the main focus of discontent; the traditionally strong textile and railway unions, seeing their industrial pre-eminence wither in the face of foreign competition, lack of investment and – in the case of railways, cuts and closures – were probably wise to consent to an orderly decline. In the face of the increasing levels of industrial action across the country in the later 1960s, the Labour government's 1969 white paper 'In Place of Strife', promoted by that daughter of Northern ethical socialism Barbara Castle, was an honourable attempt to provide a better framework for resolving disputes. But it was greatly disliked by the unions and was never passed into law. The Conservative government subsequently elected in 1970 marked the definitive end of the post-war labour truce with its enactment of anti-union legislation and the ensuing strikes. Although its 1971 Industrial Relations Act was repealed by the Labour government elected in 1974, disputes between that government and the unions continued throughout its term of office. In 1979 the Thatcher government was elected, and the postwar consensus that had been fracturing for some years was finally laid to rest. In particular for the purposes of this argument, the Thatcher government had no interest in maintaining Britain's manufacturing base. But in the North few saw the writing on the wall. The traditional concentration on heavy industry – the iron and steel industries with their great plants at Consett, Irlam, Tees-side; the mining industry, textiles – all were giants with feet of clay, and the foundations were beginning to crumble.

The early 1970s also saw instances of highly innovative and radical thinking in some of the left-dominated unions. Mike Cooley, general secretary of the white collar union TASS, did more than anyone to map out a vision for how working people could take an active role in shaping their industries. The Lucas Shop Stewards' plans for workers control and 'socially useful production' trod ground which had last been covered by the syndicalists and guild socialists back in the early 1900s, in engineering, railways and mining.[7] But these initiatives were not widespread, and large sections of the labour movement regarded issues of industrial democracy as irrelevant.

It would be hard to argue that there was a strongly distinctively 'regional' pattern in trade union activity during the Heath years and the ensuing Labour government; but there was a continuing importance for local traditions. For example, Liverpool, with its culture of poor industrial relations, had waves of strikes on the docks, in car-making and other sectors. The re-emergence of militancy on the Liverpool docks was captured in the powerful Ken Loach film *Big Flame*, which inspired a radical left group of the same name – a group which attempted to reclaim a libertarian left tradition. The miners' strike of 1974, which was widely credited with bringing down the Heath government, was a national dispute, but it was very much driven by an increasingly militant Yorkshire area NUM – led by a young ex-communist called Arthur Scargill.

The left appeared to be flourishing from 1968 to the early 1970s. New ideas were starting to emerge outside the Labour Party, particularly in the Communist Party. The Italian Communist Party, and to a lesser extent the French, were developing their own distinctive strategies – dubbed 'Eurocommunism' – based on radical democracy and alliances with non-communist forces. Even in Francoist Spain, under the leadership of Santiago Carrillo, the underground PCE turned decisively away from its Stalinist past. In Britain, encouraged by the new editorial direction of the CPGB's journal *Marxism Today*, the legacy of the past began to be shed. The main strength of the 'Eurocommunist' wing of the CPGB lay in the North West and London. Far from being a movement of the intellectual middle class – as is so often alleged – the North-West reformers were mainly based in the engineering industry. Manchester-based academics such as Dave Purdy and Pat Devine developed radical ideas for economic policy which involved rejecting many sacred cows of the left, including 'free' collective bargaining and complete total nationalisation. In *Out of the Ghetto*, published in 1979 on the eve of Thatcher's victory, Purdy and Mike Prior argued for a new approach to socialist politics which involved working through the Labour Party to create a broad coalition of social-ists, trades unionists and community activists.[8] These paths not taken could perhaps have led to a different future.

LOCAL GOVERNMENT RENEWAL

Towards the tail end of the 1964-70 Wilson government, the Redcliffe-Maud Report was published, setting out recommendations for the reform of local government. It suggested moving towards strong, directly-elected sub-regional authorities in heavily-populated 'metropolitan' areas. Within the proposed two-tier structure, metropolitan districts would administer metropolitan borough councils. The Heath government that was elected soon after its publication kept some of the report's recommendations, but, crucially, the size of many of the proposed metropolitan counties was slimmed down. The Merseyside authority, for example, lost Chester; and West Yorkshire lost Harrogate. Nevertheless, the 1972 Local Government Act was still a significant move towards regional government, and most of the new metropolitan county councils were in the North; Greater Manchester, Merseyside, South and West Yorkshire, Tyne and Wear, along with West Midlands and Strathclyde. The metropolitan county councils, established in 1974, had considerably greater powers than the shire counties, and had substantial resources to implement policies on strategic planning and transport, education, social services, fire and waste disposal. The metropolitan county councils took on increasing powers over public transport, and invested heavily in both bus and rail, and in some cases – notably South Yorkshire – established low fares policies to attract people onto the buses. Many of the municipally-owned bus companies merged into county-wide enterprises owned by the metropolitan counties, for example GM Buses, owned by Greater Manchester County Council, or 'Busways', owned by Tyne and Wear. All of the metropolitan counties had Labour majorities, and in many cases had highly talented teams. As they were new authorities, many bright young Labour politicians were able to achieve positions of power, whereas they had been stymied in attempts to win positions of influence within the established Labour-controlled local authorities. Socialist feminists such as Val Stevens won senior positions in Greater Manchester, whilst radical pro-public transport activists such as Michael Simmons were elected onto the West Yorkshire body. Badges proudly proclaiming 'The People's Republic of South Yorkshire' suggested that perceptions of place and region were starting to shift, albeit slowly.[9]

NOTES

1. Steven Fielding, *England Arise! The Labour Party and Popular Politics in 1940s Britain*, 1995.
2. Stuart McIntyre, *Little Moscows: Communism and Working Class Militancy in Inter-war Britain*, 1980.
3. T.E. Nixon, *Workers' Control for the Railways*, c 1949.
4. *Labour's Northern Voice*, August 1947.
5. *Labour's Northern Voice*, 'Miners' Special', Spring 1953.
6. *Labour's Northern Voice*, July 1953.
7. Hilary Wainwright, *The Lucas Plan*, 1981.
8. Dave Purdy and Mike Prior, *Out of the Ghetto*, 1979.
9. Martin Boddy and Colin Fudge, *Local Socialism?* 1984.

7. Thatcher, Blair and the Regions

The Callaghan government proved to be the last sigh of 'old' Labourism, falling apart on the rocks of trade union rigidity and its own inability to re-interpret socialism in the light of changing values and economics. Nowhere were these tendencies more apparent than in the Labour 'heartlands' of the North of England. Cites like Liverpool and Newcastle had long had Labour administrations, and their boss-style politics had become notorious. It was Newcastle that reached the nadir of Labour corruption with the Poulson saga. A characteristic of much Labour local politics during this time was an almost childish contempt for tradition. Thus many of Newcastle's finest buildings were demolished, to make way for new roads and office blocks which would be out-dated eyesores within a few years. And many other Labour-dominated cities suffered similar fates. An unhealthy obsession with car-oriented transport policies resulted in cities like Leeds and Birmingham being sacrificed to the private car.

Whatever energy Labour still had in government was rapidly becoming exhausted; the Callaghan government sank even as it made desperate attempts to hold on to power, including doing deals with Ulster Unionists and anyone else they could persuade.

THE MINERS' STRIKE: END OF THE LINE

The miners' strike of 1984-5 was the most significant industrial dispute since the general strike of 1926 and, as in 1926, it quickly became highly politicised. The strong regional distinctiveness of the NUM came into clear focus during the strike, when the older, Communist Party-dominated areas (South Wales and Scotland) became increasingly at odds with the Young Turks of the Yorkshire and Kent areas over the strategy and tactics of the dispute. The traditionally conservative Nottinghamshire and Lancashire areas proved completely resistant to the NUM leadership's strike calls, and many carried on working.

The strike was unquestionably a fight for survival – not just for workplaces but for entire communities that were dependent on coal mining. There are remarkable parallels here with the situation facing the Lancashire and Yorkshire weavers in the early nineteenth century, when there was an equally ferocious struggle in the shape of Luddism, and a similarly ruthless response from the state. The defeat of the strike led to the destruction of dozens of mining villages across the North, Scotland, South Wales and the Midlands. 'Destruction' is an emotive term, but this is really the only way to describe what happened to so many places, which were plunged into high unemployment, poverty and – more difficult to define – sheer demoralisation.[1]

The demoralisation of entire communities was apparent in increasing levels of drug abuse and anti-social behaviour, and the breakdown of community mores that had been built up over decades, through pit, union lodge, school, social club and a network of institutions which had now become redundant. If the results of the defeat were most strongly visible in pit communities like Grimethorpe, Ashington, Easington and Featherstone, the overall impact on the North was not hard to discover beneath the surface. The defeat of the NUM and the dismantling of coal mining in Britain had a wider impact on the economies of the North, and the way we lived. The end of the strike was the last gasp of a way of life which had been constructed in working-class communities, and across the regions of the North, over a period of more than a century. Many of the tendencies that now became dominant had been developing for some time but had been almost un-noticed: a 'privatised' life style, valuing home-based entertainment rather than collective recreation; the diminishing power of the unions and declining membership; lack of interest in politics reflected in low voter turn-out and loss of party membership. Looking back on the year 1985, we can see that at the time, though the defeat of the strike was felt as a bitter blow, we probably didn't realise just quite how serious it was. Certainly some of the newly emerging trends would have happened anyway, but the pace of change might not have been so rapid or – for the communities directly affected – so catastrophic.

LOCAL GOVERNMENT UNDER ATTACK

Within a short time of coming to power, the Thatcher Government began to impose swingeing cuts in local authorities' budgets, soon to be followed by forcing them to sell off assets and put out many services to compulsory competitive tender. There was a clear agenda – to weaken the size and power of the public sector and to bolster the non-unionised private sector by offering public contracts to private forms on the basis of the lowest bid. Thus, as regional inequality was growing, the ability of local government to defend working people was also being undermined.

There were two particularly well-known centres of local government resistance to the Thatcher government: the Greater London Council, led by Ken Livingstone, and Liverpool City Council led, in effect, by its deputy leader Derek Hatton. The two approaches, whilst sharing a common hatred of Thatcher and the Tories, could hardly have been more different. Under Livingstone, the GLC did much to empower a wide range of community organisations, and brought the capital's diverse communities together. Highly innovative approaches to economic development, spearheaded by the Greater London Enterprise Board, created thousands of jobs – many in the new 'green' technologies. On Merseyside, whilst the less-glamorous Merseyside Metropolitan County Council undoubtedly did much to try to stimulate the local economy through similar approaches, attention was very much focused on the activities of the 'Militant' group, which had won control of the Labour Group on Liverpool City Council. The Trotskyist-inspired group, formed out of the shadowy Revolutionary Socialist League, was highly secretive and centralist. Whilst Livingstone's GLC welcomed diversity and never expected slavish loyalty from the plethora of groups it supported, Militant in Liverpool was paranoid about any individual or group which they did not control. Militant saw 'Stalinism' as the ultimate crime, but their political methods and mentality were straight out of Stalinism at its worst. Their model of 'socialism', if it could be called that, was rigidly centralist and brooked no opposition; it verged on gangsterism.[2] Ultimately, however, neither the GLC model, with its interesting pointers to a new form of pluralist and ethical local politics, nor the last-gasp Leninism of Militant in Merseyside, could continue to hold out against the onslaught of Thatcherism.

For a few years the Militant policy of confrontation was electorally popular in parts of Liverpool, and Labour continued to win local ward by-elections. But before long, the Militant adventure in Liverpool began to fall apart due to its own contradictions. Meanwhile the GLC, along with the successful metropolitan county councils, was abolished, in an act of stunning authoritarianism. The local popularity of the GLC and Militant was partly due to the same factors that made Thatcher popular: a radical determination to effect change and some strong personalities who could manipulate the media. Both authorities were also able to deliver results. For example during the period of Militant ascendancy, Tony Byrne, the non-Militant but left-wing councillor responsible for housing, achieved huge improvements to the city's housing stock. And in greater London, the GLC made dramatic improvements to transport and created thousands of quality jobs in 'growing' industries. Mainstream Labour rejected both these models.

Some on the left continued to think through new approaches to socialism, and these found an echo in some local authority policies as well as in trade union strategies. As Thatcher's assault on the age-old certainties of the left continued, people such as Manchester-based Hilary Wainwright developed creative approaches to socialism that had echoes of classic libertarian socialism. *The Workers Report on Vickers*, co-authored with Huw Beynon, presented a deliverable but radical strategy to shift from arms production to 'socially useful' production.[3] The Centre for Local Economic Strategies, again based in Manchester, developed some of the most creative thinking in local authority-led economic development. Reports such as Robin Murray's *Breaking with Bureaucracy* charted alternative approaches to local economic development which were community-based and democratic.[4] Some of the most radical approaches to democracy and economic development came from outside the Labour tradition. The anarchist writer Colin Ward in particular wrote authoritatively on transport and housing issues. Ward was a very practical anarchist and his essay on 'Federalism, Regionalism and Planning' in *The Raven* highlighted the huge creative potential of democratic regionalism to economic growth, citing examples from Switzerland and Italy.[5] But these ideas were being discussed in the context of a shattering defeat for the left.

RADICAL REVIVALS

The search for new ways of renewing the old traditions, particularly through social and cultural activities, could be seen in initiatives such as the modest revival of the Clarion Cycling Club that took place in the 1980s. Bolton Clarion re-formed and played an active part in supporting the miners during the strike. It made contact with surviving members of the club, both in Bolton and in other parts of Lancashire, and a new generation of Clarion socialists was created. In spite of growing internal opposition, the National Clarion Cycling Club had retained its commitment to socialism – though the halcyon days of distributing socialist propaganda on village greens had gone. In the late 1980s the Workers Educational Association in Manchester ran a course on 'Cycling to Socialism', which covered the history of the Clarion movement and included cycle rides to old Clarion destinations in the Cheshire countryside. In 1982, the Winter Hill Mass Trespass of 1896 was celebrated by a march over Winter Hill of 1500 ramblers and socialists, organised by the Bolton Socialist Club – who had planned the original event eighty-eight years previously. Around 2,500 people participated, and the marchers were led off by a brass band, as the original march had been. Before the 'big day' a series of performances of a specially-written play *Will Yo' Come O' Sunday Mornin'?* were performed around Bolton, and a street theatre performance took place in Bolton's main square. Benny Rothman, one of the last surviving leaders of the Kinder Scout Trespass, took part in the celebrations. For the centenary in 1996 another commemorative march was organised, which attracted a crowd of over a thousand. On subsequent years a more modest group has marched over the moors – now part of an 'open access' area. A stone monument stands by the site of the old gate which once barred the way across the moors.[6]

The same venerable institution revived the annual 'Whitman Day' celebrations each May, with socialist feminist Sheila Rowbotham and a number of American Whitman scholars being guests at some of the earliest revivals. Working-class writing in the North was encouraged by the Manchester-based *Voices*, published by the Federation of Worker-Writers. In Lancashire, the county association of trades councils (LATC) obtained funding in the mid-1980s for an arts development officer, who did excellent work in building links between unions and local communities through a diverse approach to culture that involved music, drama, photography and dance, as well as assistance for revived May Day festivals. In recent years, socialists on both sides of the Pennines have come together each May Day to celebrate the great Chartist gathering on Blackstone Edge. These, and the continuation of events like the Durham Miners' Gala, reflect the popularity of celebrating our socialist culture, past and present. Wigan celebrated its 'Digger' connections through George Winstanley at an event in September 2011, and there are plans to make it an annual celebration.[7]

THE NORTH UNDER BLAIR AND BROWN

The election of a Labour government under Tony Blair in 1997 was greeted with relief as much as rejoicing in many parts of the North. Whilst many Labour Party members were overjoyed to have got rid of the Tories and won power, the 'New Labour' project had only qualified support outside the debating parlours of Hampstead. The view of many activists prior to Blair's election was that 'New Labour' was a price worth paying to keep the Tories out, with the oft-whispered comment that 'once we're in power we can be more radical'.

The distinction between 'old' and 'new' Labour was never clear cut. Blair was undoubtedly right to attempt to move on from the centralised and statist approach of 1945. He embodied a spirit of renewal which touched all aspects of life, including women's equality, gay rights, support for art and culture and devolution for Scotland and Wales. Within Blair's team, John Prescott, a long-time advocate of regionalism, was given a key role as part of a 'super department' covering Environment, Transport and the Regions.

But what of 'old Labour'? Was Blair rejecting a traditional Labour Party commitment to 'real' socialism, perhaps most strongly rooted in the North, the central belt of Scotland and South Wales? In some ways he was, and in some ways he was right to do so. The Morrisonian model of state ownership, typified by British Rail in the 1960s, was long past its sell-by date. The old state corporations were much too heavily tied to the Treasury and often lacked entrepreneurial leadership – though within BR there were certainly some initiatives. Where Blair was profoundly wrong was to accept that the private sector was the only alternative. The long tradition of co-operative and mutual enterprise simply did not figure in his thinking; neither did a different approach to the state at both national and regional levels.[8]

The Blair government did support some useful 'supply-side' initiatives which had a major impact on the North. The newly established Regional Development Agencies provided substantial support to existing businesses, and helped new start-ups, investing in training and business advice, either directly or through sponsored organisations such as Business Link. The biggest drawback of the RDAs was their governance. They were appointed bodies with no local or regional democratic accountability; their governing boards were business-dominated, and in general they were less innovative than many of the enterprise boards and even local economic development units of cities like Manchester and Sheffield had been in the 1980s.

Within the Blair cabinet, Prescott presented strong arguments for directly-elected regional government, which would have addressed the RDAs' lack of accountability and re-created the positive dynamic of the abolished metropolitan county councils. Scotland and Wales were to get referenda on devolved powers, and Prescott argued that the English regions should be allowed to set up their own regional governments if they chose to do so. The region which seemed to have the strongest aspirations for regional devolution was the North East. Yet the 2004 referendum was lost. The pro-devolution campaign suffered from a combination of effective propaganda by the 'anti' lobby – who suggested that the new region would be just another tier of bureaucracy – and the lack of powers proposed for it: it would have had less power than even the defunct metropolitan counties. These two factors guaranteed defeat. Regional government would be dead in the water for years to come.[9] Since then, local authorities in the major conurbations have explored the scope for 'city region' authorities as an alternative to traditional regional government; but the intention has been to have delegated representation from districts to the city region body, rather than directly elected authorities. Whilst this may be better than nothing, all the evidence from Europe and within the UK (Scotland, Wales, London) suggests that directly-elected regional government is what really works – the combination of sufficient size, resources and accountability. Furthermore, 'city regions' implicitly exclude rural and semi-rural areas. Whilst metropolitan government can work for particular sectors (e.g. city transport), a regional approach needs to include urban and rural areas, given that the two are more and more dependent on each other. Thousands of people live in rural North Yorkshire and commute to Leeds each day; while the Yorkshire Dales and English Lakes are crucially important for the recreational needs of Manchester and Leeds.

From the point of view of the argument in this book, New Labour can be seen as making some progress on issues of regionalism and decentralisation. But its failure to explore more fruitful alternatives to top-down government, particularly those of its own rich mutual and co-operative tradition, and its frequent resort to centralising initiatives, especially within the party itself, meant that what could have been promising developments often foundered. However, while those on the left would have plenty of criticisms of the 1997-2010 Labour governments, we shouldn't ignore their achievements. Just before the 2010 general election, one comrade in local government argued that we may come to look back on the Blair and Brown years as a golden age of urban regeneration. Initiatives such as Sure Start, and their large-scale investment in the NHS and schools, made Britain a better place during those years – and we're now seeing many of those achievements destroyed.

DEVOLUTION WORKS

Scotland and Wales

Whilst the English regions were toying with 'city region' structures, the devolved administrations for Scotland and Wales were getting on with developing their nation's economies and infrastructure. The referenda on devolution showed varying degrees of support for devolution in the two nations. Scotland had previously had a referendum, in 1979, in which, although 52 per cent had voted in favour, less than 40 per cent of the electorate had actually voted, which meant that the proposition fell. But by 1997 support was much greater and 74.3 per cent of those who voted wanted a parliament, with a smaller majority of 64 per cent agreeing to tax-varying powers, which would allow the devolved government to increase revenue through taxation. The 'spoiling' condition of a minimum number of voters did not apply. Scotland would get its parliament. Wales voted the following week, on a simple yes or no to the question of whether voters wanted a Welsh Assembly. A narrow 52 per cent said yes, but that was enough to go forward. Since 1997, both nations have made remarkable progress with what would, in most parts of continental Europe, be seen as classic 'regional' government. The powers of the Scottish Parliament were stronger than those of the Welsh Assembly, but the 2011 referendum saw the people of Wales agreeing that the Assembly should have legislative power in more areas. Elections in both countries were conducted using the 'additional member' system, with a mix of first-past-the-post and proportional representation. In Scotland this led initially to a Labour-led coalition with the Liberal Democrats and Greens; in Wales Labour also had the biggest share of seats without an absolute majority, and governed with the support of the Liberal Democrats and Greens. The world has yet to collapse as a result.

Both Scottish and Welsh governments have developed a popular momentum which many would not have foreseen in 1997; even Conservatives would not now be heard calling for the scrapping of devolved government.

The achievements of devolved government in both Wales and Scotland have been considerable, with Scotland having gone furthest down the road towards independence. Both countries have strong nationalist traditions, but the left's response in Scotland and Wales has been markedly different. In Wales, under its former leader Rhodri Morgan, Labour developed a more inclusive form of socialism which allowed it to share power with Plaid Cymru up to the last election, but in Scotland Labour's vituperative hatred of the SNP has limited its scope for alliances.

Rhodri Morgan made clear in 2002 his determination to place 'clear red water' between Wales and England, in effect limiting the impact of 'New Labour' on Wales. Labour MP Paul Flynn has observed 'a permanent irritation at Westminster that a Labour-controlled body can stray from the revealed truth of the fashionable, often short-lived, nostrums of New Labour, giving as examples of such straying the rejection of the private finance initiative (PFI) and the retention of community health councils.[10] The Welsh Assembly has enshrined 'sustainable development' into the Government of Wales Act, which provides the legislative framework for the Welsh Government. In a key speech in November 2006, '21st century Socialism – a Welsh Recipe', Morgan developed a distinctive Welsh approach. Whilst noting the electoral success of the Blair project, he proceeded to set out something very different, not only in style but in content. As Nick Davies and Darren Williams commented, the recipe was distinctly unappetising to New Labour supporters:

> One by one, the nostrums of New Labour and its Thatcherite predecessors were emphatically rejected as Morgan reasserted the role of the state as a force for good in politics, emphasizing the importance of universality and the solidarity of interest that is reinforced by

universal provision. The Welsh socialism of the 21st century would be 'more participative than passive'...[11]

Morgan's speech was, and still is, remarkably radical. It not only challenged Blair and New Labour, it also struck at the foundations of the earlier post-war 'Labourism' and took us back to the heroic years of the ILP, and still earlier – even quoting Robert Owen. Morgan's emphasis on culture was particularly notable:

> At the start of the 21st century, our sense of socialism here in Wales will be shaped by a greater appreciation of the importance of culture, as well as of class. It is not good enough, I think, simply to shake our heads at the way that 'identity politics', as it is known, appears to have colonised the place which, fifty years ago, was occupied by political parties. We know that, in very large numbers, individuals identify themselves with causes from eliminating global poverty to keeping open their village post office or pub. We know that individuals understand their own place in the world on the basis of personal characteristics – be that race, or gender or disability.
>
> Socialism, traditionally, has had a rather ambivalent relationship with these social movements. 21st century socialism in Wales will need to reshape that way of thinking. We need to demonstrate the alignments which exist between the issues which motivate people and the politics which we represent ... In an era of globalisation our physical environment here in Wales, our cultural assets and our language all represent ways of securing that sense of distinctiveness and identity which provides an essential anchor in times of such rapid change. Reinforcing the links which bind progressive people together, including class, but going beyond it, has to be part of our renewed mission.[12]

Labour in Wales has been able to act as a hegemonic force in the real Gramscian sense, developing a progressive national culture with which forces beyond Labour's traditional constituencies can identify with. By championing a modern sense of Welsh identity Labour has been able to go beyond the sort of sterile sectarianism which has damaged Labour in other parts of the UK. Davies and Williams comment that the kind of socialism espoused by Morgan has deep roots, but potentially can take the nation forward:

Welsh Labour's detractors think the 'clear red water' agenda is old-fashioned. But while it has its origins in Wales' radical traditions, the refusal to regard the users of services as 'serial shoppers', the emphasis on equality of outcome and the commitment to sustainability are a glimpse into a democratic socialist future, beyond the dysfunctional, unequal and frequently violent neo-liberal present. Welsh Labour then, has one foot in the future, and the other in the past.[13]

The Welsh Labour agenda has much to offer socialists in the North of England, and the other English regions, by drawing on radical traditions and re-interpreting them for the twenty-first century.

London

The Blair government held a referendum on devolution for London in 1998. The proposal for an elected assembly with a separately elected mayor was supported by 72 per cent of voters, with strongest majorities in inner London. Elections were held in May 2000, with the result that Ken Livingstone was elected mayor with a Labour majority amongst the twenty-five assembly members. As with the Welsh and Scottish elections, a former of 'additional member' voting system was used, with 14 members elected through first past the post, and a further 11 by a proportionally-based all-London top-up system. The results saw the election of nine Labour members and nine Conservative, four Liberal Democrats and three Greens. In 2008 Boris Johnson was elected mayor and the Conservatives won the largest number of assembly seats, with eleven to Labour's nine, while the Liberal Democrats had three, the Greens two and the BNP one.

The most tangible evidence of the benefits of devolution for London is in transport. Livingstone's administration began a process of investment in the capital's decaying transport infrastructure that radically tilted the balance away from the priority previously given to the private car, and towards one which put sustainable modes at the top. Alongside major investment in the heavy rail and underground network, Livingstone promoted bus transport, cycling and walking. Congestion charging was an intelligent way of ensuring that the money was there to pay for it. Unlike other cities which decided to have a referendum on the issue (such as Manchester and Edinburgh), Livingstone bit the bullet and did it, in the teeth of bitter opposition from the Tories and many within the Labour Party. The system has proved such an obvious success that the Johnson mayoralty is unable to reverse it.

This extended discussion on devolved government demonstrates two things. Firstly, that forms of proportional representation can work perfectly well in the UK as they do in many other countries. They can have the effect of encouraging efforts to find common ground rather than focusing on division and confrontation. Secondly, that they do not result in 'weak' government. Both the devolved nations and London have used their powers to invest in better infrastructure, health and social care. Further tangible benefits of devolution have been free prescriptions and abolition of student fees. London's Development Agency, established under Livingstone's administration, has recaptured some of the dynamism of the GLC's enterprise boards, with support for local businesses including co-operatives and other social enterprises.

ENTER THE COALITION: GOODBYE ENGLISH REGIONS

The election of a Conservative/Liberal Democrat Coalition government in May 2010 surprised the many political commentators who had assumed David Cameron would 'walk it' and get a clear majority. Prior to the election, the Tories had sent out misleading impressions about whether they would, or would not, abolish the RDAs. The impression amongst many people in industry and local government was that those RDAs with strong local support, such as Yorkshire Forward, One North-East and the NWDA, would survive, though perhaps in a slimmed-down format. This was given encouragement by the Liberal Democrat presence within government. They had for long been the strongest advocate of regional government amongst the three main parties, and whilst the RDAs were not accountable bodies, they were a half-way house to so being. Despite all that, Eric Pickles, when appointed secretary of state in the Department for Communities and Local Government, wasted no time in announcing not only the abolition of the RDAs, but also the Government regional offices. These had been set up by Michael Heseltine in the 1980s, and had proved a very useful way of keeping central government more in touch with the English regions, with teams of civil servants based in each regional centre in close touch with local authorities and the business community.

In place of the RDAs, 'Local Enterprise Partnerships' have been established, covering smaller areas. Like the RDAs they are 'business led', but they have far fewer resources and powers, and economic development professionals expect them to have not much impact, especially given that the scale of cuts in local government is so great.

The last vestiges of regional administration in England, outside of London, have disappeared. The 'north-south divide' is once again being talked about: house prices continue to plummet in many parts of the North whilst in some parts of the South they are rising. Given the higher dependency on public sector employment and spending in the North, the economic gap is likely to grow. Many private sector businesses are dependent on local authority contracts for their existence and these are starting to dry up.

One of the encouraging aspects of the 2010 election campaign was the cross-party support for social enterprises and 'mutuals'. However, this is seen by the government as little more than a means of transferring public sector facilities into the private sphere. 'Social enterprise' is a nice term, but successful social enterprises are usually the result of steady organic growth, public sector encouragement and experienced leadership, rather than panic transfers. And to be sustainable and 'sellout proof' they need to be protected against hostile takeovers.

It could be so much better. As Scotland, Wales and London move on with their programmes of investment, the North of England is facing years of decline, as public sector jobs disappear and a weak private sector is unable to bridge the gap.

The Labour Party has a new leader, who has made clear a willingness to 'move on' from the Blair years. Decentralisation, co-operatives and community empowerment are on the agenda, coupled with a sense of realism that what Labour offers has to be deliverable, financially as well as politically. As John Prescott argues in his foreword, this is not about ignoring the role of the state, but using its enabling power – at regional as well as national levels – to promote sustainable development.

NOTES

1. Paul Routledge and Francis Beckett, *Marching to the Fault Line*, 2009.
2. Martin Crick, *Militant*, 1984; and *The March of Militant*, 1986.
3. Hilary Wainwright and Huw Beynon, *The Workers Report on Vickers*, 1980.

4. Robin Murray, *Breaking with Bureaucracy: ownership, control and nationalisation*, 1987.
5. Colin Ward. 'Federalism, Regionalism and Planning', *The Raven*, vol. 8 no. 3, Autumn 1995.
6. See Salveson, *Will Yo' Come O'Sunday Mornin'?* op. cit.
7. The Durham Miners Gala has enjoyed a renaissance. In 2011 socialists in Wigan organised a commemoration of Gerard Winstanley in September 2010 and the intention is to make it an annual event. The Tolpuddle Festival goes from strength to strength, despite persistently poor weather.
8. See Mike Davis, 'Modernisation means Democratisation', in Chris Wearmouth (ed.), *Beyond Blair: prospects for a New Socialist Left*, 2006.
9. Andy Croft 'A Profoundly Reactionary Moment in British Politics' in *Red Pepper* December 2004/January 2005
10. Paul Flynn, Foreword to Nick Davies and Darren Williams, *Clear Red Water: Welsh Devolution and Socialist Politics*, 2009.
11. N. Davies and D. Williams, ibid.
12. Rhodri Morgan speech to Compass conference, Swansea, 30 November 2006. The speech can be accessed at http://www.compassonline.org.uk/news/item.asp?n=338.
13. Ibid.

PART 3

The North Resurgent

8. Radical Regionalism: Will the North Rise Again?

This book's meander around the branch lines of Northern socialism hasn't just been an exercise in nostalgia. There is much in the heritage of the socialist movement which has relevance to modern-day socialist politics – though of course some that is less so. The emphasis on a 'larger socialism' that includes culture, the outdoors, the environment and even an element of spirituality has something to say to us today. The stress on values and a truly 'ethical socialism' must have relevance to us in an age in which the public are heartily sick of the corruption of public life, especially following the MPs' expenses scandal and the News International revelations.

The pride in regional identity expressed through dialect may seem less relevant, but in Wales and to some extent Scotland, language is a crucial part of a progressive national identity. And promotion of different linguistic traditions need not be exclusive: my grand-daughter Iona, brought up in south London and now living on Skye, has recently won gold prizes for Gaelic poetry. I visited a literary festival in Co. Mayo a few years ago, and some of the best entrants in the children's category were young Polish kids. And in many working-class areas of Bradford and Rochdale you will hear young children of Asian ancestry speaking with strong local accents. So a new Lancashire and Yorkshire dialect literature, which isn't just about the past, cobbled streets and smoking mills, might have more to it than it at first sight seems. The 'death of dialect' has been pronounced for the last two hundred years and more, and I'm not going to risk being proved wrong by suggesting that it finally *has* died out. It hasn't! But dialects are subject to many new influences, and reflect the complexity and ethnic make-up of today's Northern working class: English, Irish, Polish, African-Caribbean, Asian. A progressive Northern culture can still have room for some dialect, brass bands, the Huddersfield Choral Society and the Halle, as well as the likes of The Fall. Wasn't it Mark E Smith who wrote 'The North Will Rise Again'? Maybe he would be a candidate for first president of a Northern People's Republic.

But returning to reality ... we need to build a radical regionalist agenda which is sensitive to people's identities and which makes the most of our heritage, without wallowing in it. That's why this book has been about 'Socialism with a Northern Accent'. It is not about retreating into a cosy world of 'Northern-ness', to strains of 'Coronation Street'. It is about creating a modern, diverse regionalism that can appeal on economic but also on social and cultural levels.

If 'socialism' is to have any relevance in the twenty-first century, it must be more de-centralised, community-based and diverse – and with a sense of humour. What better guide to help us down that road than that upper class gay man from Brighton, Edward Carpenter, whom the Northern working class took to its heart? Can Labour recapture some of the radicalism and passion which informed the early years of the ILP and the Clarion movement over a hundred years ago, of which Carpenter was such a great figurehead?

But let's combine passion with some analysis. In many ways socialism was still an immature movement at the turn of the twentieth century, and the realities of office in the 1920s led to a retreat from the fun and tomfoolery, and quasi-religious appeals, of the early days. Labour's economic strategy was a particularly unimaginative version of classic Liberalism. But there are things we can learn from those early days. If we can find ways of reconnecting with people's lives and culture in the widest sense, there may be a better chance for socialism to rebuild itself as a popular force across Britain.

Simply attacking the government will not win over the numbers of people to whom Labour needs to appeal if it's to form a viable government. We need to have something positive to offer, that is both radical and popular. As we saw in the previous chapter, Rhodri Morgan, the former leader of the Labour Party in Wales, summed up the issue very clearly. For him it was about creating a twenty-first century socialism to a Welsh recipe. This book is saying we need something similar for the North of England – a twenty-first century socialism with a Northern accent, with a toe or two in the past but above all looking to the future. What would it look like? And what can we really learn from the past?

VALUES, DEMOCRACY, INCLUSIVITY

Comparisons between past and present can easily come across as trite and simplistic. The North of England is a very different place now than it was even thirty years ago, let alone a hundred and fifty years ago. How can we compare the Manchester of Peterloo with the city of today? So any comparisons need to be made with care. Yet there are some that can be made. There was never a 'golden age' of a radical socialist Labour Party post-1900, and trying to conjure one up is pointless and dishonest. But there was much of value in the ILP and co-operative tradition from which we can learn – as well as from the post-1945 period. Perhaps above all, the 'ethical socialism' of the ILP offers the foundations of a values-based socialism that could be rebuilt in a form that resonates with people today.

The Chartists have much to tell us too; above all about the importance of grass-roots democracy. The tens of thousands of working class Chartists wanted the vote so that they could change society – it was 'a knife and fork' question, combining the struggle for democracy with a wider social agenda. A modern-day 'Chartism' should be about deepening democracy at local, regional and national level, linking with economic democracy in the form of social enterprise, greater control over the provision of public services and greater democracy in the workplace.

Any serious democratic advance in voting systems should be based on some form of proportional representation. But the UK-wide referendum on the 'Alternative Vote' in 2011 demonstrated the limitations of current political debate in Britain as a whole. The quality of the debate was poor, while in any case the Alternative Vote model has very little semblance to proportionality; if enacted, it would have represented at best a very modest improvement on the current system. Elections to the Scottish Parliament, Welsh Assembly, Greater London Assembly and the Northern Ireland Assembly are already based on PR and have proved successful. A similar voting system for Westminster elections would have much more potential support than AV.

Austin Mitchell, the quirky but perceptive MP for Grimsby, summed up the issues as far back as 1989:

> Proportional representation – representing the people's wish in parliament – should be the central part of a wider process; entrenching rights, in the constitution, at work, to services, as citizens: decentralisation of power by breaking down the dominance of The Great Wen and establishing regional governments, not only in Scotland and Wales but in all the English regions with powers transferred down from the centre and up from the counties ...[1]

Alongside the need for strong regional government and a fairer electoral system, the case needs to be made for a root and branch reform of how government actually functions. Men still outnumber women by a huge majority in Parliament and local government, and our elected representatives are becoming increasingly alike, regardless of party. It's time to breathe new life into British politics, and a big part of that is widening the pool of talent for councillors and MPs. And here, class needs to re-emerge alongside gender, sexuality and race as an area of political concern.

The Labour Party has done more in this field than the other main parties. It has agreed a range of policies which strengthen women's role within the party, including all-women shortlists. Yet few would say that real equality has been achieved. The leadership election candidates in 2010 consisted of five men and one woman, though there are a number of strong women politicians in the Labour leadership. These include Yorkshire MPs Yvette Cooper and Mary Creagh, and Doncaster's Rosie Winterton, who is Chief Whip; not forgetting Lancashire's Louise Ellman, who has great expertise in transport and local government. (By contrast, the visibility of women in the Coalition Government is remarkably low, for all Cameron's 'modernising' rhetoric. Compare this with countries such as Norway, Switzerland, Spain and Denmark where women make up a majority of cabinet ministers or represent a very large minority.) But Labour could do much better. Further shifts towards gender equality within the Labour Party are needed, in promoting talented women activists and targeting women for membership. Here there are some great role models from the past, as we've seen – Katharine Glasier, Carrie Martyn, Hannah Mitchell, Selina Cooper and scores more.

A REGIONALIST INTERNATIONALISM

'Regionalism' is often dismissed as parochial and lacking interest in anything that happens beyond its boundaries. Yet, as we have seen, in the North of England there is a long and honourable internationalist tradition, stretching back to support for the French Revolution, through anti-slavery, to support for Irish independence and the republic forces in the Spanish Civil War. A 'Socialism with a Northern accent' would have little difficulty in being a socialism which celebrates a genuine internationalism – one that is based not on hero worship of a particular pseudo-revolutionary state, but on support for international struggles for democracy and freedom. The support of Lancashire workers for the anti-slavery forces of Abraham Lincoln, the opposition to tyranny in Europe expressed by some of the North's working class dialect writers, and the its support for democracy in Spain, make up a heritage to be proud of. Some of that selfless sacrifice for a just cause remains today, amongst the thousands of people who still raise money and support for liberation struggles and anti-poverty campaigns around the world.

Immigration from Asia, Africa and Eastern Europe has radically altered the culture, and economy, of the North. In some ways it has made us more aware of international issues, though cities like Bradford, Leeds, Liverpool, Salford and Manchester have always had a strong cosmopolitan culture, reflecting generations of immigration – often people fleeing from oppression and poverty. The huge response to the Pakistan Flood Appeal of 2010 – not just from Pakistani communities but from a wide range of non-Asian people – is a positive example of such solidarity. It would be wrong to say this is a purely 'Northern' phenomenon, but it is notable that many Northern local authorities, such as Bradford, have been to the fore in organising support for the appeals.

Internationalism is also about building progressive networks between people in different countries, where experience and ideas can be shared. For example the experience of regional government in Spain's Basque Country and Catalonia, as well as the Swiss cantons and French regional councils and the German Länder, has much to tell and guide us. EU-sponsored networks, particularly the 'Europe of the Regions' programme, can also be of enormous value for learning about what has worked elsewhere, and for helping to create collaborative networks in a huge range of areas – including education, arts and culture, environmental best practice, local economic development and new forms of democracy. A democratic 'Europe of the Regions' is a strong and potentially popular alternative to the increasingly strident anti-Europeanism of the Tories.

A NEW UNIONISM

What of unions in the North today? The days of local or regional unions ended decades ago, and a process of merger and consolidation has meant that many once-powerful sectoral unions are part of mass unions such as Unite, GMB and Community. Thatcherism, and ensuing de-industrialisation, had a dramatic impact on union membership across the country, and it was inevitable that the most noticeable decline would be in areas of traditional, strongly unionised industries that were in headlong decline: mining, textiles, iron and steel, shipbuilding and railways. This meant that the North was hit proportionately harder. It is in the remaining public sector that unions retain a stronger membership.

The unions have moved a long way from the cautious respectability of earlier generations. Their leaderships have become much more diverse and responsive to the needs of today's members. Allegiance to the Labour Party has become more qualified: the RMT, probably the most 'left' of the main unions, disaffiliated from the party in the 1980s. Those which stayed in have had many hopes frustrated by Blair's love affair with the private sector, but the current leadership is taking a more balanced approach, which is right. The old days of 'beer and sandwiches' at No. 10 may have gone, symbolising what was too close a link between unions and the Labour Party. But a new settlement in which Labour sees the trades unions as friends and allies in a common struggle for extended democracy, sustainable economic development, individual rights and improved living standards would be good not only for the labour movement but for the UK as a whole.

The 2010 Trades Union Congress, held in Manchester, where the first TUC met in 1868, had an intelligent debate about strategies to limit the Coalition's cuts agenda. The importance of linking up with a wide range of partners came over clearly. Opting for strike action in isolation was seen by many delegates as a dead end which would risk further isolating the trade union movement, and finishing off the job which Thatcher started. Can a new unionism develop which goes beyond the traditional, and shrinking, confines of industry, and links up with local communities who are at the sharp end of Coalition attacks?

My own union, the Transport Salaried Staffs Association (TSSA) has appointed two 'community organisers' to work with grassroots organisations outside the railway industry, on issues around service cuts and building local campaigns for better facilities. The union's assistant general secretary, Manuel Cortes, has been working with community transport providers FreeBus in Bristol, a non-profit organisation funded by memberships and donations from Bristol residents. Whilst passengers are encouraged to become members or donate, the service is free at the point of use:

> FreeBus aims to develop a model that communities across the UK can use to take control of their transport systems. If you live or work in Bristol, I would urge you to become a member. Your support will help provide a comprehensive, environmentally friendly and free public transport system for the city. Even though the service is only a few hours old, it is already proving incredibly popular. The first two buses were standing room only. Passengers are delighted with this new free friendly service. FreeBus is also very positive about unions. They have already signed a recognition agreement with us. This shows that by working with our communities we can also aid union growth. Let's hope that the Bristol experience is replicated elsewhere![2]

There is much more scope for trades unionists to build links with communities, not least on environmental issues. The TUC Education service has begun to develop courses on environmental issues for union representatives, but these are no more than drops in the ocean. The trade union movement has the potential to put itself at the head of a strong grass-roots based movement to campaign for 'green jobs' and recruit in new areas of employment such as the growing number of businesses working in the environmental sector.

Socialists and trades unionists should avoid a simplistic view that 'business' is the enemy; quite the contrary, we need to cultivate allies in the private sector. Labour and the unions can learn from business and unite around a shared need to manage the economy in a more sustainable way. A regionalist approach, based on accountable regional development agencies, would be a key weapon in achieving that. The old RDAs achieved a lot, but could have done more if they were democratically accountable to elected regional councils. Their own governance should reflect a public, private and voluntary sector mix, so that the best of each is exploited.

Unions should also be a core part of the 'cultural socialism' that is a recurring theme in this book. The employment by Lancashire Association of Trades Councils of an Arts Development Officer in the 1980s (see p166) offers one model. More recently, the RMT has been sponsoring Easington Colliery Band, and in October 2011 the band led off the 'Jarrow Youth March' to London.

We need more initiatives such as these, through individual unions sponsoring their own members' cultural activities, and the TUC at regional level supporting a wider cultural agenda. Such activities need focus and organisation – and unions like Unite, Community and GMB are big enough, and have sufficient resources, to employ a small team of 'cultural workers'.

LABOUR AND THE IMPORTANCE OF ALLIES

The structure of the Labour Party that emerged in 1900 was unique amongst socialist and social democratic parties in Europe. The organic link with the trades unions was at once its strength and – to some on the left – its weakness. The unions exerted a brake on some of the more radical elements within the Labour Party, and for decades remained uneasy about even describing the party as 'socialist'. Yet without that link to the unions it is unlikely that working-class voters would have made the break with Liberalism in such numbers. Socialism in Britain could well have remained a much smaller force, with a handful of MPs in the North, Wales and Scotland. The price of compromise was a diluted social democracy, which, for all its faults, appealed to a much wider audience. From some of the examples in this book, it's clear that 'socialism' to many activists in the past was about *collective* solutions to the great issues of the day, but this did not necessarily involve state-led solutions. Co-operation, municipal enterprise and trades unionism are the obvious examples of that.

In the twenty-first century the link with the unions remains vital to the success of the Labour Party, but, in a turn-round from the early 1900s, many unions are now further to the left of Labour: during the

Blair years they became increasingly frustrated with New Labour's love affair with the banks and big business. The size of the trade union movement has been much reduced from the heady days of the 1960s and 1970s, and their influence is weaker. If there is to be a serious challenge to the Coalition, Labour and the unions need to agree a new version of the historic compromise that led to Labour's formation in 1900. This means both widening and deepening a progressive movement.

Labour should become the core of an alliance which includes other political forces, notably the Greens and the progressive wing of the Liberal Democrats. It's easy to see the Liberal Democrats only in their role as part of a Coalition government imposing a radical right-wing agenda of cuts and privatisation, and as reflecting the neoliberal nostrums in the Orange Book published by leading Liberal Democrats before the 2010 general election. But not only is this approach anathema to many Liberal Democrat party members and supporters, it also flies in the face of the radical tradition of Liberalism exemplified by people like Thomas Newbigging, Joseph Cowen and Solomon Partington. There is a large section of the Liberal Democrats who are part of a progressive centre-left of which Labour should be the keystone.

This is not about Labour diluting its principles, or its values, to get into power. Socialists have co-operated with radical Liberals in the past, and we should do so now and in the future, on areas where we are in agreement at local and possibly national level. Some local authorities already have a Labour-Liberal Democrat Coalition, and many are working well given the climate of cuts. Within the Liberal tradition there is a seam of radicalism which finds natural allies with Labour and the socialist tradition. By looking for common ground, rather than pushing Liberal Democrats into a corner with accusations of 'betrayal', the potential for a radical and progressive coalition will be infinitely stronger.

There are also newer political forces, particularly the Greens, who should be our natural allies. They bring a particular approach to politics, locally and nationally, which is valuable, fresh and practical. It's the wrong response to say they should join Labour. Why should they? At times, Labour has not shown itself particularly interested in environmental issues. Having a lively Green Party pushing Labour on issues which it has traditionally seen as 'fringe' can only be a good thing. It doesn't mean that we should not fight them at local elections, but when they do win council seats, we should not see them as enemies but as possible partners.

Writing at the end of 2011, it's clear that the Conservatives have cleverly corralled the Liberal Democrats into being junior partners of a very right-wing government; time will tell how long this will last. It is important not to take from this experience the idea that any form of coalition is inevitably bad. People want to see politicians working together for the common good. That happens in many parts of the country at local level already, as we have seen with Scotland and Wales, as well as in English local authorities like Bradford and Kirklees. This kind of co-operation needs to happen much more. Labour can become a truly 'national' party if it can reach out in a spirit of co-operation and generosity towards many different traditions – not least the Liberal tradition, which has been so powerful and influential in the North. And anyone who says that the Conservative tradition has absolutely nothing to teach us is ignorant of history. The party of Disraeli was far from being a bunch of reactionary, self-interested bigots. Radical Tories such as Huddersfield's Richard Oastler, who fought against child labour in the 1830s, were in many ways 'to the left' of most politicians of their time. The modern-day Conservative Party isn't entirely composed of hidebound reactionaries. Like the Labour Party, there is an internal coalition; some of it is liberal and progressive though much of it is right-wing and reactionary. The Conservative Co-operative Movement, led by Hereford MP Jesse Norman, is one example of a progressive Toryism which should not be dismissed.

There are other forces in society that are instinctively 'progressive' and to which Labour should reach out. For example the voluntary sector is a huge force in society, and has been hard hit by cuts in public expenditure. In areas such as community development, social care, environment and heritage Labour can offer practical policies; but it can also learn from the perspectives of the voluntary sector.

Labour has got to win more members and supporters, making itself attractive to the many people who do not want to be hardened political activists, 'out on the knocker' day and night, but are willing to do something to help. It's a myth that we have become a nation of 'non-joiners'. Look at the size of charities like the National Trust and RSPB. It's just that people are picky about *what* they join. Labour's biggest allies outside the labour movement itself – (i.e. the Labour and

Co-operative Parties, the trades unions, and the Co-operative movement) are in the voluntary sector. This is an incredibly diverse sector involving tens of thousands of organisations, ranging from bodies such as the National Trust with three million members, though to tiny community groups with a handful of supporters. It is immensely powerful and is facing common threat through the current climate of cuts and recession. The 'Big Society', whilst it may not have started out as a cynical exercise to get the voluntary sector to do public jobs more cheaply, is now looking increasingly threadbare, as thousands of voluntary organisations face major funding cuts.

PRACTICAL SOCIALISM – THE CO-OPERATIVE REVIVAL

The biggest challenge facing Labour is being able to present a credible alternative to free market capitalism. Calling for nationalisation of manufacturing industry carries less and less conviction. But there is an alternative, and it has been around a long time. Co-operation was seen by many in the mid to late nineteenth century as 'practical socialism'. The hard-headed working men and women who provided the leadership of the Co-operative movement often had an innate suspicion of the state – it was seen as a hostile external force, or at best as irrelevant to co-operation, as long as it left them alone and free to get on with their co-operating. 'Municipal socialism' in the form of local authority ownership of tramways, gas and water supplies and the like, was seen as complementary. Indeed, by the turn of the twentieth century many co-operators would be involved in local government. Experience in co-op committee work would have provided invaluable skills for running local authorities, as Labour took control of a growing number of councils by the 1920s. However, nationalisation was viewed by many with a degree of scepticism bordering on hostility. It might perhaps have been appropriate for railways and mines, but productive industry was in the main seen as future 'co-operative' territory.

The Co-operative movement has continued to grow world-wide, though it has not succeeded in challenging the basic model of free-market capitalism to any great extent. There are successful examples of co-operative businesses in many advanced capitalist countries, not least our own Co-op retail stores. Whilst the 'co-operative world' which supplied every conceivable need has fragmented, the Co-op remains an important, even iconic, feature of British life. And there are good examples of industrial, as well as consumer, co-operatives in several sectors, including several 'new' industries such as communications.

On a political level, the Co-operative Party offers an alternative model to the increasingly threadbare post-war model of social democracy, which was based on state ownership and a 'passive' population eagerly and gratefully receiving the beneficence of the welfare state.

The Co-operative ideal is perhaps the North's greatest gift to Britain and the world. It is alive and well, and there are some exciting shoots of new growth – in small-scale producers' co-operatives as well as in new areas for consumer co-ops (e.g. the Phone Co-op); but there is also new potential in its democratic ideals. In Labour's 2010 Manifesto, the importance of mutualism and social enterprise re-emerged. These can take many forms, but the co-operative model provides a tried and tested solution for many industrial sectors. If state socialism is dead, co-operative models of socialism, offering diversity, decentralisation and genuine popular participation, have huge potential. This isn't to say that the state doesn't have a role: a sensible left-of-centre approach would see the state as having a more important and more interventionist role than it currently has. It simply wouldn't be the all-encompassing state dreamt of by socialists of old.

Manchester remains the world headquarters of modern co-operation. The statue of Robert Owen, dubbed 'the father of co-operation', is a familiar sight to commuters arriving at Manchester's Victoria station. The sculpture, with Owen comforting a young child, stands outside the Co-op's headquarters building, fronting one of the most successful businesses not just in Britain, but the world.

MUNICIPAL ENTERPRISE RENEWED

Labour today should be building alliances with the voluntary sector, not only to resist cuts here and now, but to work out new ways in which a future Labour government might work with the voluntary sector. There is nothing inimical to the socialist tradition in local social enterprises running parks, creating new public places, operating local bus services, or running post offices, tourist information offices or theatres and libraries. What is anathema is using such opening up as a backdoor means to letting the big private sector 'facilities providers' take over these services. The period of 'employee ownership' of the bus industry, following the break-up of the local authority-owned bus companies in the 1980s, lasted a few years at most, before they were bought out by the likes of Stagecoach and First group. Unless a service is protected against private take-over, the 'social enterprise honeymoon' is always likely to be very short.

Labour should be looking at new forms of municipal enterprise, doing more with the local state. The municipal socialism of the 1890s saw hundreds of councils running tramways, gasworks, power stations and other services, and they made a good job of it. Some local authorities still own substantial businesses, including bus companies, airports and docks – and in Blackpool trams.

How should municipal enterprise develop in the twenty-first century? Some of the thinking in Labour-led local authorities (e.g. the GLC, Manchester, Sheffield, Southampton) in the 1970s and 1980s would benefit from a dusting-down, to look again at some of the imaginative ideas that local government at that time was generating. Their support for local workers' co-operatives and employee participation in major enterprises, and their bottom-up approaches to economic regeneration – often in the face of national Labour indifference or even hostility – still have great relevance. Strong democratic local and regional government is the way to really drive such initiatives forward. Local authorities, supported by powerful regional agencies, could do much to support emergent industries, which may need little more than an initial leg-up. Taking shares in developing businesses could be part of a more interventionist approach that would bring a range of benefits to local communities, through jobs, business development and the wider multiplier effect of growth.

LOCAL GOVERNMENT AND COMMUNITY LEADERSHIP

The dilemmas faced by socialist councillors in the 1930s, and in the 1980s, have parallels with the situation facing local government today. The budget cuts imposed by the Coalition government shift the responsibility for implementing cuts to local authorities, just as happened in the 1930s and 1980s. Labour-controlled councils are in the invidious position of having to implement cuts at the behest of an increasingly unpopular government. Public sector workers are furious at the sight of Labour Party elected members voting through the most stringent cuts for decades, with many vulnerable communities having services and facilities cut. We have got to learn the lessons of the past and avoid futile gestures. Labour politicians today do not have the option of a 'Poplar' style revolt. 'Revolutionary' tactics such as refusing to set a budget and allowing the Council to go bankrupt would do a lot more harm than good, and primarily to the least well-off constituents. Equally, walking away from the problem would only leave Tories and Liberals with the freedom to implement even more regressive cuts. There is only one option, that taken by Selina Cooper in the 1930s: to stay in there and fight to get the least-worst deal for our communities.

Labour has frequently showed much more radicalism in local government than when it held power nationally. There were visionary local authority leaderships, such as those in Manchester, Leeds, Newcastle, Sheffield, and even little Farnworth and Nelson, exercising power in the first three decades of the twentieth century, and the 1970s saw some exciting developments, with local authorities working in partnership with communities and worker co-operatives in many towns and cities. Labour can rebuild its popularity, even in the face of huge cuts in public funding, by re-connecting with some of its radical traditions. The next few years are likely to see Labour taking control of many councils across the country, but perhaps in the North in particular. Cities and towns like Newcastle, Sheffield, Hull, York, Stockport, Bury and many others are within Labour's grasp. On the one hand power might seem a poisoned chalice, and dozens of Labour authorities have already had to impose swingeing cuts to council budgets. But on the other it offers an opportunity to empower local communities and work collaboratively with community groups and businesses to minimise the impact of Coalition cuts. But nobody is saying that will be easy. The alternatives are to refuse power – political madness by any standard – or meekly implement cuts without mounting a grassroots challenge to them.

Labour-controlled local authorities will need to get out of their comfort zones and build alliances. The Coalition has made great play of the 'Big Society', and Labour's response needs to be measured. Talk of 'empowering local communities' whilst cutting funding to the voluntary sector is a cynical exercise. But the 'Big Society' should not be dismissed simply as a veil for cuts. Over the last fifteen years the voluntary sector has done well from Labour, both in terms of national support and help for Labour local authorities. It could have done more, but it was moving in the right direction; in the coming years Labour needs to present itself unequivocally as the defender of the voluntary sector.

Over the next few years, Labour in local government should make a leap in imagination and re-connect with a diverse range of communities, acting as a focus for a new kind of local politics. It needs to position itself as the party of the voluntary sector, and to see community organisations, locally and nationally, as allies who can help deliver some of Labour's goals. A whole range of environmental, cultural and social activities could develop which are delivered by community groups and supported by local government and local sponsorship. The emerging 'community foundation' movement is a clear example of how this might work.

At a local political level, Labour should not be afraid of working with constituencies who may traditionally be seen as natural allies of the Tories – particularly local businesses. Neither should it be afraid of building progressive alliances with Greens and Liberal Democrats, many of whom feel let down by their national leaders.

Bradford – where the Independent Labour Party was founded in 1893 – is a very different place from the city of Fred Jowett and J.B. Priestley; but they would recognise some recurring aspects. It is – and arguably always has been – the North's most diverse city, with several distinct communities from the Asian sub-continent as well as the Caribbean and Eastern Europe. Writing of his early years in Bradford, Priestley said:

> Bradford became at once the most provincial and yet one of the most cosmopolitan of English provincial cities ... there was this curious leaven of intelligent aliens, mostly German Jews ... there was then this odd mixture in pre-war Bradford. A dash of the Rhine and Oder found into our grim tunnel. Bradford was determinedly Yorkshire and provincial, yet some of its suburbs reached as far as Frankfurt and Leipzig.[3]

The Labour Party took control of the City Council in May 2010, on the same day that Labour lost power nationally. The leader, Ian Greenwood, describes himself as 'an old-time politico' steeped in the socialist tradition. He embodies the Bradford Labour tradition of Jowett. But his deputy leader, Imran Hussain, is a young lawyer from Bradford's large Pakistani community. Many of the councillors – Conservative as well as Labour – are from Asian backgrounds. But this diversity goes well beyond the Council chamber. It is very obvious in the streets – the city has a dynamic Asian culture the like of which you don't see in Leeds, Manchester, Sheffield or Liverpool. The city also has two BNP councillors, reflecting the fears and prejudices of some parts of the white community. In August 2010 the right-wing English Defence League attempted to stage a highly provocative march through the city – which on the day ended in farce with the EDL directing its anger mainly towards the police. What has emerged from the widespread and shared anxieties preceding the march is a real sense of unity and co-operation. And this was nurtured and supported by a Labour Council, which – no doubt imperfectly – represents the diversity of this city. The council has reached out to the faith communities, to the voluntary sector and to the business community; and they have been inclusive towards the Conservatives and Liberal Democrats on the council. This is how Labour should be working across the country. It harks back to the days of the late 1930s and 'The Popular Front' against emerging fascism.

Local government, for all its faults and weaknesses, is the most democratic form of government we have. Elected politicians are in close touch with the people who elected them, and whom they represent. They live and work in their communities and understand how their place 'ticks'. This position does not mean that they should have responsibility for everything, but it does point towards a future role of local government that is 'hegemonic' in the sense intended by the Italian Marxist Gramsci. The local authority should 'lead' by winning hearts and minds, and act as a unifying and democratic force in the community. It should not be afraid of allowing other accountable bodies (community foundations, residents' organisations, amenity groups) to go off and do things which benefit communities, and it must recognise the incredibly strong and creative power of voluntary action. But local government has a central role as a democratic, funded body which represents everyone and not just a sectional interest, however important. Getting that relationship right, between responsible and accountable local government and a flourishing non-governmental sector, is vital.

NORTHERN IDENTITY

The Northern socialist culture of the late nineteenth century reflected the world of which it was part, above all the industries which dominated the North: textiles and mining. Much of its symbolism related to nonconformist religion, and its dialects reflected the homogenous nature of an industrial working class. Northern dialect literature of a century ago, particularly the writings of Allen Clarke and Ben Turner, showed how using local speech made socialism 'belong' to local people; it was distinctive to a particular place or county and not the 'alien creed' that its opponents claimed. The lessons from that incredibly effective movement are not that we should all start talking 'broad Lancashire' or 'gradely Yorkshire' (lots do already), but that we should do more to celebrate locality and tradition.

Many people, way beyond the Labour Party, value local culture. Local history continues to be immensely popular, and local festivals show no sign of decline. But we need a new socialist culture which speaks to people in the world we are in now, not a world we might like to be in. Certainly within that we can allow ourselves a degree of nostalgia, a celebration of a heritage that is distinctly ours. But we need to do more than that; otherwise socialism will become a heritage theme park. Creating a sense of place and identity that is genuinely popular is entirely achievable. It requires inclusive approaches to the arts and local history, more community festivals, and the development of interactive media which can build up a vibrant local culture.

The North has a huge range of talented, progressive artists, musicians and writers who have no particular political allegiance. Painters such as Anthony Turner, a committed supporter of the labour movement, whose excellent work has been on tour around the North during 2010, are the exception. Turner has re-invented the political banner, using a mixture of irony and heroism to promote trade unionism. A modern Northern socialist culture must also include bands like the Fall, as well as poets such as Simon Armitage and the great array of talent in Asian and African-Caribbean communities in cities like Bradford, Manchester and Sheffield.

We have moved on from the days of 'institutional' socialist art, which was perhaps too closely (but understandably) linked to party and trade union. But regional art does need nurturing, and that requires funding. At a time when the arts are under concerted attack there is a risk that the arts will revert to elitist obscurantism, with funding only possible through big business sponsorship. There is a role for local government in arts sponsorship, but also for non-state bodies such as the unions and co-operative movement. There is also a very strong relationship between art and economic and social regeneration. The renaissance of some major cities, like Bilbao with its Guggenheim or even Middlesbrough, Wakefield and Walsall with their galleries, has been arts-led. The cultural industries have great potential in creating jobs and new businesses, and at the same time in laying the foundations for a distinctive local and regional culture.

Politics needs to be a bit quirky at times. There is no doubt that the annual Whitman Day celebration in Bolton fits that description. It grows in popularity each year, with people attending from Manchester's gay community, together with Labour Party members and other socialists from around Lancashire. The complex mosaic of regional currents in socialism needs celebrations like Whitman Day. There are other events which we still commemorate, such the Tolpuddle Martyrs, the great Chartist meeting on Blackstone Edge in 1848, and the Burston School Strike. But there could be many more. Our history is full of inspiring events, many lying forgotten and waiting to be re-discovered. Let's celebrate them and discover more.

BUILDING A NORTHERN VOICE TODAY

The extent and range of mass communication has changed immeasurably since the heroic days of the early socialist press. The internet has transformed communication and social networking sites have made it easier to get simple messages across to large audiences. The 'traditional' left can learn a lot from the use of Twitter and Facebook by anti-capitalist protesters and other campaigns; at present we are hopeless amateurs.

But these new media have their limits. They are useful for building up awareness of meetings and demonstrations, but less helpful for developing ideas or putting across more in-depth news and opinion. We still need to talk to each other, face to face, and not just through a keyboard. There undoubtedly is still a role, though a different one, for traditional media – Labour, or left-inclined, newspapers which have a local circulation. But they need to understand what Blatchford and Clarke took as second nature: that people don't want to be bombarded with 'serious' politics all the time. Socialist messages need to be transmitted in ways which are accessible and entertaining. It's very unlikely we will see a return of the campaigning community magazines which flourished in the 1970s and 1980s – *Tameside Eye, Leigh People's Paper, Rochdale Alternative Paper* and many others. But we can learn a lot from their style – cheeky, unserious, gossipy and provocative.

Local Labour websites can help; they need to be lively, up to date and accessible. It isn't difficult to set one up but the challenge is in making people not only aware of it but having them want to look at it. A simple catalogue of the misdeeds of the Coalition is only for the dedicated. We need to get better at using the web to put across a lively progressive message which is strongly local. And doing that is a lot easier than traipsing round streets in the rain distributing papers which go straight into the bin.

GREEN LABOUR?

Back in the 1890s Allen Clarke was pointing out the enormous damage to people's lives that came from unregulated industrial capitalism. The pollution from belching factory chimneys was seen by many at the time as 'natural', in much the same way as today we tend to regard car-borne pollution as a price that has to be paid for mobility. Labour politicians still don't always see the contradiction between calling for cheaper fuel and curbing carbon monoxide emissions. The Labour Party in the past has had an uncomfortable relationship with environmental issues, despite the great work of SERA (Socialist Environmental Resources Association). Yet a growing number of party leaders and activists are recognising that climate change poses huge threats which are going to require radical solutions. This is where the role of the central state becomes incredibly important. We can't solve the problems of world climate change through local action on its own; it needs a co-ordinated response internationally, and Britain's record under Labour was actually very good.

The countryside has long been a 'political' issue. Winter Hill in 1896 and Kinder Scout in 1932 showed how passionately working-class people in the North feel about their countryside. And this isn't 'just' a middle class issue. Although the fight for access to the countryside has largely been won, there are still some areas of land barred to the public, and a real risk of the gains made in recent years being slowly rolled back. Organisations like the Ramblers Association do an excellent job in fighting for walkers' rights and challenging local infringements. It's an issue that a lot of people feel strongly about. The first big victory against the Coalition in 2011 was their u-turn on the sale of woodlands. This was a real mass campaign, strongly supported by Labour, but with support also going way beyond the traditional anti-Tory sectors. This demonstrated clearly that English people's love of the countryside can be mobilised in directly political ways. The enjoyment of our countryside is one of our most precious rights, and any meaningful radical political programme should have the defence of our countryside, and access to it, high up the agenda.

Transport is another key area where Labour can win massive political support. The early pioneers of the ILP wanted a nationally-owned rail system and municipally-owned trams and buses. Today, a sustainable transport policy should be delivered by well-resourced regional authorities accountable to directly-elected regional councils (see below). These regional authorities should determine the shape of an integrated public transport network, making the most of rail, bus and tram. New forms of social ownership need to be applied to the national rail network, including train operating companies structured as co-operatives. Network Rail, as owner of the nation's infrastructure, may well work best as a state-owned company with a high level of employee and stakeholder participation. The huge semi-monopolies controlling Britain's bus operations need to be reformed, with encouragement given to smaller, mutually and/or municipally owned operators.

The decline of cycling in the 1960s and 1970s has come to an end and both 'utility' and recreational cycling are on the increase. Socialism has a natural affinity with cycling, through its historical ties with the Clarion movement. The newspaper, the cycling club, choirs, ramblers and scouts, did a million times more to create socialists than Fabian and Marxist pamphlets. Cycling is a bit like railways: it has been in and out of vogue. Today, both are back in. The London bike hire scheme is proving a huge success; sales of bikes are growing and membership of the Cyclists' Touring Club is on the increase. Cycling is part of the solution to urban traffic problems, but it's more than that. It is part of a 'healthy living' agenda which includes social as well as physical health.

NEW FORMS OF POLITICAL LIFE

To be able to build a new form of Labour politics needs plenty of talk. In the past we have been scared of this, and the ultimate put-down for any group is that 'it's just a talking shop'. Where we are at, we need more talking shops, and a stepping-back from old assumptions which have not served us well. Some Labour Party branches and constituencies have 'political education officers', but most education is limited to what is in effect basic training for political cadres. Trade union education is also largely 'training' for union representatives – valuable in itself, but there is such a bigger world out there.

A huge gap has opened up for the provision of that wider education to nourish the mind and the soul – be it politics, history, culture, science, economics – all the things which the nineteenth-century pioneers deemed important. A generation of political and trade union activists is growing up with precious little knowledge or understanding of the tradition of which they form a part.

One of the most promising developments for years is the quite sudden growth of informal discussion circles. The 'philosophy in pubs' network, formed in Liverpool but extending beyond the Mersey, is one example. The Raymond Williams Foundation is supporting the spread of a network of informal political discussion groups, again based in pubs, where the group selects a topic and each person has their say – without any formal 'tutor'. My own village – Slaithwaite – or 'Slawit' – has recently formed 'The Free University of Slawit' with similar aims. These groups don't need funding, just interest and enthusiasm. Most pubs are more than happy to provide a room for free on quiet weekday evenings. Long may they continue, with no requirement for targets, inspections, or fees.

Political life would benefit from applying some of the ideas of the old ILP socialists and 'Clarionettes'. The socialist clubs which sprang up across Labour's Northern heartlands provided not only a political base but a social and educational one too. Many became cheap drinking clubs but are now struggling to survive changing lifestyles and commercial competition. Can the traditional 'Labour club' re-invent itself as a social and cultural community centre? If it doesn't, it will disappear, and very soon.

The popularity of cycling has come full circle, and its social, environmental and health benefits for group leisure are widely recognised.

Local Labour Party members and their friends could set up informal cycling and walking groups, offering a healthy social activity and getting out of the endless meetings. If the Labour Party is serious about building a strong membership it has to do more than improve the interest level at its monthly meetings. Offering a social and cultural dimension to party life, which could include bike rides and family walks and excursions, would make such a difference. Regular social events, using the talent which exists amongst party members, would help re-create the sort of vibrant culture which characterised the early years of the socialist movement. The socialist choral tradition has continued and is enjoying a modest revival; Bolton Socialist Club has its own Clarion Choir, and a sister group exists in East Lancashire, performing for labour and socialist movement events across the North. People's choirs are singing away in Sheffield, Huddersfield, Tyneside and other parts of the North.

REGIONAL DEMOCRACY

It's time for the English regions to get the sort of devolution that other parts of the UK have benefitted from over the last ten years. Some significant steps have been taken towards devolution, in Scotland, Wales and Northern Ireland. Keir Hardie and many of his comrades believed in 'Home Rule all round', including Ireland, Scotland, Wales and also England. The idea of regional devolution took many decades more to surface but both socialists and radical Liberals of the 1890s would have recognised its value. Perhaps the reason it didn't develop was that the North was such a strong economic and political force anyway; regionalism had little to 'hold on to' – certainly there was a very strong regional consciousness, reflected in the dialect literature of Lancashire, Yorkshire and the North East. But it did not translate into an overtly regional political consciousness which demanded devolved political power from the centre. By contrast, both Scotland and Wales have had nationalist movements, which, though they may had fluctuating fortunes over the last 150 years, were able to provide a focus for national aspirations and to nudge the Labour Party to make concessions to nationalist demands.

Today, London has its own mayoralty with extensive powers. Yet the English regions have an increasingly weakened local government, with what semblance there was of regional government dismantled in the first few months of the Coalition government. All the experience of regional government in Europe suggests that it can have a trans-formative effect, providing it is directly elected and takes power away from the centre. The experience in Scotland and London shows that devolution can bring vastly improved services, including new railways and infrastructure. The 'clear red water' which separates Wales from England is becoming deeper and more pronounced, with a Welsh government becoming increasingly confident of its power and inde-pendence, following the 2011 referendum on gaining greater powers.

The problem with the regional system which had built up in the last few years was that it was messy and unaccountable. The regional development agencies did much that was positive, but they had no real political accountability to the regions they served. The Government Regional offices were also a good idea and enabled cross-departmental working. But they answered to Whitehall, not to Manchester, Newcastle or Birmingham. John Prescott had great ideas for demo-cratic regionalism, but they were less than enthusiastically championed by Tony Blair. The referendum on devolution for the North East seemed almost specifically designed to be lost, with only limited powers on offer for the proposed regional assembly, and the impression that it would simply be another tier of bureaucracy.

The solution which followed, to have 'city region' governments covering smaller areas, was a classic compromise, with a serious demo-cratic deficit. 'City regions' are simply too small – all the development over the last thirty years has been for the economy and the transport system to outgrow cities or even city regions. People travel ever longer distances into work, and supply chains get bigger and bigger. People's leisure has extended over much longer distances, bringing the city and countryside into much closer contact, and this is compounded by more and more professional and business people working perhaps part of their week in a city centre but living fifty or sixty miles away in the countryside. This is no longer just a London phenomenon.

Regions are realities, and the need for a new form of regional government will, sooner or later, re-assert itself. Labour needs to develop some innovative approaches to regional government which ensure that it is accountable, has real power ,and above all takes power from the centre not from the locality. Regional government is vital for economic growth. The American academic Robert Putnam makes the point that:

… the regions characterised by civic involvement in the late twentieth century are almost precisely the same regions where cooperatives and cultural associations and mutual aid societies were most abundant in the nineteenth century, and where neighbourhood associations and religious confraternities and guilds had contributed to the flourishing communal republics of the twelfth century. And although these civic regions were not advanced economically a century ago, they have steadily outpaced the less civic regions both in economic performance (at least since the advent of regional government) and in quality of government.[4]

Back in the early 1990s Robin Murray explored the relationship between a progressive regionalism and local government in *Local Space: Europe and the New Regionalism*.[5] A central point in Murray's argument was the importance of democratic involvement beyond simply casting your vote at election times. To be fully effective, local and regional democracy needs active involvement of employees and communities as part of a dynamic municipal enterprise. It's a sad reflection on the times that, twenty years on from the publication of Murray's report, much of the innovation and enterprise which characterised some British local authorities has all but disappeared. It can, and should, be revived.

Labour and its allies need to work out a radical but deliverable plan for local and regional government which learns from best practice abroad. Regional government has been shown to deliver – in the UK as well as in Germany, France, Spain and the Scandinavian countries. But it needs to be democratically elected, not just a jumble of indirectly elected councillors and unelected business people and local worthies.

Nowhere is the need more pressing than in the North of England, where we are seeing the return of mass unemployment, swingeing local authority cuts and worsening public services.

Coming up with policies for a new regionalism – and with it real 'localism' – needs lots of debate and discussion, within and beyond the Labour Party. There needs to be a symbiotic relationship between regional authorities and local government. Local authorities should be encouraged to be pro-active in economic development, and to host district-based agencies (possibly developed from the proposed 'local enterprise partnerships', which look like being a geographical rag-bag).

These should include practical but visionary people from the business community and voluntary sector. 'Localism' is a hugely abused term, and it is hard to see much in the current government agenda that is giving real power to local authorities. But that is a challenge which Labour has got to take up, showing that it means business now – not in the few months before a general election.

The Labour Party – and it doesn't have to wait until it gets back into power – should set up pilot 'regional commissions' which are genuinely representative of each region concerned – to look at the options. Such projects should include an examination of the successful models of regional government in Germany, the USA and other OECD countries, including their funding models and the kinds of activities in which they engage. There should be no assumption that any new regional bodies would be like traditional 'glorified county councils', with a simple elected chamber. Is there scope to involve not only the business community but also the voluntary sector and faith groups? How would that work and how would it be truly accountable? Some suggestions are floated at the end of this chapter, but the fundamental point must be devolution from Whitehall and Westminster, not from the local or county level; and any new form of government must be elected on the basis of proportional representation, using the model that has proved itself in the Scottish, Welsh and London elections.

ETHICAL SOCIALISM WITH A NORTHERN ACCENT

Labour's defeat in 2010 was a disaster, not just for the Labour Party but also for large swathes of communities across Britain. But it is also an opportunity for the Party to rebuild, learning from what is a very honourable tradition but applying the lessons in a creative way to the needs of the future. It has got to become more inclusive, more tolerant and more willing to engage enthusiastically in coalitions and partnerships at local, regional and national levels.

Paul Richards, in *Labour's Revival*, seeks to reclaim the ethical socialist inheritance:

> the ethical socialist pioneers gave the Labour Party a socialism which was non-Marxist, often Christian, rooted in values, passionate about tackling poverty and disadvantage, and concerned with the brother-

hood and sisterhood of humanity rather than a preconceived economic doctrine.[6]

And he's right. The political model that equates socialism with state ownership is dead, and the Labour Party needs to unite behind a modern, progressive model which includes that old-fashioned concept and term, a 'mixed economy', using the resources of the state at national, regional and local level to protect the most vulnerable.

Of course all economies are mixed. What we have seen in recent years has been a marked swing towards traditional private ownership and away from public ownership. A new socialism needs to shift the pendulum back towards the centre, with an emphasis on co-operatives and different models of social enterprise. In some industries and services there are strong arguments for state ownership, including the major utilities and railways, but these must be managed in a way that incorporates the best democratic practice found in mutuals, with real user and employee involvement.

At the same time, there are many dynamic, socially responsible businesses out there which Labour should be building links with. Instead of cosying up to the great and powerful simply because they are great and powerful, Labour should identify allies in the private sector who share Labour's ethos of social responsibility. Austin Mitchell, writing at a time when Labour found itself out of power and unable to present a robust ideological challenge to Thatcherism, said that Labour should not revert back to old certainties but instead work with other forces – Liberals and Social Democrats – to aim for a 'new settlement ... more state, less market in the environment, health and education, but not excluding either when they serve the paramount purposes of the people rather than ideology'.[7]

So what would 'ethical socialism' look like in the twenty-first century? In his 2006 speech on 'Twenty-first-century Socialism' Rhodri Morgan concluded by stressing the intertwined importance of freedom and equality, 'two of the most enduring and important goals which remain for a renewed Left':

> Inequality is the most insidious form of injustice because it prevents individuals from achieving their full potential. And every time inequality prevents any of our fellow citizens from exercising their talents, or accessing the services to which they are entitled, the total

stock of freedom available to all of us is diminished. More equal societies enjoy greater economic success. As even the World Bank now agrees, inequality matters because it is as inefficient as it is unjust. More equal societies enjoy better health. Health isn't simply a matter of spending more and more money. It is about the under-pinning sense of social capital which more equal societies provide and which produce a sense of being cared for by others.

When Raymond Williams wrote about a common culture, what he meant was culture based on full democratic participation and the celebration of diversity which equality brings, not some homogenized uniformity. 21st century socialism in Wales means blending a culture of cohesion, participation and mutual aid at the community level, with the promotion of freedom and critical revolt at the level of the individual.[8]

This is fundamental. Wales and Scotland currently enjoy more of the democratic foundations to take the twin pillars of freedom and equality forward – though both Welsh and Scottish socialists would say there was still a long way to go. In the North, we haven't even got to the starting line, and are moving towards an ever-increasing dependence on a centralised Whitehall and Westminster government. Creating a values-led socialism which is democratic, ethical and rooted in its communities is necessary if Labour is to become a credible force for change, and an electable political party.

Paul Richards is an unapologetic Blairite, and would see himself as a long way politically from Rhodri Morgan. Yet his arguments for a twenty-first century socialism have much in common with Morgan's vision. He argues that the party should have three 'foundations' that could provide the framework for the development of more detailed policy. These are: 'Creating a democratic politics – Creating a fairer society – Creating a mutual economy'. He goes to point out that:

each reinforces the other; none can be tackled in isolation. A true democracy creates by definition a fairer society. A fairer society means that the economy works for the benefit of all ... each aspect of the programme feeds into the others. Running through a democratic politics, a fairer society and a mutual economy is the imperative need to tackle the greatest issues of the age: environmental protection, equality for women, trade justice, and preventing the spread of ideologies of hate ...[9]

Richards is right about the foundations. A modern democratic socialism cannot have any one of them without the others. The issue is to translate each of these into meaningful policy. The argument of this book is that the next stage in democratising Britain must be a new political settlement for the English regions, based on the success of devolution in Wales, Scotland and London. Wales and Scotland are nations, London isn't, and neither is the North of England. The powers appropriate for English regional government will be less perhaps than those of the Scottish Parliament, but would be similar to those currently enjoyed by the Welsh Assembly and elected on the same basis as the devolved governments for Scotland, Wales, Northern Ireland and London.

WHAT WOULD A NORTHERN ASSEMBLY DO?

A new Northern Assembly must have strong powers backed up by appropriate resources from the start, though it could gradually take on a wider range of responsibilities over time. There is no contradiction between strong, democratic local government and regional government. Regionalism must be about devolving power from the centre, not take power away from a local or county tier. The last four decades have seen power taken away from local government, mostly by Conservative governments. The pendulum now needs to swing back, but it's important to be clear on what is right for what level. If the starting point is serious devolution of powers currently exercised by Whitehall, it's worth considering the main powers of the Welsh Assembly. They include agriculture and rural development; culture, sport and recreation; economic development and tourism; education and training; the environment; health; transport; housing; social welfare; and town and county planning. This is an extensive range of powers. But it leaves Westminster with substantial responsibilities, including constitutional affairs, defence, foreign affairs, energy (electricity, coal, oil, gas, nuclear), employment, financial and macroeconomic matters; and social security.

A Northern Assembly might want to select which initial responsibilities it takes from central government. An obvious priority ought to be economic development and tourism (without removing local tourism powers from local authorities), as well as education and training, town and country planning, environment and transport. 'Culture' would be a good issue to start with, and is a field where a real difference could be made. Each of these themes is closely related, and is vital to the economic, social and environmental health of the region. Taking these powers away from Whitehall could begin a radical transformation of the North based around the principles of sustainable development.

A Northern Assembly could make a major local contribution to the really challenging global issue of climate change. This is a perfect example of a 'world' issue where part of the solution is local and regional. More investment needs to go into 'green industries', and there is a need to develop sustainable transport networks at local and regional level. A Northern Assembly could address the historic under-investment in the rail network, ensuring better links within the North, rather than just the main routes to London. This should involve, as is currently happening in Scotland and Wales, investment in both infrastructure and rolling stock.

The Scottish Parliament, through its executive arm Transport Scotland, is re-opening the railway to the Borders and electrifying the main Edinburgh-Glasgow Line. It has already funded the re-opening of the Edinburgh to Glasgow via Bathgate Line. The equivalent for the North of England would be a 'Transport North' executive accountable to the Northern Assembly. Electrification of the main TransPennine route between Leeds and Manchester would be the equivalent of electrifying the Edinburgh to Glasgow main line, though the populations covered would be considerably greater. Re-opening routes such as Skipton to Colne (linking East Lancashire and North and West Yorkshire), and York to Beverley and Hull, would be of similar scale to re-opening the Borders Railway, but connecting much larger populations.

'Transport North' should become the franchising body for the 'Northern Rail' passenger franchise, but ought also to have the power to abandon the expensive and bureaucratic franchising approach altogether, either itself taking direct ownership of local and regional passenger services, or creating a social enterprise to operate services, with any surplus generated being ploughed back into service improvements, instead of shareholders' pockets. The example of Spain's Basque

Country, where the regional government owns the local rail network, should be closely studied. Since the dilapidated network was taken over from the central state in 1982 there has been a major programme of investment, resulting in a local rail network which is of high quality, with passenger numbers growing year on year.

A Northern Assembly should have major powers to invest in emerging industries, including through full or partial ownership. A huge gap has been left by the destruction of the regional development agencies, and a new 'Enterprise North', accountable to the Assembly, would take over some of their former functions, as well as new responsibilities aimed at kick-starting a Northern industrial revival. Providing direct financial support to social enterprises, through grants and soft loans, and advice and training (perhaps through a network of local development agencies with strong local authority, business and community involvement), would encourage a flourishing mutual sector.

WHY NOT AN 'ENGLISH' GOVERNMENT?

The idea of having devolved government for 'England' alongside similar arrangements for Scotland, Wales and Northern Ireland sounds like a logical solution to the current muddle, not least to the 'West Lothian' question, which highlights the silliness of Scots, Welsh and Northern Irish MPs being able to vote on issues which are of purely 'English' concern, whilst English MPs don't have the same power to influence a wide range of policy areas in the devolved nations.[10] But there's a huge problem that has escaped the notice of many of the (mostly London-based) commentariat who push the idea of 'English' government. The biggest problem is that it would remain massively oriented towards London and South East. The governments of Wales, Northern Ireland and Scotland have been able to reverse centuries of centralised government that was often ignorant and uncaring about what went on in those places – unless it really had no choice but to intervene (such as in Northern Ireland in 1969). The last thing the North, or the other English regions, need is another London-based government which thinks it understands the problems of the regions beyond the Home Counties. And the problem would not be solved by locating an 'English' government in Birmingham, York or Manchester. Manchester would no more understand the needs of the South West or East of England than a government in London.

Regional government needs to be big enough to provide an over-arching strategic polity but small enough to have a clear identity which reflects a meaningful 'community of interest'. An English government would no more do that than the system we have at present. As a mate of mine said of the idea, 'There's nowt in this for us'.

There is a further problem. Some well-meaning socialists (Billy Bragg amongst others) enthuse about the importance of 'reclaiming' English patriotism. This is a very dangerous horse to ride and has a nasty tendency to lurch uncontrollably to the right. The political entity of 'England' as it is now has centuries of experience in throwing its weight around with surrounding nations, and fine-tuning a sense of 'Englishness' which is exclusive and reactionary. I'm not insensible to the many good things that have happened in England, including the Levellers, the Chartists and more recent achievements (with a few friends) in defeating Hitler. However, the whole dynamic of 'English nationalism' pulls heavily to the right, as we see with the 'English Defence League', the English Democrats and similar reactionary organisations. It's a dangerous road to take, and there really is an alter-native which could potentially lay the way towards a genuinely progressive England within a federal Britain: an England of the Regions.

Clearly 'The North' is part of England, as much a part as London and the South East, Midlands, the South-West, and the East of England. It isn't a nation and is unlikely (within the next few genera-tions) ever to have any aspiration towards 'nationhood'. It has lots in common with Scotland and Wales, reflecting both a shared industrial and political history in some respects, as well as a common awareness that 'London' government has not always been in our interest.

A new democratic Britain needs a fresh settlement between the three historic nations, with the current devolution of powers enjoyed by Scotland, Northern Ireland and Wales extended to the English regions, effectively creating a federal United Kingdom. This would resolve the West Lothian question: MPs at Westminster would concern themselves with issues of concern to Britain and Northern Ireland as a whole, allowing a range of devolved powers to be dealt with by the Scottish and Welsh nations and English regional governments.

A strong devolved North within a reformed England is an attractive concept, which would settle the West Lothian question once and for all and allow the North – and the rest of England – to break free from the centralised clutches of Westminster and Whitehall, and it would also allow central government to get on with the tasks it can do best. It opens up the prospect of a federal Britain, with the nations and regions of the UK respecting each other's traditions and working together where and when everyone wants to. A 'Federal Britain' presupposes a much reduced central government, with fewer MPs and a much smaller civil service. Regions should take over much of the powers currently based within central government, reflecting the arrangements for Wales and Scotland, which could include tax-varying powers.

To get to that point, a progressive majority needs to be won in the Westminster Parliament we have now, and the one we will have following boundary changes and the reduction in the number of MPs. Labour will not win if it is just seen as the 'Northern Party'. But what would be fatal is a Labour Party which assumes 'the North' will carry on voting Labour and instead focuses on 'the South', along the lines of the 'Southern Comfort' arguments of Giles Radice, first articulated in the early 1990s and re-stated more recently by John Harris.[11] Labour does need to win in the South, and that means having policies which make sense to voters in that part of England. But that does not necessitate taking a traditional right-wing approach – on which the Tories will always have the advantage. Livingstone won London on the basis of strong, centre-left policies, and but this didn't dilute his appeal to the centre ground. There are big issues around the local economy, transport, the environment and housing where Labour could make real gains in the South East by developing an appropriate regional strategy.

What Labour shouldn't do is assume that 'the North' will carry on dutifully voting Labour whatever happens. It didn't do that in 2010 and won't do in the future unless the party has something different to offer. That's why it needs to connect with people's Northern identities (and in other regions to their Welsh, Scots, East Anglian, Cornish, London and other identities). This is a cultural as much as an economic issue. It is not about trying to breathe life into an expired culture of 'northern-ness' that excludes the diverse array of communities which are now firmly established in the North. It is about celebrating a diverse regional identity which can reach out to every section of the community, coupled with a radical but deliverable plan for the economy. The two are directly linked. Regional government would act as a catalyst for genuinely sustainable development, in the same way that regional government has delivered across Europe and devolved government is delivering in Wales and Scotland.

And this takes us back to Bradford, where it all began, in 1893. Bradford is a great Northern city that has lots of divisions and lots of economic problems that may get worse before they get better. Its Labour-led council is struggling to unite the city's communities, businesses and faiths to build a Bradford which does justice to the municipal ideals of its late nineteenth century pioneers. If a Northern regional government could not succeed in making a difference to the problems it is facing, it wouldn't be worth bothering with. 'Socialism with a Northern Accent' has nothing old fashioned or sentimental about it. It is the radical future for socialism in the North. A socialism which is open, tolerant, decentralist, and enterprising.

NOTES

1. Austin Mitchell, *Beyond the Blue Horizon*, 1988, p160.
2. See *TSSA Journal* May/June 2011.
3. J.B. Priestley. *English Journey*, 1934, pp158-160.
4. Robert Putnam, *Making Democracy Work: civic traditions in modern Italy*, 1993, quoted in Colin Ward, 'Federalism, regionalism and Planning', in *The Raven*, autumn 1995, p301.
5. See Robin Murray, *Breaking with Bureaucracy* (op. cit., Chapter 7); and Mike Davis et al, *Go Local to Survive: Decentralisation in Local Government*, Labour Co-ordinating Committee, 1984.
6. Paul Richards, *Reforming Labour*, 2011.
7. Austin Mitchell, op. cit., p179.
8. Rhodri Morgan, Speech to Compass Conference, Swansea, 1 December 2006, available at Compass website.
9. Ibid.
10. See Mark Perryman (ed.), *Breaking Up Britain: Four Nations After a Union*, 2009, esp. John Harris, 'An English re-alignment', for an intelligent discussion of some of the issues, but one which manages to avoid any mention of regional devolution.
11. Giles Radice, *Southern Discomfort*, 1992; and John Harris, op. cit.

The Hannah Mitchell Foundation

The Hannah Mitchell Foundation is a forum for the development of a distinctive democratic socialism in the North, rooted in our ethical socialist traditions of mutuality, co-operation, community and internationalism. It was formed in November 2011 by a group of socialists from across the North of England. Its prime focus will be to develop the case for directly elected regional government for the North of England – either as a whole or for the three regions which make up 'the North' (North East, Yorkshire & Humber and North West).

The foundation is named in memory of an outstanding Northern socialist, feminist and co-operator, who was proud of her working-class roots and had a cultural as well as political vision.

For more information visit www.hannahmitchell.org.uk.

APPENDIX I

The Socialist Ten Commandments

1. Love your school companions, who will be your co-workers in life

2. Love learning, which is the food of the mind; be as grateful to your teachers as to your parents

3. Make every day holy by good and useful deeds and kindly actions

4. Honour good men and women; be courteous to all, bow down to none

5. Do not hate nor speak evil of any one; do not be revengeful, but stand up for your rights and resist oppression

6. Do not be cowardly. Be a good friend to the weak, and love justice

7. Remember that all good things of the earth are produced by labour. Whoever enjoys them without working for them is stealing the bread of the workers

8. Observe and think in order to discover the truth. Do not believe what is contrary to reason, and never deceive yourself or others

9. Do not think that they who love their country must hate and despise other nations, or wish for war which is a remnant of barbarism

10. Look forward to the day when all men and women will be free citizens of one community, and live together as equals in peace and righteousness

APPENDIX 2

England, arise!

Edward Carpenter

England, arise! The long long night is over,
Faint in the east behold the dawn appear;
Out of your evil dream of toil and sorrow
Arise, O England, for the day is here.
From your fields and hills
Hark! the answer swells:
Arise, O England, for the day is here.

Long, long have been the anguish and the labour,
Dark, dark the clouds of unbelief unrolled,
Dreadful the night when no man trusted neighbour,
Shameful the nightmare-greed of gain and gold;
Yet from fields and hills
Hark! the song now swells:
Arise, O England, for the day is here.

By your young children's eyes so red with weeping,
By their white faces aged with want and fear,
By the dark cities where your babes are creeping
Naked of joy and all that makes life dear;
From your wretched slums
A voice of pity comes:
Arise, O England, for the day is here.

By all your workshops where men sweat and sicken,
Foredone to death, in toil and hope deferred,
Where cheeks are flushed and pulses start and quicken,
Not with glad life but by dark hatred stirred;
From each bench and forge
A sound comes like a surge:
Arise, O England, for the day is here.

By your high homes of wealth and wasteful living,
By your rich tables piled, without good cheer,
By the ennui, ill-health, and sickly striving –
Not great to be, but only to appear;
O'er the weary throng
Strangely floats the song:
Arise, O England, for the day is here.

By your rich orchards, lands of corn and pasture,
Where all day long the voice of joy should ring,
Now mute and desert, by land-grabbers wasted,
Robbed of the love the peasant longs to bring;
From the stricken land
Hark! the words ascend:
Arise, O England, for the day is here.

People of England, all your valleys call you,
High in the rising sun the lark sings clear;
Will you dream on, let shameful slumber thrall you?
Will you disown your native land so dear?
Shall it die unheard –
That sweet pleading word?
Arise, O England, for the day is here.

Over your face a web of lies is woven,
Law that are falsehoods pin you to the ground;
Labour is mocked, its just reward is stolen,
On its bent back sits Idleness encrowned;
How long, while you sleep,
Your harvest shall it reap?
Arise, O England, for the day is here.

Out of your ruin rich men thrive and fatten,
Your merchants rub their hands when food is dear,
Capital says your claims are not forgotten
If wages keep you just starvation-clear;
People of England, when
Will ye rise like men?
Rise and be freemen, for the day is here!

Hear, England, hear! Deliverance is within you;
Though like a man whom death is very near,
Though sick the head, the whole heart faint within you,
Dare to be true! – and even from the bier
Where your body lies
A new life shall arise,
England shall rise again to life sincere.

Yet thus I warn you: long shall be the struggle,
Not one but many men in it shall die;
This cancerous disease and devil's juggle
Shall not pass in the twinkling of an eye;
To undo their wrong
The people shall strive long:
O that they fail not! for the day is here.

Forth then, ye heroes, patriots and lovers!
Comrades of danger, poverty and scorn!
Mighty in faith of Freedom, your great Mother,
Giants refreshed in joy's new-rising morn!
Come and swell the song
Silent now so long –
England is risen and the Day is here!

APPENDIX 3

A Gradely Prayer

Allen Clarke/Teddy Ashton

Give us, Lord, a bit o' sun,
A bit o' wark, an' a bit o' fun.
Give us aw in th' struggle an' splutter,
Eaur daily bread – an' a bit o' butter.

Give us health, eaur keep to make,
An' a bit to spare for poor folk's sake;
Give us sense, for we're some of us duffers,
An' a heart to feel for them that suffers.

Give us, too, a bit of a song,
An' a tale an' a book to help us along;
An' give us eaur share o' sorrow's lesson
That we may prove heaw grief's a blessin'.

Give us, Lord, a chance to be
Eaur gradely best, brave, wise, an' free;
Eaur gradely best for eaursels an' others,
Till all men larn to live as brothers.

Timelines: A Northern Chronology

1789:   French Revolution
1791:   Publication of Paine's *Rights of Man*
1798:   United Irishmen uprising crushed
1799:   Combination Acts passed outlawing trades unions
1812:   Luddite attacks on factories in the North
1819:   Peterloo massacre
1830:   Opening of Liverpool and Manchester Railway
1833:   First Co-operative Conference, Manchester
1834:   Poor Laws enacted
1838:   People's Charter Published
1839:   Chartist insurrections in Bolton, Huddersfield, Newport
1842:   Chartist General Strike across North
1848:   Publication of Communist manifesto
1853:   Preston Cotton Workers Lock-Out
1861:   American Civil War; start of Lancashire Cotton Famine
1868:   TUC founded in Manchester
1878:   Weavers' strikes in Blackburn
1881:   Democratic Federation (DF) founded by H.M. Hyndman
1884:   DF becomes Social Democratic Federation (SDF)
1886:   Socialist League formed from split with SDF
1887:   Bolton Engineers' Strike
1890:   Manningham Mills Strike, Bradford
1891:   Clarion newspaper founded by Robert Blatchford
1892:   Keir Hardie elected MP for West Ham; George Garside elected as first ILP county councillor
1893:   Independent Labour Party officially founded in Bradford
1894:   Clarion Cycling Club formed
1896:   Winter Hill Trespass in Bolton
1899:   TUC votes narrowly to establish independent working-class party
1900:   Labour Representation Committee founded as forerunner of Labour Party

1901: First 'Teddy Ashton Picnic' in Bolton attracts 10,000
1903: Formation of Women's Social and Political Union
1906: LRC becomes The Labour Party; 29 MPs elected
1907: Victor Grayson elected as MP for Colne Valley
1911: General strikes in Liverpool and Salford; British Socialist Party formed
1914: Outbreak of First World War; Labour movement split
1918: War ends; some women get the vote
1920: Communist Party of Great Britain formed
1921: Major wave of strikes; Poplar revolt against poor relief
1924: First Labour government formed; lasts until October
1926: General Strike lasts 9 days
1929: Labour government elected; Macdonald is prime minister
1931: Collapse of Labour government: Macdonald and Snowden join in National Government
1932: ILP votes to leave Labour Party; weavers' strikes in east Lancashire
1933: Walter Greenwood's *Love on the Dole* published; Hitler seizes power
1936: Jarrow March; Outbreak of Spanish Civil War
1939: War declared
1941: Hitler invades USSR; Russia enters war
1945: War ends: election of Labour government with huge majority
1950: Labour elected with small majority but lose power the following year
1956: Invasion of Hungary by USSR; Suez Crisis
1964: Labour wins general election; Wilson is prime minister
1966: Wilson wins again
1969: Troops sent to Northern Ireland; USSR invades Czechoslovakia
1972: National Miners' Strike
1984: Start of Miners' Strike over pit closures
1985: End of Miners' Strike
1989: Berlin wall comes down
1997: Labour wins general election; Tony Blair is prime minister
1999: Regional Development Agencies established
2010: Labour loses general election; Conservative-led Coalition formed with Liberal Democrats

Select Bibliography

The work of regional history groups is extremely valuable. The North West Labour History Society and their North-East colleagues publish excellent newsletters and reports.

Good general introductions to the history of the labour and socialist movement include:

Davies, A.J., *To Build a New Jerusalem: The Labour Movement from the 1880s to the 1890s*, 1992.

Callaghan, John, *Socialism in Britain Since 1884*, 1990.

Laybourn, Keith, *The Rise of Socialism in Britain c 1881-1951*, 1997.

Pugh, Martin, *Speak for Britain: a new history of the Labour Party*, 2011.

Thorpe, Andrew, *A History of the British Labour Party*, 3rd ed., 2008.

DEMOCRATIC STRUGGLES

Bamford, Samuel, *Passages in the Life of a Radical.*

Chase, Malcolm, *Chartism: A New History*, 2007.

Thompson, E.P., *The Making of the English Working Class*, 1963.

BETWEEN CHARTISM AND SOCIALISM

Bonner, Arnold, *British Co-operation*, 1961.

Black, L. and N. Robertson (eds.), *Consumerism and the Co-operative Movement in Modern British History: Taking Stock*, 2009.

Brooke, Alan, *The Hall of Science; Co-operation and Socialism in Huddersfield 1830-1848*, 1993.

Harrison, Royden, *Before the Socialists*, 1965.

Moody, T., *Michael Davitt and Irish Revolution, 1846-1882*, 1981.

Turnbull, J. and J. Southern, *More Than Just a Shop: A History of the Co-op in Lancashire*, 1995.

THE NEW PARTY IN THE NORTH

Clark, David, *Colne Valley; Radicalism to Socialism*, 1981.

Clark, David, *Labour's Lost leader: Victor Grayson*, 1985.

Cohen, Gidon, *Failure of a Dream: The Independent Labour Party from Disaffiliation to World War II*, 2007.

Davies, Sam, *Liverpool Labour*, 1996.

Dowse, R.E., *Left in the Centre: The ILP 1893-1940*, 1966.

Groves, Reg, *The Strange Case of Victor Grayson*, 1975.

Howell, David, *British Workers and the ILP: 1888-1906*, 1983.

James, D., T. Jowitt and K. Laybourn, *The Centennial History of the ILP*, 1992.

Laybourn, Keith, *Philip Snowden: a biography*, 1994.

Liddington, Jill, *The Life and Times of a Respectable Rebel: Selina Cooper, 1864-1946*, 1997.

Morgan, K.O., *Labour People – Hardie to Kinnock*, 1992.

Norris, Jill and Jill Liddington, *One Hand Tied Behind Us*, 1978.

Rowbotham, Sheila, *Edward Carpenter: A Life of Liberty and Love*, 2008.

Thompson, Laurence, *Robert Blatchford: Portrait of an Englishman*, 1951.

Turner, Ben, *About Myself*, 1930.

A NORTHERN SOCIALIST CULTURE

Foley, Alice, *A Bolton Childhood*, 1973.

Frow, Ruth and Edmund, *The General Strike in Salford in 1991*, 1990.

Harrison, Stanley, *Poor Men's Guardians*, 1974.

Gorman, John, *Banner Bright*, 1986.

Klaus, Gustav, *The Literature of Labour: 200 years of Working Class Writing*, 1985.

Klaus, Gustav, *The Rise of Socialist Fiction*, 1987.

Liddington, Jill, *Rebel Girls: Their Fight for the Vote*, 2006.

Mitchell, Hannah, *The Hard Way Up*, reprinted, 1967.

Pye, Denis, *Fellowship is Life: the National Clarion Cycling Club 1885-1995*, 1995.

Robertson, Michael, *Worshipping Walt – The Whitman Disciples*, 2009.

Salveson, Paul, *Will Yo' Come O' Sunday Mornin'? The 1896 Winter Hill Trespass*, 1996.

Salveson, Paul, *Lancashire's Romantic Radical: the life and writings of Allen Clarke/Teddy Ashton*, 2009.

Salveson, Paul, *With Walt Whitman in Bolton: spirituality, sex and socialism in a Northern Mill Town*, 2009.

BETWEEN COMMUNISM AND LABOURISM?

Edwards, Hazel, *Follow the Banner*, 1988.

Feaver, William, *Pitmen Painters: The Ashington Group 1934-1984*, 1993.

Frow, Ruth, *Edmund Frow: The Making of an Activist*, 1999.

Greenwood, Walter, *Love on the Dole*, 1935.

Hannington, Wal, *Unemployed Struggles*, 1974.

Hikins H. (ed.), *Building the Union: Merseyside 1756-1967*, 1973.

Hill, Howard, *Freedom to Roam*, 1980.

Reynolds, J. and K. Laybourn, *Labour Heartland: a history of the Labour Party in West Yorkshire 1918-1939*, 1987.

Rowbotham Sheila, *Dreamers of a New Day: women who invented the 20th Century*, 2010.

Stephenson, Tom, *Forbidden land: the struggle for access to mountain and moorland*, 1989.

Thompson, Willie, *The Good Old Cause: British Communism 1920-1991*, 1992.

Wilkinson, Ellen, *The Town that was Murdered*, 1939.

Worley, Matthew, *Labour Inside the Gate: a history of the Labour Party between the wars*, 2005.

THE HIGH TIDE OF SOCIAL DEMOCRACY

Eatwell, Roger, *The 1945-1951 Labour Governments*, 1979.

Fielding S., P. Thompson and N. Tiratsoo, *England Arise! The Labour Party and Popular Politics in 1940s Britain*, 1995.

Morgan, K.O., *Labour in Power 1945-1951*, 1984.

THATCHER, BLAIR AND THE REGIONS

Beckett, F., and Hencke, D., *Marching to the Fault Line*, 2009.

Crick, Michael, *The March of Militant*, 1986.

Kogan, D., and M. Kogan, *The Battle for the Labour Party*, 1982.

Mitchell, Austin, *Britain: Beyond the Blue Horizon*, 1989.

Pearmain, Andrew, *The Politics of New Labour*, 2011.

Perryman, Mark (ed.), *Breaking Up Britain: four nations after a union*, 2009.

Prior, M., and D. Purdy, *Out of the Ghetto*, 1979.

GENERAL

Russell, Dave, *Looking North: Northern England and the national imagination*, 2004.

Todd, Nigel (ed.), *The Right to Learn: The WEA in the North-east 1910-2010*, 2010.

Walton, John, *Lancashire: A Social History 1558-1939*, 1987.

Index